Jim Rodewald

Given to me at the Calvin Studio Colloquium at
Columbia Theological Seminary by Dr. Hesselink
on March 2, 2002

Calvin's First Catechism

COLUMBIA SERIES IN REFORMED THEOLOGY

The Columbia Series in Reformed Theology represents a joint commitment of Columbia Theological Seminary and Westminster John Knox Press to provide theological resources for the church today.

The Reformed tradition has always sought to discern what the living God revealed in scripture is saying and doing in every new time and situation. Volumes in this series examine significant individuals, events, and issues in the development of this tradition and explore their implications for contemporary Christian faith and life.

This series is addressed to scholars, pastors, and laypersons. The Editorial Board hopes that these volumes will contribute to the continuing reformation of the church.

EDITORIAL BOARD

Columbia Theological Seminary wishes to express its appreciation to the following churches for supporting this joint publishing venture:

First Presbyterian Church, Tupelo, Mississippi

First Presbyterian Church, Nashville, Tennessee

Trinity Presbyterian Church, Atlanta, Georgia

Spring Hill Presbyterian Church, Mobile, Alabama

St. Stephen Presbyterian Church, Fort Worth, Texas

COLUMBIA SERIES IN REFORMED THEOLOGY

Calvin's First Catechism

A Commentary

I. JOHN HESSELINK

Featuring Ford Lewis Battles's translation of the 1538 Catechism

Westminster John Knox Press
Louisville, Kentucky

Book and cover design by Drew Stevens

First edition

Published by Westminster John Knox Press
Louisville, Kentucky

This book is printed on acid-free paper that meets the American National Standards Institute Z39.48 standard. ♾

PRINTED IN THE UNITED STATES OF AMERICA

98 99 00 01 02 03 04 05 06 — 10 9 8 7 6 5 4 3 2

Library of Congress Cataloging-in-Publication Data

Hesselink, I. John, date.
    Calvin's first catechism : a commentary : featuring Ford Lewis Battles's translation of the 1538 Catechism / I. John Hesselink.
        p.   cm. — (Columbia series in Reformed theology)
    Includes bibliographical references and indexes.
    ISBN 0-664-22055-X
    1. Calvin, Jean, 1509–1564.   Instruction et confession de foy.
    2. Reformed Church—Catechisms—History and criticism.
    3. Reformed Church—Catechisms—English.   I. Calvin, Jean, 1509–1564.
    Instruction et confession de foy. English. II. Title. III. Series.
BX9429.G4H47   1997
230' .42—dc21   97-23142

Dedicated to the memory of
Ford Lewis and Marion Davis Battles,
gifted Calvin scholars and
faithful servants of the Lord

CONTENTS

PREFACE

This is the product of a long, interesting process. It goes back to my missionary days in Japan, when I was asked by a group of lay people in our Japanese church to introduce them to the thought of Calvin. An ideal vehicle toward that end was Calvin's first catechism, originally written in French in 1537. The French version bore the title *Instruction in Faith.* An English translation by Paul T. Fuhrmann was then available and, more important, a Japanese version, *Shinkō no Tebiki,* translated by Nobuo Watanabe.

I began writing a simple commentary in English, which was then translated into Japanese. Later this was expanded and used in the introductory course on Calvin which I taught for several years at Tokyo Union Seminary.

In 1973 I was invited to become president of Western Theological Seminary in Holland, Michigan. During the twelve years I was president, I continued to do some teaching. One of the courses was on Calvin's life and theology. The substance of this volume was used as one of my texts for the course. This book, however, is a considerably expanded version of that text and reflects my continual reading of Calvin's works and the secondary literature. In the meantime, the Fuhrmann edition of *Instruction in Faith* went out of print (it is now available again from Westminster John Knox Press). Even prior to my return to the United States, I had become acquainted with the great American Calvin scholar and translator of the *Institutes,* Ford Lewis Battles. He showed me his translation of Calvin's Latin edition of the same work written the following year and now simply called *Catechism 1538.* He had published this privately while at Pittsburgh Seminary and kept making revisions and corrections until his death. One of my most precious bibliographical possessions is the bound copy he gave me during our last visit in Butterworth Hospital in Grand Rapids, dated November 18, 1979. He died four days later.

Prior to his death we had agreed that we would publish his translation and my commentary together. This would serve the purpose of providing in one volume an original text of Calvin's plus an introduction to his theology for nonspecialists. It is not intended to compete with standard works on Calvin's theology by scholars such as Wilhelm Niesel or

François Wendel or the fine collection of essays, *Readings in Calvin's Theology*, edited by Donald K. McKim (Baker Book House, 1984). There is also the recent study by T.H.L. Parker, *Calvin: An Introduction to His Thought* (Westminster John Knox Press, 1995), but it is largely a summary of the *Institutes* with recent secondary literature.

It should be noted that although this commentary is based primarily on the 1538 Catechism and follows its structure, I have utilized freely other writings of Calvin's, particularly the *Institutes* and the commentaries. Also, keep in mind that this is intended as a relatively simple introduction, although some of the notes are more technical. Moreover, I have appended a chapter which seeks to illustrate the oft-repeated thesis that Calvin is above all a theologian of the Holy Spirit.

Subsequent to Ford Battles's death, I kept in touch with his wife, Marion, who was also a good friend. She was very supportive of this whole venture and looked forward to the publication of this book. Her sudden death in December 1994 was a shock and a blow to all of those who knew and loved her. As a result, this book is now dedicated to the memory of both of these dear friends.

Various friends have been helpful and encouraging as this book has developed. I am particularly grateful to the following people: Elton Bruins, emeritus professor of religion at Hope College, Holland, Michigan; Donald K. McKim, dean and professor of theology at Memphis Theological Seminary; Richard Muller, professor of church history at Calvin Theological Seminary, Grand Rapids, Michigan; and A. van de Beek, professor of dogmatic and biblical theology, the University of Leiden, the Netherlands.

I also want to thank our former faculty secretary and now assistant to the president, Marilyn Essink, who deserves the credit for typing the last drafts of this manuscript. Toward the end of this venture she was assisted by Kari Trumpie, our receptionist at Western Seminary. Without their help this would have been a lost cause.

I am also indebted to the editorial board of the Columbia Series in Reformed Theology for their willingness to accept this volume in the series. Finally, I would like to thank Timothy Staveteig, formerly at Westminster John Knox Press, who worked with me in the initial days of the production; and Stephanie Egnotovich, managing editor, both of whom have been gracious and helpful in this venture. Thanks also to Carl Helmich, production editor, and Jan Richardson, copyeditor, for their excellent work in the editorial process and for their role, along with the other unknown collaborators at Westminster John Knox, for bringing this project to fruition. And finally I want to express my gratitude to my son Nathan and several special friends who assisted in proofreading.

I. John Hesselink

Western Theological Seminary
Holland, Michigan

JOHN CALVIN: *CATECHISM 1538*

Translated by Ford Lewis Battles

CATECHISM or INSTITUTION OF THE CHRISTIAN RELIGION,[1] accepted by the common approval of the Church of Geneva recently reborn in the gospel, and previously published in the vernacular, but now also in Latin in order that the sincerity of that faith may be manifest also to other churches everywhere.

By John Calvin, author.
At Basel, in the year of our Lord 1538.

To all who devotedly honor the gospel of Christ, the ministers of the church at Geneva pray grace and peace, and the increase of true godliness from the Lord.

Lest anyone expect an extraordinary statement in this Catechism of ours, we freely admit it to be such that to some it might seem more advantageous to keep it within the boundaries of our church, and not to publish it more widely. For, as it has been drafted more out of pious willingness than keen and lofty learning, so there is no very great hope that some benefit of teaching can be gathered from it, especially among Latin speakers. Nor obviously would we have published it if some other reason to commend it had impelled us than that of trying to sell our product among foreign nations. This I would therefore like to explain to you, lest anyone might interpret the purpose of this edition otherwise than we intended.

Because we know it befits us especially that all churches embrace one another in mutual love, there is no better way to attain this than for all parties to work out an agreement and testify to it in the Lord. For us there is no closer bond than this to keep minds in harmony. But if it at any time was expedient otherwise, in our time it is surely most necessary, an era which we see steeped in such wickedness that there is no innocence sufficiently safe from false charges, no simplicity free enough from suspicions.

Concerning others we say nothing. But we ourselves have already been taught by more than enough experiences how wicked denunciation is effective not only in dividing the minds of otherwise good men, but also almost in uprooting churches themselves, as often as it can spread sinister rumors about a matter not clearly investigated. Indeed, as a fire which has already burned far and wide is not extinguished offhand, so it is too late, once such evils have arisen, for us to try to cope with them. Wonderful it is in how short a time the poison of false charges oozes forth, so that you are never able to cure it before the minds of many become infected. Moreover, the remedy itself is exceedingly difficult: obviously it is even more difficult to cleanse again the mind of a man steeped in vicious opinions than it is to befoul it with them. Indeed, there is nothing we are more ready to do than grasp the first signs; once received, we lay them aside most reluctantly. When therefore troubled at various times by empty accusations, we have learned we must fear them very much: insofar as permitted we prefer to cut off the occasion for these until the next day, rather than wait for them, while we ought to struggle with them in hand-to-hand combat.

Since we seemed to be able to attain this by no shortcut more readily than if some sure model of our doctrine—or, rather, catholic attestation thereof—were to stand forth publicly, we considered that this Catechism, which had a little while ago been put out in the vernacular, ought also to be published among other churches, and having been received as a guarantee, they may become more certain of our union with them. Also, if the pastors of the churches, whom we very highly esteem for their piety, holiness, and learning, both previously furnished and continue to furnish no ambiguous evidence of their goodwill and sincere love toward us. That it may appear they have been no less securely persuaded concerning the purity of our religion than if it were to be sealed a hundred times over with votive offerings.

But they are not the only ones with whom it is expedient to deal; and we must have no fear of exceeding the measure in this matter in which nothing can be excessive. Moreover, the doctrine with which we are instructing the people entrusted to us by the Lord we believe to be so in accord with holy truth, that there will be no one of the godly who does not recognize in it what awareness of religion he has, seeing that we have endeavored not to pour forth our own views but to dispense things taken soberly and faithfully from God's pure Word. But especially those who do not wish to judge most unfairly could easily have determined how unjust that one would be toward us, who attempted to belabor us before good men with suspicion no less obscure than devious; as if our opinion concerning the distinction of persons in the one God disagreed somewhat with the orthodox consensus of the church. And that one indeed, according as not only his ungodliness but also his most wicked life deserve, has escaped men's judgment for a time in order to be saved for divine vengeance, the clear marks of which all men see already appearing in him. The Lord, moreover, has shown himself in time the vindicator of our innocence, having speedily closed the way to such shameful falsehood, lest it either crawl more deeply into or occupy longer the hearts of the godly. Surely we, by the Lord's grace, are not so badly trained nor so miserably versed in the Scriptures that we go about blindly in such bright light. For however involved, and yet not obscure, this proof may seem to others, we nevertheless know that there in the one essence of God the Trinity of persons is more clearly indicated.

Indeed, we have with good reason caused a confession published with solemn oath-taking by the whole people to be adjoined. Just because our senate asked us to draw up a plan to administer this oath, some people are thoughtlessly circulating rumors about us as an innovator. This is the kind of thing that usually happens when a matter has not been clearly disclosed. Actually, in our opinion, the fairness of what we have done shines too brightly to need any defense, at least among prudent and sagacious men. Yet not even thus could the calumnies of such men be escaped. So great is the peevishness of ignorance that even in the most tested of matters there is always something to blame. We therefore who consider it to be our duty to satisfy all to the best of our ability will indicate to a few how firm our reason for this plan really is.

Even though, after the abomination of papalism had been laid low here by the power of the Word, a decree had been published to the effect that, removing superstitions and their tools, the religion of the city be composed to the purity of the Gospel—still that form of the church seemed not to exist among us which lawful administration of our office required. For however others may appraise it, we certainly do not think our function confined within such narrow limits that, having assembled for preaching and as it were having discharged one's duty, one is allowed to be idle. Those whose blood is required of us if it should fail through our idleness ought to be cared for much more closely and with more vigilant effort.

If this solicitude in other respects kept us anxious, then as often as the Lord's Supper was to be distributed it burned and tormented us. For even though we might have doubts and even grave mistrust of many, yet all were rushing in indiscriminately. And they were even devouring God's wrath rather than partaking in the sacrament of life. Yet ought one not to consider that the pastor who has no delight in communicating it is himself profaning this great mystery?

For this reason we could obtain peace and repose with our own consciences on no other condition than to give allegiance to Christ by public profession—we who wished to be reckoned among his people and admitted to that spiritual and most sacred banquet! That, they assert, had been done once for all in baptism. But some had defected from their baptismal profession. If they aver that the first oath of military service is sufficient for a deserter, an oath he has violated by his treachery, we will not say a word in defense of our cause.

Yet we are destitute of neither illustrious examples nor of the support of Scripture. The ancient folk had the covenant of circumcision impressed upon their bodies, whom Moses exhorted to make a new covenant. The same renewal of the covenant by the holy kings, Josiah and Asa, was afterward accomplished by those remarkable defenders of liberty, Ezra and Nehemiah. Can our act, fortified by so many classical authors, be now exposed to this accusation?

Driven, therefore, by such great need, we appealed to our Senate on this matter, and having offered a formula of confession, earnestly requested that in professing his truth they should not be reluctant to give glory to the Lord. It is proper that the magistrates should in such a holy action precede their people, for whom they knew they ought to be the pattern of all virtue. We readily obtained what was a fair request, that the common people, called together in groups of ten, might subscribe to this confession. Their eagerness to take this oath was no less than the diligence of the Senate in publishing it. And they were bidden by oath to promise to observe the divine law, something from which they can in no way be excused. Those who are clamoring so heedlessly against it are not paying attention to those with whom they have undertaken the struggle.

Of what sort was the covenant that Josiah, with the Lord's approval, made in his own and the people's name? It was "to walk after the Lord, to keep his commandments and testimonies and statutes with all his heart and soul." To these conditions all the Jews, not without oath-taking, bound their faith. Under Asa the covenant was ratified by the same laws, "was sworn to wholeheartedly with shouting, with a great voice, with the blare of the trumpet, and the sound of horns." The same oath, with Ezra and Nehemiah covenanting, was administered, in which even parents took vows for their tender children, and older brothers for those not yet grown up.

Scripture testifies that by oaths of this sort, whereby men are constrained to keep God's law, the Lord has charge over them. And no wonder, seeing that under that eternal covenant was continued what once for all, with him as Ruler, Founder, and Author, immediately after the law was promulgated, had been ratified. With therefore so many chief men of the church, with the prince of all prophets Moses, with God himself, let them dispute—these persons who allow themselves to rail with such licentious cursing against this form of the promise.

But by what right will the Lord, who by exacting the observance of his Law, was wont to promise mercy in return and the pardon of sins, be thought to have led his people into the fraud of perjury? Why will the people be charged with perjury who by binding themselves were at the same time grasping the grace offered to them? Yet were they to compare that formula of the oath written by us with the Mosaic one, in the face of condemning so many holy men, they will be forced to absolve us. For we are the mediators of the covenant which the Lord, when he promised it through Jeremiah, declares will be inviolable.

Indeed, to us has been commanded the word of reconciliation whose sum is: that Christ who knew not sin was for us made the purgation of sin that we may by the righteousness of God be in him. This is not exacted by men, that they may strive eagerly after law-righteousness, but that, deprived of their own righteousness, they may be clad with Christ's righteousness. But in our confession is contained the statement that observance of the divine law is impossible. Nevertheless, there are those who openly grumble that we have simply forced people to promise fulfillment of the law by oath. And they do not have regard for what is taught there in clear words concerning the law.

Now we turn our discourse especially to you, brethren, who have been appointed under the auspices of the Holy Spirit, to rule and pasture Christ's churches. If for the one Leader we struggle in the same army against the same enemy in a single war, let us remember to arouse ourselves in no slight degree to concord and unanimity with all these. It is surely of no slight honor that such a great leader deigned us for his ranks. Accordingly, we are most ungrateful if we do not devote ourselves wholly to him. As it usually happens, it is fitting not only in good faith to strive zealously to carry out his business, but also with both eyes to look to his command. Both are indeed very necessary. For the reason conflicts boil over exceedingly is that each man seeks himself, not Christ. Meanwhile, those who, intent on following faithfully with a zealous heart their own duties, kindle just as serious contentions, yet follow their own inclination rather than the standard of their Leader. Yet, if it is decided to judge truly, the beginning of right conduct for soldiers is this: having laid aside all obstinacy, to depend utterly on the leader's authority. For a person who in one way or another is devoted to himself is indeed zealous for himself.

But if we desire to prove our obedience to Christ our Leader, we must enter into a godly compact among ourselves and foster mutual peace, which he not only commends to his own, but also inspires in them. Why? Ought not the enemy also, the devil himself, to shoot his arrows to make us achieve reconciliation? For even if he is a beast of many heads, still we see, don't we, how he would hunch himself into a thick wedge to attack Christ's kingdom? If in the prince of hatreds, factions, schisms, this is agreement, how much more tightly is it fitting for us, who contend against him on behalf of the King of Peace, to join purposes and forces? To this end this sort of combat urges us. With what arms are we equipped against Satan's falsehoods but God's truth? When this is removed, we are left bare and unarmed. Yet as God's truth is one and consistent with itself, so will it not suffer itself thus to be withdrawn from our struggles. Finally, since we have been stationed to guard this same fortress, what do we want for ourselves when we are agitated with internal battles?

Yet if so many reasons do not affect us at all, at least let us turn our attention to what Christ proclaims: "A wound cannot be inflicted on one's servants without the master's considering it as inflicted upon himself." O, if this thought came to our mind, that there is danger lest we dash against Christ, how often are we inveigled into taking up a conflict with those in whom even one spark of piety appears? How many sprouting seeds of contentions would this thought snuff out? How much boiling anger would it extinguish? How many upspringing quarrels would it suppress?

But we ourselves, on the other hand, are also God's servants. How much more, therefore, must we see to it that we revere and cherish our Lord's insignia and ornaments wherever they appear? Thus it is right that a man for his own sake by his own right voluntarily yield and forgive much, unless by fiercely contending we wish to rend and tear apart God's gifts, by which one's own honor is unable to be kept without at the same time condoning vices inextricably bound with them. But since our fair-mindedness and moderation ought to proceed to this point, how gravely do we offend, when on account of uncertain and sometimes worthless little suspicions, we leap away from those whose piety, sincerity, and probity we know full well by the clearest proofs?

We are aware of two kinds of suspicion from which the church in the past sustained and today sustains very many evils. Either when we interpret the things done by our brethren and leaders on the left side, which if they got right and kindly judges, could be taken in the best part, or surely at least be excused. Or when we too readily incline ourselves to quaff and imbibe rumors. What evils may follow from all this we prefer to imagine rather than to experience! For that reason let us ponder how to expend every effort to avert them. Accordingly, because it is going to be for us an incredible boon, let us struggle rather in mutual goodwill and love, let us contend to provide with protection, let us both by example and exhortation call one another forth to duty.

By forms of conflicts and contentions such as these the church is not fatigued, troubled, nor afflicted; rather it grows, flourishes, and is strengthened with new increases. If there is zeal for cooperation and peace, let us urge unity of doctrine and minds rather than insist somewhat peevishly on ceremonies conforming to the letter. For it is most unworthy of us to seek a servile conformity, having passed over edification, in those whom the Lord leaves freedom in order that there might be a greater readiness to be edified. And yet when that last judgment-seat will have been reached, where once for all an account of our performance will have to be made, it will not at all be a question of ceremonies nor conformity in external matters, but the lawful use of freedom will be strictly reckoned: lawful at last will that be considered which has contributed most to edification. Therefore, let all our care, watchfulness, industry, attention press toward this edification, which we know will succeed to the degree that it advances in sober fear of God, sincere piety, and unfeigned holiness of morals.

END

CATECHISM
OR INSTITUTION OF THE CHRISTIAN RELIGION
Of the Church of Geneva previously published in the vernacular,
and now at last rendered also in Latin, by
John Calvin

1. All Men
Have Been Born for Religion

No human being can be found, however barbarous or completely savage, untouched by some awareness of religion. It is evident, consequently, that all of us have been created in order to acknowledge our Creator's majesty and to receive it and esteem it, once acknowledged, with all fear, love, and reverence.

But, leaving aside the ungodly who are bent upon one thing only—to blot out of memory the notion of God sown in their hearts—those of us who claim to be godly must deem this fleeting life, soon to fall into ruin, to be nothing but a meditation upon immortality. Now, nowhere but in God can one find eternal and immortal life. Hence the chief concern and care of our life ought to be to seek God, to aspire to him with our whole heart, and to rest nowhere else but in him.

2. The Difference between
False and True Religion

It is a matter of common agreement that without religion we live a most miserable life, not above the level of brute beasts, and consequently there is no one who wishes to appear completely alien to piety and the worship of God. Yet there is a great difference in the way men declare their religion, for the majority goes untouched by an earnest fear of God. But, whether they want to or not, they are repeatedly brought up short by this thought, that there is a divinity by whose decision they stand or fall. Consequently, struck by the notion of such great power, they venerate it after a fashion in order not to call it down upon themselves by excessive contempt.

Yet in the meantime they lead a most depraved life completely devoid of all zeal for uprightness, and display utter nonchalance in their contempt for God's judgment. Then, because they measure God not by his infinite majesty but by the foolish and stupid vanity of their own nature, they fall away from the true God. Accordingly, with however much care they afterward weary themselves over worshiping God, they get nowhere, since it is not the eternal God but the dreams and ravings of their own heart they are adoring as God. But true godliness does not consist in a fear which willingly indeed flees God's judgment, but since it cannot escape is terrified. True godliness consists rather in a sincere feeling which loves God as father as much as it fears and reverences him as Lord, embraces his righteousness, and dreads offending him worse than death. And whoever have been endowed with this godliness dare not fashion out of their own rashness any God for themselves. Rather, they seek from him the knowledge of the true God, and conceive him just as he shows and declares himself to be.

3. What We Must Know of God

Now since God's majesty in itself far outstrips the capacity of human understanding and cannot even be comprehended by it at all, it is fitting for us to adore rather than to investigate its loftiness, lest we be utterly overwhelmed by such great splendor. Accordingly, we are to search out and trace God in his works, which are called in the Scriptures "the reflection of things invisible," because they represent to us what otherwise we could not see of the Lord. This is not something that keeps our minds in suspense with vain and empty speculations, but something that is beneficent for us to know and which begets, nourishes, and strengthens perfect godliness in us, that is, faith joined with fear. For in this universe of things we contemplate the immortality of our God, from which flow the beginning and origin of everything; we contemplate his power which both framed this great mass and now sustains it; we contemplate his wisdom which composed in definite order this very great and confused variety and everlastingly governs it; we contemplate his goodness, itself the cause that these things were created and now continue to exist; we contemplate his righteousness marvelously preferring itself to defend the godly but to take vengeance of the ungodly; we contemplate his mercy which, to call us back to repentance, tolerates our iniquities with great gentleness.

From all this we ought abundantly to have been taught—as much as is sufficient for us—what God is like, but for the fact that our sluggishness was blinded by such great light. And not only do we sin out of blindness alone, but such is our perversity that in reckoning God's works, there is nothing it does not interpret badly and wrongheadedly, and it turns completely upside down the whole heavenly wisdom which clearly shines in them. Therefore, we must come to God's Word, where God is duly described to us from his works, while the works themselves are reckoned not from the depravity of our judgment but the eternal rule of truth. From this, therefore, we learn that God is for us the sole and eternal source of all life, righteousness, wisdom, power, goodness, and mercy. As all good flows, without any exception, from him, so ought all praise deservedly to return to him. And even if all these things appear most clearly in each part of heaven and earth, yet we at last comprehend their real goal, value, and true meaning for us only when we descend into ourselves and ponder in what ways the Lord reveals his life, wisdom, and power in us, and exercises toward us his righteousness, goodness, and mercy.

4. Man

Man was first formed to God's image and likeness, that in his adornments, with which he had been resplendently clothed by God, he might look up to their Author and might worship him with fitting gratitude. But since, relying on the very great excellence of his own nature, and forgetting its origin and ground, he tried to elevate himself beyond the Lord, he had to be deprived of all God's benefits on which he was stupidly priding himself, so that stripped and bare of all glory, he might recognize God whom he, rich with God's bounty, had dared despise. Therefore, all we who take our origin from Adam's seed, when God's likeness is wiped out, are born flesh from flesh. For although we consist of soul and body, we savor of nothing but flesh. Consequently, whatever way we turn our eyes, we can see nothing but what is impure, profane, and abominable to God. For man's prudence, blind and entangled in limitless errors, ever wars against God's wisdom. Our depraved will, stuffed with corrupt feelings, hates nothing more than his righteousness. Our strength, weakened for every good work, madly dashes off into wickedness.

5. Free Will

That man is enslaved to sin the Scriptures repeatedly testify. This means that his nature is so estranged from God's righteousness that he conceives, desires, and strives after nothing that is not impious, distorted, evil, or impure. For a heart deeply steeped in sin's poison can bring forth nothing but the fruits of sin. Yet we are not to suppose for that reason that man has been driven by violent necessity to sin. He transgresses out of a will utterly prone to sin. But because on account of the corruption of his feelings he utterly loathes all God's righteousness and is inflamed to every sort of wickedness, it is denied that he is endowed with the free capacity to choose good and evil which men call "free will."

6. Sin and Death

In the Scriptures sin is called both that corruption of human nature, the source of all vices, and also the origin of wicked desires and the evil deeds which come forth from these desires, such as murder, theft, adultery, and the like. We are, therefore, sinners from the womb, born all of us for God's wrath and vengeance; grown up, we subsequently heap upon ourselves a heavier judgment; at last we proceed through our whole life to death. For if there is no doubt that all iniquity is hateful to God's righteousness, what do we poor folk expect from his sight save the surest confusion, such as his indignation bears toward us who are both pressed down under a huge weight of sins and befouled with limitless dregs? This knowledge, though it strikes man with terror and overwhelms him with despair, is nevertheless necessary for us in order that, stripped of our own righteousness, cast down from confidence in our own power, deprived of all expectation of life, we may learn through the knowledge of our own poverty, misery, and disgrace to prostrate ourselves before the Lord, and by the awareness of our own wickedness, powerlessness, and ruin may give all credit for holiness, power, and salvation to him.

7. How We Are Restored
to Salvation and Life

From this knowledge of ourselves, which shows us our nothingness if it seriously lodges in our hearts, is provided a ready access also to a truer knowledge of God. Indeed, it has already opened the first door into his kingdom, when it has overthrown those two most harmful plagues of all, carefree disregard of his vengeance and false confidence in our own capacity. For we then begin to lift our eyes, formerly glued to earth, heavenward; and we who were resting secure in ourselves now long for the Lord. Although our wickedness deserved something far different, yet on account of his inexpressible kindness he, the Father of mercy, willingly offers himself to us thus afflicted and stricken. And he knows by what steps to extricate us from our weakness, and calls us back from error to the straight path, from death to life, from disaster to safety, from the devil's sway into his own kingdom. When the Lord therefore establishes this first step for all those whom he deigns to restore into the inheritance of heavenly life, in order that they, wounded with the consciousness of their own sins and wearied by their weight, may be aroused to fear him, he sets forth his law first of all for us, to exercise us in that knowledge.

8. The Law of the Lord

In God's law is given the most perfect rule of all righteousness, which is for the best of reasons to be called the Lord's everlasting will. For in its two tables has been included fully and clearly all that we need. The first table has in a few commandments set forth the worship appropriate to his majesty; the second, the duties of charity owed to one's neighbor. Let us therefore hear it, and afterward we shall see what sort of teaching we are to grasp from it as well as what fruits we are to gather.

Exodus 20
i. I am the Lord your God who led you out
of the land of Egypt from the house of bondage.
You shall not have other gods before my face.

Part of this commandment is a sort of preface to the whole Law. For while he declares himself the Lord our God, he implies that it is he who has the right to give commandments, and that his commandments are to be obeyed. As he says through his own prophet: "If I am a Father, where is love of me? If I am a Lord, where is fear of me?" At the same time he recalls his benefit in order to prove our ungratefulness, unless we pay heed to his voice. For by that kindness he once set the Jewish people free from Egyptian bondage; by the same kindness he also frees all his servants from the everlasting "Egypt" of believers, that is, from the power of sin.

His forbidding us to have other gods means that we are not to give to another than himself what belongs to God. And he adds: "before his face" in order to make clear that God wills himself to be acknowledged not only by outward confession but also to be held in truth within the depths of the heart. Now these things belong to the one God and cannot be transferred to another without sacrilege; that we are to worship him alone; we are to rely upon him with complete faithfulness and hope; whatsoever is good and holy we are to recognize as received from him; and we are to direct all praise for goodness and holiness to him.

*ii. You shall not make for yourself a graven image
or likeness, etc.*

As in the previous commandment God declares himself to be one, so
now he states what he is like and how he is to be worshiped. Therefore he
forbids us to fashion any likeness of him. In Deuteronomy 4 and in Isaiah
the reason for this is given: that spirit and body are in no way alike. Accordingly, he forbids us to honor any image for the sake of religion. Let us
therefore learn from this precept that the worship of God is spiritual, for
as he is Spirit, so he bids us worship him in spirit and in truth. Then he
adds a dreadful threat, by which he suggests how gravely he is offended
by the breaking of this commandment, I AM THE LORD GOD, etc. It is as if
he were saying that it is he alone to whom we should cleave, nor can he
bear an equal. Also he will be the vindicator of his own majesty and glory.
If anyone transfers it to graven images or to other things, that vengeance
is not to be a brief and simple one but one that is to extend to grandchil-
dren and great-grandchildren, who will obviously be imitators of their fathers' impiety. Just as lasting also does he show his mercy and kindness
to be for long generations to those who love him and keep his law. While
he commends the wideness of his mercy to us, which he extends to a thou-
sand generations, he has assigned only four generations to his vengeance.

*iii. You shall not take the name of the Lord
your God in vain.*

Here he is forbidding us to misuse his holy name in oaths, to confirm
either vain things or lies. For oaths ought not to serve either our lust or our
desire, but right necessity: when either God's glory is to be vindicated or
something is to be declared with intent to edify. He utterly forbids us to
pollute his holy name in any respect, but rather would have us use it with
reverence and the greatest dignity as befits his holiness, whether we may
be taking an oath or may be saying something about him. But since the
chief use for taking this name lies in calling upon him, let us understand
this is here commanded of us. Finally, he decrees a punishment in order
that those who have profaned the holiness of his name with perjuries and
other blasphemies may not trust they can escape his vengeance.

iv. Remember the Sabbath Day, etc.

We observe that there were three reasons for this commandment. For
the Lord willed under the repose of the seventh day to represent spiritual
rest to the people of Israel, by which believers ought to take holiday from
their own work to let the Lord work in them. Secondly, he willed that a

day be set to gather together to hear the law and carry out the ceremonies. Thirdly, he determined that a day of rest be provided for servants and for those functioning under the authority of others in order that they might have some surcease from toil. As for the first reason, there is no doubt that it ceased in Christ. For he is truth at whose presence all figures disappear. He is body at whose advent shadows are left behind. On this account Paul declares that the Sabbath was the shadow of the reality to come. The truth of this he explains elsewhere, when he teaches that we have been buried with Christ in order that through his death we may die to the corruption of our flesh. That comes to pass not in one day but throughout the course of our life, until utterly dead to ourselves, we become filled with God's life. Superstitious observance of days ought therefore to be far from Christians. But since the two latter reasons ought not to be reckoned with the old shadows but fit all ages equally, after the Sabbath was abrogated, among us it still has this place: that on set days we gather together to hear the word, to break the mystical bread, to pray publicly; secondly, that servants and workers be given surcease from their toil. Yet such is our weakness that it cannot be arranged for meetings of this sort to take place daily. Accordingly, because it was expedient to avoid superstition, the day observed by the Jews was set aside. Because it was necessary to maintain peace and order in the church, another was designated in its place. Therefore, as truth was conveyed to the Jews under a figure, so is it commended to us without shadows: first, that we might throughout life meditate on an everlasting Sabbath from our works in order that the Lord may work in us through his Spirit; secondly, that we may observe a lawfully constituted order for the hearing of the Word, the administration of the sacraments, and public prayers; thirdly, that we may not inhumanly oppress those subject to us.

v. Honor father and mother, etc.

By this commandment there is enjoined upon us piety toward parents and toward those who by the Lord's ordaining are in authority over us in the place of parents, such as magistrates. That is, we are to render to them the highest reverence, obedience, gratefulness, and whatever duties we are capable of. For it is the Lord's will that we accord mutual service to those who have brought us into this life. It makes no difference whether those to whom this honor is paid are worthy or unworthy. For of whatever sort they may be, they have been set over us as parents by the Lord, who has willed us to honor them. And this indeed is the first commandment with a promise, as Paul says, by which the Lord promises the blessing of the present life to his children who reverence with fitting observance their parents. At the same time, he hints that the most certain curse hangs over all disobedient and unyielding children. However, it should be noted in passing that we are bidden to obey our parents only in the Lord. Accordingly, we are not to be required to break the law of the Lord to please them. For in that case we are not to count as parents but rather as strangers those who try to steal us away from obedience to our true Father.

vi. You shall not kill.

By this commandment is forbidden to us all violence and injury and every sort of harm which hurts our neighbor's body. For if we recall that man was created in God's image, we ought to hold him sacrosanct, as he cannot be violated without God's image also being violated.

vii. You shall not commit adultery.

By this commandment God orders every sort of fornication and lewdness to depart from us. For the Lord has joined man and woman solely by the law of marriage. And also by his blessing he has sanctified that fellowship, initiated by his authority. Hence it is evident that any union outside of marriage[2] is accursed in his sight. Therefore, those who have not been endowed with the gift of continence, a singular gift indeed and not within the power of everyone, should betake themselves to the honorable remedy of their intemperance, marriage. For marriage is honorable among all, but the Lord will judge fornicators and adulterers.

viii. You shall not steal.

By this commandment we are forbidden to waylay one another's possessions. For the Lord wills that all robberies that plague and oppress the weak, all frauds that cheat the innocence of simple persons, be far removed from his people. Therefore, if we wish to keep our hands clean and innocent of theft, we must abstain no less from all cunning and craftiness than from violent plunder.

ix. You shall not speak false testimony, etc.

Here the Lord condemns evil-speaking and reproachful wantonness by which our brother's reputation is shattered, as well as all falsehood whereby he is hurt in any part. For if a good name is more precious than any treasures whatsoever, it is no less harmful for us to be deprived of the uprightness of our name than our possessions. But in snatching away his substance false witness is no less effective than greedy hands. Therefore, just as the hand is restrained by the previous commandment, so is the tongue by this one.

x. You shall not desire your neighbor's wife, etc.

By this commandment the Lord imposes a bridle upon all our desires which outstrip the bounds of charity. For all that the other commandments forbid us to commit in deed against the rule of love, this one prohibits from being conceived in the heart. Accordingly, by this commandment hatred, envy, and ill-will are condemned, just as much as murder previously was condemned. Lust and inner filth of heart, just as much as fornication, are forbidden. Where previously rapacity and cunning were restrained, here avarice is; where cursing, here spite is curbed.

We see how general the scope of this commandment is and how far and wide it extends. For God requires a wonderful affection and a love of the brethren of surpassing ardor, which he does not wish even by any desire to be aroused against a neighbor's possessions and advantage. This then is the sum of the commandment: we ought to be so minded as not to be tickled by any longing contrary to the law of love, and be prepared utterly freely to render to each what is his. We must reckon as belonging to each man what we owe him out of our duty.

9. The Sum of the Law

The direction in which all the commandments of the law tend, Christ our Lord sufficiently declared when he taught that the whole law was comprised under two heads: "We are to love the Lord our God with all our heart, all our soul, and all our strength. Then, we are to love our neighbor as ourselves." He took this interpretation from the law itself. For the first part is read in Deuteronomy 6; the second, in Leviticus 19.

10. What Comes to Us from the Law Alone

Here is the true pattern of a righteous and holy life and even the most perfect image of righteousness itself. If anyone expressed in his life the law of God, he would lack nothing for perfection in the Lord's sight. But to quote his own testimony, he promises to those who fulfill his law not only signal blessings of this present life which also Leviticus 26 and Deuteronomy 27 recount, but also the reward of eternal life. Conversely, he pronounces the vengeance of eternal death on all those who do not fulfill by deed the things he has commanded. Moses, also, having published the law, called heaven and earth to witness that he had set before the people good and bad, life and death.

But even if he shows the way of life, we must still see what he can provide us with by thus showing it forth. Obviously, if our whole will were to be formed and composed to obedience to the divine will, clearly knowledge of the law alone would suffice for salvation. But since our nature, carnal and corrupt, wars violently against God's spiritual law, and nothing is improved by its teaching, it remains that the law itself which had been given for salvation, if it had met with suitable hearers, would have turned into an occasion of sin and death. For since all of us are proved to be transgressors of the law, the more clearly it discloses God's righteousness, the more it unmasks on the other hand our iniquity. Conversely, the greater the transgression it holds us guilty of, at the same time the heavier the judgment to which it makes us answerable. And when the promise of eternal life has been taken away, the curse alone remains, which hangs over us from the law.

11. The Law Is a Step toward Christ

But just because the iniquity and condemnation of us all is sealed by the law's testimony, this is no reason for us to fall into despair and with despondent heart to dash to destruction. That we have indeed been condemned by the law's judgment the apostle testifies, "that every mouth may be stopped and the whole world may be subject to God." He teaches the same thing elsewhere: "God has consigned all to unbelief," not to lose them or even to let them perish, "but that he might have mercy on all." The Lord, therefore, with the faithfulness of his power and mercy consoles us, having warned us through the law both of our weakness and our impurity. And this is in his Christ, through whom he shows himself a kindly and propitious Father to us. For in the law he is recompenser of perfect righteousness alone, of which we are all destitute. On the other hand, he appears as a severe judge of crimes. But in Christ his countenance shines full of grace and kindness even toward poor and unworthy sinners. For he has given this wonderful example of his boundless love, by showing us his own Son, and in him has disclosed all the treasures of his mercy and goodness.

12. By Faith We Grasp Christ

Just as our merciful Father offers us his Son by the word of the gospel, so by faith we embrace him, and as it were recognize him given. Indeed the very word of the gospel calls us all to share in Christ; but most men, blinded and hardened by unbelief, spurn such singular grace. Therefore, Christ is enjoyed only by believers, who receive him sent to them, who do not reject him given to them, who follow him calling them.

13. Election and Predestination

Now in this difference [between believers and unbelievers] we must consider the sublime secret of the divine plan. For the seed of God's Word takes root and bears fruit only in those whom the Lord has by his eternal election predestined as his children and heirs of the kingdom of heaven; for all the rest, who were condemned by this same plan of God before the foundation of the world, the utterly clear preaching of truth can be nothing but the stench of death unto death. Now why should the Lord deem the former worthy of his mercy but exercise his severe judgment on the latter? Let us leave the cause in his hand, for he has for the best of reasons willed to hide it from us. Indeed, our sluggish intelligence cannot bear such great light nor can our slender powers grasp such great wisdom. Anyone at all who strives to lift himself to this point or refuses to restrain his own rash mind will experience how true what Solomon says is: "The investigator of majesty will be pressed back from glory." Only let us acknowledge among ourselves that this dispensation of the Lord, although hidden to us, is nonetheless just and holy. For if he were to destroy all mankind, he would only be doing so by his own right. In those he calls back from perdition one can see nothing but his supreme goodness. Let us therefore recognize the elect to be the vessels of his mercy; the reprobate the vessels of his wrath, but a just wrath indeed. From these two let us take proof and substance to proclaim his glory. On the other hand, let us not—in order to fix the assurance of our salvation (something that commonly happens with many persons)—seek to penetrate into heaven itself and to fathom what God from eternity decreed for us. Such thinking can only vex us with miserable anxiety and trouble. Rather, let us content ourselves with the testimony wherewith the Lord has amply confirmed that certainty for us. Just as all who before the foundation of the world were foreordained to life were chosen in Christ, so it is he in whom the pledge of our election is set forth to us. Accordingly, we receive and embrace him in faith. For what do we seek in election save that we may share in eternal life? Yet we obtain it in Christ who from the beginning was life and was set before us as life, that all who believe in him may not die but enjoy eternal life. But if while possessing Christ in faith, we at the same time possess life in him, we have no business investigating anything beyond this concerning God's eternal plan. For Christ is not simply the mirror wherein God's will is shown to us, but the pledge wherewith it is, so to speak, sealed.

14. What True Faith Is

Now we are to conceive the Christian faith as no bare knowledge of God or understanding of Scripture which rattles around the brain and affects the heart not at all. Such is the common view of matters of this sort confirmed to us by some rational proof or other. But it is a firm and staunch confidence of the heart by which we securely repose in God's mercy promised us through the Gospel. For it is from the substance of the promises that the definition of faith is to be sought, which so rests on that foundation that once it is removed, utterly falls or rather vanishes. Accordingly, while the Lord bestows his mercy upon us through the promise of his gospel, if we surely and unhesitatingly have confidence in the Promiser, we are said to grasp his Word by faith. And not different from this definition is that of the apostle where he teaches that it is "the substance of things hoped for, the evidence of things not seen." For Paul means a sure and secure possession of those things which have been promised by God, and an evidence of things not seen, namely, of life eternal, whose expectation we grasp by confidence in the divine goodness offered us through the Gospel. But since all God's promises are confirmed in Christ, and, so to speak, are presented and fulfilled, it is beyond a shadow of doubt that Christ himself is the everlasting object of faith, in whom we are to contemplate all the riches of divine mercy.

15. Faith, God's Gift

If we duly ponder both how much our minds are blinded to God's heavenly mysteries and with how much unfaith our hearts labor in all things, we will have no doubt that faith far surpasses all our natural powers and is an excellent and singular gift of God. For if, as Paul reasons, no one is witness to the human will save the spirit of man which is in him, what man is sure of the divine will? And if God's truth among us wavers even in those things which we at present behold with our eyes, how could it be firm and steadfast when the Lord promises such things as neither eye can see nor human understanding can grasp?

Therefore, it is perfectly clear that faith is the enlightenment of the Holy Spirit by which our minds are illumined and our hearts confirmed in a sure persuasion within, which establishes that God's truth is so sure that he cannot but supply what he has promised he will do by his Holy Word. On this account it is also called a pledge which establishes in our hearts the assurance of divine truth, and a seal whereby our hearts will be sealed unto the day of the Lord. For he it is who testifies to our spirit that God is Father to us, and we in turn are his children.

16. We Are Justified in Christ through Faith

After it becomes commonly known that Christ is the perpetual object of faith, we cannot know what we should follow through faith in any other way than if we gaze upon him. He has been given us by the Father that in him we may obtain eternal life. As he says: "This is life eternal, to know the one God the Father and him whom he has sent, Jesus Christ" (John 17:3). Likewise, "He who believes in me will never die, but if he die, he will live" (John 11:26). But in order for this to come to pass we who are sullied with the soil of sins, will have to be cleansed in him, for nothing filthy will enter God's kingdom. Accordingly, he makes us sharers in himself, that although we in ourselves are sinners, we may be adjudged righteous before God's throne. Thus stripped of our own righteousness, we are clad with Christ's righteousness; unrighteous in our own works, we are justified by faith in Christ. For we are said to be justified by faith, not because we are inwardly imbued with any righteousness, but because Christ's righteousness—just as if it were ours—is said to have been received by us, while our own iniquity is counted as nothing against us, so that (in a single word) one may call this righteousness truly "forgiveness of sins." This the apostle very clearly states when he quite often compares works-righteousness with faith-righteousness and teaches that the one is overturned by the other. Now in this way Christ has merited this righteousness for us, and we shall see in the Creed the various parts of this doctrine. In that place will be taken up individually the parts upon which our faith has been founded and now is supported.

17. Through Faith We Are Sanctified
unto Obedience to the Law

Just as Christ by his righteousness intercedes on our behalf with the Father, that with him as our sponsor we may be reckoned as righteous, so by participation in his Spirit he sanctifies to all purity and innocence. Indeed, the Spirit of the Lord rested upon him without measure, the spirit, I say, of wisdom and understanding, of counsel, of strength, of knowledge, of the fear of the Lord, that from its fullness we all may drink, and grace for grace.

They are deceived, then, who boast in their faith in Christ while utterly stripped of the sanctification of his Spirit. Scripture teaches that for us Christ was made not only righteousness but sanctification as well. Accordingly, his righteousness cannot be received by us with faith, unless we embrace at the same time that sanctification. For in the same way the Lord, because he covenants with us in Christ, promises he will be kind toward our iniquities and will engrave his law on our hearts. The observance of the law does not therefore require our capacity, but rather spiritual power whereby it comes to pass that our hearts are cleansed of their corruption and softened to the obedience of righteousness. Now Christians make a far different use of the law than those without faith can make of it. For where the Lord has engraved on our hearts the love of his righteousness, the outward teaching of law, which previously was accusing us of nothing but weakness and transgression, is now a lantern for our feet to keep us from wandering away from the straight path. It is our wisdom by which we are formed and instructed to complete uprightness. It is our discipline which does not permit us to abandon ourselves in more wicked license.

18. Repentance and Regeneration

Hence we are now ready to understand why repentance is always joined with faith in Christ, why also the Lord affirms that no one can enter into the kingdom of heaven unless he is reborn. For repentance signifies conversion, by which, having said farewell to the perversity of this world, we betake ourselves into the Lord's way. Moreover, Christ is not the minister of sin, and for that reason he does not clothe with participation in his righteousness those cleansed of the corruptions of sins in order that we may profane with new filth repeatedly his great grace, but that we, adopted as God's children, may consecrate our lives forever to our Father's glory. But this effect of repentance depends upon our regeneration, which consists of two parts: the mortification of our flesh, that is, the mortification of the corruption inborn in us, and spiritual quickening. We must press with our whole life toward this meditation, that dead to sin and to ourselves, we may live to Christ and his righteousness. And since this regeneration is never fulfilled so long as we sojourn in the prison of the mortal body, there must be an unflagging pursuit of repentance even unto death.

19. How the Righteousness of Good Works and the Righteousness of Faith Fit Together

There is no doubt that good works which proceed from such purity of conscience are acceptable to God. Since he recognizes his righteousness in them, he cannot but approve and commend them. Yet we must beware of becoming so puffed up with vain confidence as to forget we are justified by faith in Christ alone. Surely in the Lord's sight there is no works-righteousness save what corresponds to his righteousness. Therefore, one who seeks to be justified by works does not do enough by merely performing one work or another, but has need of reaching perfect obedience to the law, from which those who completely surpass all others in keeping the Lord's law are as yet very far away.

Then, even if it were possible to satisfy God's righteousness by only one good work, the Lord could not find a single work in his saints to credit with righteousness on its own merit. For even though this fact could seem incredible, it is nonetheless very true: no work at all leaves our hand accomplished with complete perfection, and unmarred by some defect. Accordingly, since we are all sinners and sprinkled with very many traces of vices, we must needs be justified outside ourselves. Namely, we always have need of Christ, by whose perfection our imperfection is covered, by whose purity our uncleanness is cleansed, by whose obedience our iniquity is wiped out, finally on account of whose righteousness, righteousness is freely imputed to us, without any reckoning of our works, which are in no way great enough for us to stand up in God's judgment. But when our spots, which otherwise could have befouled our works in God's sight, are thus covered, the Lord sees in them nothing but the highest purity and holiness. Accordingly, he honors them with preeminent names. For he both calls and regards them as acts of righteousness, and promises for them the fullest recompense. To sum up, we must conclude that fellowship with Christ has such great power because on its account we are not only freely reckoned righteous, but our works are also imputed to us as righteousness and will be recompensed with an everlasting reward.

20. The Creed

We spoke above of what we obtain in Christ through faith. Now we must hear what our faith ought to look to in Christ and to ponder how it is to be strengthened. This is explained in what is called "the Creed." That is to say, in what way Christ was by the Father for us made wisdom, redemption, life, righteousness, and sanctification. Who the author was or rather who wrote down this epitome of the faith is not of great concern to us, for it contains nothing merely human but has been assembled from very sure testimonies of Scripture. Lest anyone may be perturbed that we confess we believe in Father, Son, and Holy Spirit, we must say a few preliminary things about this matter. When we name Father, Son, and Spirit, we are not fashioning three Gods, but in the simplest unity of God and Scripture and the very experience of godliness we are showing ourselves God the Father, his Son, and Spirit. Our understanding cannot conceive of the Father without including the Son at the same time, in whom his living image shines; and the Spirit in whom his might and power are visible. Let us cleave with the total concentration of our mind upon the one God; yet in the meantime let us contemplate the Father with his Son and Spirit.

i. I believe in one God, Father Almighty,
Creator of heaven and earth.

By these words we are not simply taught to believe in God but rather to recognize him to be our God and to trust that we are among the number of those to whom he promises he will be God and whom he receives as his people. Omnipotence is attributed to him, by which is signified both that he administers all things by his providence, governs by his will, and directs by his power and hand. When he is named "Creator of heaven and earth," we are at the same time to understand that all he once created he everlastingly nourishes, sustains, and quickens.

ii. And in Jesus Christ his only Son our Lord.

Earlier we taught that Christ is the proper object of our faith. From this it readily appears that in him are represented all parts of our salvation. We call Him "Jesus," by which title he has marked himself as the heavenly oracle, for he was sent to make his people safe from sins. Consequently, the Scriptures affirm that no other name has been given to men to save them. The title "Christ" designates that he was endowed with all the graces of the Holy Spirit, which are marked in the Scriptures with the name "oil" for the reason that without them we waste away, dry and barren.

Now by this anointing he was first appointed King by the Father, to subject to himself all power in heaven and on earth, that in him we might be kings, having sway over the devil, sin, death, and hell. Then he was also consecrated priest to placate by his self-sacrifice and reconcile the Father to us, that in himself we might be priests, with him as our intercessor and mediator, offering our prayers, our thanks, ourselves, and our all to the Father. Moreover, he is called "Son of God," not as believers are, merely by adoption and grace, and consequently "only" to distinguish him from others. He is, moreover, our Lord, not only according to the divinity which he holds together with the Father from eternity, but also in that flesh in which he was set forth to us. "For there is one God, from whom are all things," says Paul, "and one Lord Jesus Christ, through whom are all things."

iii. Who was conceived of the Holy Spirit,
born of the Virgin Mary.

Here we have how he became for us the Son of God, and Jesus, that is, Savior; and Christ, that is, anointed as King, to protect us; and Priest, to reconcile us to the Father. Indeed, he put on our flesh in order that having become Son of Man he might make us sons of God with him; having received our poverty in himself, he might transfer his wealth to us; having submitted to our weakness, he might strengthen us by his power; having accepted our mortality, he might give us his immortality; having descended to earth, he might raise us to heaven.

He was born of the Virgin Mary that he might be recognized as the true son of Abraham and David, who had been promised in the Law and the Prophets; as the true man, like us in all things, save only sin, who having been tried by all our infirmities learned to bear with them. Yet that same one was conceived in the Virgin's womb by the wonderful and ineffable (to us) power of the Holy Spirit, that he might not be fouled by any physical corruption, but might be born sanctified with the highest purity.

iv. Suffered under Pontius Pilate, crucified, dead and buried,
he descended into hell.

By these words we are taught how our redemption, for the sake of which he was born a mortal man, was accomplished. For because God was provoked to wrath by man's disobedience, by Christ's own obedience he wiped out ours, showing himself obedient to his Father even unto death. And by his death he offered himself as a sacrifice to his Father, in order that his justice might once for all be appeased for all time, in order that believers might be eternally sanctified, in order that the eternal satisfaction might be fulfilled. He poured out his sacred blood in payment for our redemption, in order that God's anger, kindled against us, might be extinguished and our iniquity might be cleansed.

But there is nothing without mystery in that redemption. He suffered under Pontius Pilate, condemned indeed by the judge's sentence as a criminal and wrongdoer, in order that we might by his condemnation be absolved before the judgment seat of the highest Judge. He was crucified, that on the Cross (which had been cursed by God's law) he might bear our curse which our sins deserved. He died, that by his death he might conquer death which was threatening us, and might swallow it which was to have swallowed us. He was buried, that through his grace we might be buried to sin, freed from the sway of the devil and of death. It is said that he descended into hell. This means that he had been afflicted by God, and felt the dread and severity of divine judgment, in order to intercede with God's wrath and make satisfaction to his justice in our name, thus paying our debts and lifting our penalties, not for his own iniquity (which never existed) but for ours.

Yet it is not to be understood that the Father was ever angry toward him. For how could he be angry toward his beloved Son, "in whom he was well pleased"? Or how could he appease the Father by his intercession, if the Father regarded him as an enemy? But it is in this sense that he is said to have borne the weight of divine severity, since he was "stricken and afflicted" by God's hand, and experienced all the signs of a wrathful and avenging God, so as to be compelled to cry out in deep anguish: "My God, my God, why hast thou forsaken me?"

> *v. He arose again from the dead, ascended into heaven,*
> *sits at the Father's right hand; thence he shall come*
> *to judge the living and the dead.*

From his resurrection one may infer a sure confidence we will obtain victory over the power of death. For as he could not be held back by the pangs of death but overcame all its power, he so blunted all its darts that they cannot now prick us into destruction. Therefore, his resurrection is, first, the surest truth and substance of our coming resurrection; secondly, also of the present quickening by which we are aroused into newness of life. By his ascent into heaven he opened for us the entry into the kingdom of heaven that had been closed to all in Adam. Indeed, he entered heaven in our flesh as if in our name, that already in him we may possess heaven through hope, and hereafter may sit, so to speak, among the heavenly ones. And he is there not without our highest good, but having rather entered God's sanctuary not made with hands in accordance with the function of eternal priest, he intercedes for us as everlasting Advocate and Mediator.

The statement that "He sits at the Father's right hand" means that he has been appointed and declared King, Judge, and Lord over all, in order that by his power he may preserve and govern us; that his kingdom and glory may be our strength, power, and glorying against hell; secondly, that he has received all the gifts of the Holy Spirit to bestow them, so as by them to enrich those who believe in him. Therefore, although lifted up into heaven, he has removed his bodily presence from our sight; yet he does not refuse to be present with his believers in help and might, and to show the manifest power of his presence. This also he has promised: "Behold, I am with you even until the end of the age."

Finally, there is added that he will descend in the same visible form from heaven as he was seen to ascend, namely, on the last day, when he will appear at once to all, with the ineffable majesty of his reign, to judge the living and the dead, that is, both those still alive at that day and those who had previously been taken away by death. And he will recompense all according to their works, as each proves himself faithful or unfaithful in his works. And from this a remarkable comfort comes to us because we hear that judgment has been transferred to him whose coming could be only for our salvation.

vi. I believe in the Holy Spirit.

While we are taught to believe in the Holy Spirit, we are also enjoined to await from him what is attributed to him in the Scriptures. For Christ accomplishes whatever good there is through the power of his Spirit. Through that power he empowers and sustains all things, causes them to grow and quickens them; through it he justifies, sanctifies, and cleanses us, calls and draws us to himself, that we may attain salvation.

Therefore, the Holy Spirit, while dwelling in us in this manner, illumines us with his light in order that we may learn and plainly recognize what an enormous wealth of divine goodness we possess in Christ. He kindles our hearts with the fire of love both toward God and toward our neighbor, and day by day he boils away and burns up the vices of our inordinate desire so that if there are in us any good works, they are the fruits of his grace and his excellences. But our gifts, apart from him, are darkness of mind and perversity of heart.

vii. I believe the Holy Catholic Church,
the communion of saints.

Already we have looked at the spring where the church flows forth. At this point it is proposed that we are to believe the church with this end in view: that we may have assurance that the whole number of the elect are joined by the bond of faith into one church and society and one people of God, which Christ our Lord is Leader and Prince, and, so to speak, Head of the one body, just as in him before the foundation of the world they were all chosen to be gathered into God's kingdom.

Now this society is catholic, that is, universal, because there could not be two or three churches, but all God's elect are so united and conjoined together in Christ that as they are dependent upon one Head, they also grow together into one body, being joined and knit together as are the limbs of one body. They are made truly one since they live together in one faith, hope, and love, and in the same Spirit of God, called to the inheritance of eternal life.

It is also holy, because as many as have been chosen by God's eternal providence to be adopted into the number of the church—all these are made holy by the Lord through spiritual regeneration.

The significance of the final phrase is still to be interpreted more clearly. Namely, the communion of believers is only valid in the sense that as a particular gift is reserved for each, all are truly made sharers in it, even though by God's dispensation it has been expressly given to one, not to others. Just as the members of one body share among themselves by some sort of community, each nonetheless has his special gift and distinct ministry. For, as has been said, they are gathered and fastened together into one body. We believe the church and its communion to be holy on this condition, that, relying upon a solid faith in Christ, we too trust we are members of it.

viii. I believe forgiveness of sins.

On this foundation our salvation stands and is supported, since forgiveness of sins is the way to approach God and the means which keeps us and guards us in his kingdom. Indeed, all the righteousness of believers is contained in forgiveness of sins, which they obtain not through any merit of their own but solely by the Lord's mercy, when oppressed, afflicted, and confounded by the awareness of their own sins, they are stricken by the sense of divine judgment, become displeased with themselves, and, as it were, groan and toil under a heavy burden. And by this hatred of sin and by their own confusion they mortify their flesh and whatever derives from it. But in order that Christ may prepare for us freely given forgiveness of sins, he buys it back at the price of his own blood, in which we ought to seek the whole cleansing of, and satisfaction for, our sins. Therefore, we are taught to believe that by God's generosity, with Christ's merit interceding, forgiveness of sins and grace are provided for us who have been adopted and grafted into the body of the church. No forgiveness of sins is given either from another source, or in any other way, or to anyone else. For outside this church and communion of saints there is no salvation.

ix. I believe the resurrection of the flesh,
everlasting life.

Here we are first taught concerning the expectation of the future resurrection. It is "future" in order that the Lord may, by the same power which raised the Son from the dead, call back from dust and corruption into new life the flesh of those who were taken away by death before the final judgment day. For those who will then be found still surviving will, by a sudden change rather than by the natural form of death, pass into life. But because there will be a common resurrection of godly and ungodly together, but in a different condition, a final phrase is added to distinguish between our lot and theirs. That is to say, our resurrection will be such that the Lord will then revive us from mortality into immortality and receive us glorified both in body and in soul into blessedness which will last forever, beyond all sort of change or corruption. This will be the true and firm perfection for life, light, and righteousness, when we inseparably cleave to the Lord, who like an inexhaustible spring contains in himself the fullness of these things.

That blessedness will be the kingdom of God, crammed with all brightness, joy, power, happiness—things far removed now from human sense, and which we now see only in a glass darkly, until that day comes on which the Lord will show his glory to us to see face to face.

On the other hand, the ungodly and the reprobate, who have not sought and reverenced God with pure faith, inasmuch as they will have no part in God and his kingdom, will be cast with the devils into undying death and incorruptible corruption. Thus, outside all joy, power, and the other goods of the heavenly kingdom, condemned to eternal darkness and eternal punishment, they will be gnawed by a deathless worm and burn in an unquenchable fire.

21. What Hope Is

If faith (as we have heard) is a sure persuasion of the truth of God, a persuasion that cannot lie to us, deceive us, or vex us, then those who have grasped this assurance expect that it will straightway come to pass that God will fulfill his promises, since according to their opinion they cannot but be true. To sum up, hope is nothing else than the expectation of those things that faith believed to have been truly promised by God.

Thus faith believes God to be truthful; hope waits for him to show his truth at the right occasion. Faith believes God to be our Father; hope waits for him ever to act as such toward us. Faith believes eternal life has been given us; hope waits for it sometime to be revealed. Faith is the foundation on which hope leans; hope nourishes faith and sustains it. For as no one can expect from God anything unless he has previously believed God's promises, so on the other hand ought we by patiently hoping and waiting to sustain and cherish the weakness of our faith, lest it wearily fall.

22. Prayer

A man duly versed in true faith first readily recognizes how needy and empty of all goods he is and how all aids to salvation are lacking to him. Therefore, if he seeks resources to succor himself in his need, he must go outside himself in his need, he must go outside himself and get them elsewhere. On the other hand, he sees that the Lord willingly and freely reveals himself in his Christ, and in him opens all heavenly treasures that his whole faith may contemplate his beloved Son, his whole expectation depend upon him, and his whole hope cleave to and rest in him. It therefore remains for him to seek in him, and in prayers to ask of him, what he has learned to be in him. Otherwise, to know God as the master and bestower of all good things, who invites us to request them of him—this would be of as little profit as for a man to neglect a treasure, buried and hidden in the earth, after it had been pointed out to him.

23. What Is to Be Sought After in Prayer

Since prayer is a sort of agreement between us and God whereby we pour out before him all the desires, joys, sighs, and finally, thoughts of our hearts, we must diligently see to it, as often as we call upon the Lord, that we descend into the innermost recesses of our hearts and from that place, not from the throat and tongue, call God. Although the tongue sometimes contributes something in prayer, either to keep the mind intent by its exercise upon thinking about God, or to occupy that part of us expressly destined to proclaim God's glory, together with the heart, with meditating on the Lord's goodness—the Lord through his prophet has declared what value this has when mindlessly expressed, when he lays the gravest vengeance upon all who, estranged from him in heart, honor him with their lips. But if true prayer ought to be nothing else but a pure affection of our heart as it is about to draw near to God, we must needs forego all thought of our own glory, all notion of our own worth—in short, all confidence in ourselves, as we are admonished by the prophet: to pour out our prayers not in our own righteousness but in his great mercies, that he may answer us for his own sake, as his name has been invoked over us. Nor ought the feeling of our own misery hinder us from access to the Lord, for prayer was not ordained that we should be haughtily puffed up before God, or greatly esteem anything of our own, but by it we should confess our calamities and weep for them before him, as children intimately unburden their troubles to their parents. Rather, this sense of sin ought to be for us like a spur or goad the more to arouse us to pray.

Now there are two things that ought to impel us to seek prayer intently: the command of God bidding us to pray, and the promise assuring us we will receive whatever we ask. For those who call upon and seek him enjoy remarkable consolation because they know that by so doing they are thus rendering something acceptable to him; then, relying on his truth, they have real assurance their prayers will be heard. "Seek and it will be given you"; and Psalm 50: "Call upon me in the day of necessity; I will rescue you, and you will glorify me." There also are included briefly but beautifully two parts of prayer: invocation or petition, and thanksgiving. By the former we lay the desires of our heart before God; by the latter we recognize his benefits to us. We ought to use both constantly. For such great anxieties urge and press us from all sides that there is reason enough for all, even the holiest, continually to groan and sigh to God and to beseech him as suppliants. In short, we are well-nigh overwhelmed by so great and so plenteous an outpouring of God's benefits, by so many and mighty miracles of his, discerned wherever one looks, that we never lack occasion for praise and thanksgiving.

24. Exposition of the Lord's Prayer

Now our most kindly Father in addition warns us and urges us to seek him in every need. Yet since he saw that we did not even perceive what was fair to request, or what was profitable for us, he also provided for this ignorance of ours, and what was lacking to our capacity he supplied and made sufficient from his own resources. From this kindness of his we receive great fruit of consolation: that we know we are requesting nothing absurd, nothing strange or unseemly—in short, nothing unacceptable to him—since we are asking almost in his own words.

This form or rule of prayer consists of six petitions of which the first three have been particularly assigned to God's glory. And this alone we ought to look to in them, without consideration of "our own advantage," as they call it. The three others are concerned with the care of ourselves, and are especially assigned to those things which we should ask for our own advantage. Yet we should so pray for our own benefit as to turn our minds away from it and freely seek after the Lord's glory, the sole object of the first three petitions; on the other hand, we are allowed to ask only unto the Lord's glory that which we seek for our own advantage.

i. Our Father, who art in heaven.

First, at the very threshold one meets what we previously mentioned: all prayer ought to be offered to God by us in Christ's name, as no prayer can be commended to him in another name. For in calling God "Father" we assuredly put forth Christ's name. Since obviously no man is worthy to present himself to God and come into his sight, the Heavenly Father himself, to free us at once from this confusion (which ought to have thrown the hearts of us all into despair) has given to us his Son Jesus Christ, to be our Advocate and Mediator with him. By his guidance we may confidently come to him and with such an Intercessor, trust that nothing we ask in his name will be denied us, as nothing can be denied to him by the Father. The throne of God, also, is not only a throne of majesty, but of grace, before which in his name we dare with all confidence to appear, to receive mercy, and to find grace in timely help.

And as a rule for calling upon God has been established, and a promise given that those who call upon him shall be heard, so too we are particularly bidden to call upon him in Christ's name; and we have his promise that we shall obtain what we have asked in his name.

That he is in heaven is added. By this his unspeakable majesty (which our minds on account of their brutishness cannot conceive) has been signified, because nothing more sublime or majestic than this can come before our gaze. Accordingly, it is as if he had been said to be mighty, lofty, incomprehensible. But while we hear this, our thought must be raised higher when God is spoken of lest we dream up anything earthly or physical about him, lest we measure him by our small measure or conform his will to our emotions.

ii. First Petition: Hallowed be thy name.

The name of God is that by which he is remembered and celebrated among men for the sake of his excellences: such are his wisdom, goodness, power, righteousness, truth, mercy. Therefore, we petition that this majesty be hallowed in excellences such as these, not in God himself, to whose presence nothing can be added, nothing taken away: but that it be held holy by all, namely, be truly recognized and magnified. And whatever God does, let all his works appear glorious, as they are. If he punishes, let him be proclaimed righteous; or if he pardons, merciful; if he carries out what he has promised, truthful. In short, let there be nothing at all wherein his graven glory does not shine, and thus let praises of him resound in all hearts and on all tongues.

iii. Second Petition: Thy kingdom come.

The kingdom of God is this: by his Holy Spirit to act and to rule over his own people in order to make the riches of his goodness and mercy conspicuous in all their works. On the other hand, it is to ruin and confound the reprobate who are unwilling to be subject to his reign, and to lay low their sacrilegious arrogance, in order to make clear that there is no power which can withstand his power.

Accordingly, we pray that "God's kingdom come," that is, that the Lord may day by day add new believers to his people so that they may celebrate his glory in every way; [also] that he may pour out ever more widely upon them his rich graces, through which he may live and reign day by day more and more in them, until he completely fulfills their perfect union with himself. At the same time we pray that he will cause his light and truth to shine with ever new increases, by which to dispel, snuff out, and destroy the darkness and falsehoods of Satan and his kingdom.

While we pray in this way, that "God's kingdom come," at the same time we desire that it at last may be perfected and fulfilled, that is, in the revelation of his judgment. On that day he alone will be exalted and will be all in all, when his own folk are gathered and received into glory, but Satan's kingdom is utterly disrupted and laid low.

iv. Third Petition: Thy will be done,
as in heaven, so on earth.

By this petition we ask that just as he is wont to do in heaven, so on earth he may temper and compose all things according to his will, govern all occurrences, dispose all his creatures in accordance with his decision, and subject all wills of all beings to himself.

Indeed, as we petition this, we are renouncing all our desires, resigning and turning over to the Lord any affections that are in us, not asking solely that God void and invalidate our affections that war against his will, but rather that God create in us new minds and new hearts, having extinguished our own. We ask that no prompting of desire be felt in us, except one pure and in agreement with his will. To sum up, we ask not what we will of ourselves, but that his Spirit may will in us. While the Spirit teaches us within, let us learn to love those things which are pleasing to him, but to hate or abhor all that displeases him.

v. Fourth Petition: Give us today our daily bread.

By this petition we ask of God all things in general that our bodies have need to use under the elements of this world, not only for food and clothing, but also for everything God forsees to be beneficial to us, that we may eat our bread in peace. Briefly, by this we give ourselves over to his care and entrust ourselves to his providence that he may feed, nourish, and preserve us. For our most gracious Father does not disdain to take even our bodies under his safekeeping and guardianship in order to exercise our faith in these small matters, while we expect everything from him, even to a crumb of bread and a drop of water.

Now the fact that we say "daily," and "this day," means we are to ask only as much as is sufficient for our needs, and, as it were, from day to day. We are to do so with this certain assurance, that as our heavenly Father nourishes us today, he will not fail us tomorrow.

Consequently, however abundantly goods may flow to us, we ought always to ask for our daily bread, counting all possessions nothing except insofar as the Lord, having poured out his blessing, makes them prosper and bear fruit. And what is in our hand is not even ours except insofar as he bestows each little portion upon us hour by hour and allows us to use it.

In calling the bread "ours," God's generosity stands forth the more, for it makes ours what is by no reckoning owed to us. The fact that we ask that it be given us signifies that it is a simple and free gift of God, however it may come to us, even when it would seem to have been obtained from our own skill and diligence.

vi. Fifth Petition: Forgive us our debts,
as we forgive our debtors.

By this petition we ask that we be granted pardon and forgiveness of sins, necessary for all people without exception. We call sins "debts" because we owe penalty or payment for them to God, and we could in no way satisfy it unless we were released by this forgiveness. This free pardon comes from his mercy.

We petition that this pardon be granted, "as we forgive our debtors," namely, as we spare and pardon those who have in any way injured us, either treating us unjustly in deed or insulting us in word. This condition is not added as if by our forgiveness which we bestow on others we merit God's forgiveness. Rather, this is set forth as a sign to assure us he has granted forgiveness of sins to us just as surely as we are aware of having forgiven others, provided our hearts have been emptied and purged of all hatred, envy, and vengeance. Conversely, it is by this mark that those who are eager for revenge and slow to forgive and practice persistent enmity are expunged from the number of God's children, in order that they may not dare call upon God as Father and thus avert from themselves the displeasure they foment against others.

vii. Sixth Petition: Lead us not into temptation,
but free us from the evil one.

By this petition we do not entreat that we feel no temptation at all, for it is in our interest rather to be aroused, pricked, and urged by them the more lest, with too much inactivity, we grow sluggish—just as the Lord daily tests his elect, chastising them by disgrace, poverty, tribulation, and other sorts of affliction. Rather, this is our plea: that along with the temptation he may bring it about that we may not be vanquished or overwhelmed by any temptations, but strong and vigorous by his power we may stand fast against all hostile powers that attack us. Secondly, that received into his care and safekeeping, and sanctified by his spiritual gifts, fortified by his protection, we may stand unconquered over the devil, death, the gates of hell, and the devil's whole kingdom. We must moreover note how the Lord wills our prayers to be shaped to the rule of love, for he has determined that we are not to seek for ourselves what is expedient for us apart from concern for our brothers; but he bids us be concerned about their good just as much as about our own.

25. *Perseverance in Prayer*

Lastly, we must see to it that our intention is not to bind God to particular circumstances, as in this prayer we are taught not to make any law for him, or impose any condition upon him. For before we make any prayer for ourselves, we pray that his will be done. By these words we subject our will to his in order that, restrained as by a bridle, it may not presume to control God.

If, with minds composed to this obedience, we allow ourselves to be ruled by the laws of divine providence, we shall readily learn to persevere in prayer and, with our own desires suspended, patiently to wait for the Lord. Then we shall be sure that even though he does not appear, he is always present to us, and will in his own time declare how he has never had ears deaf to the prayers that in men's eyes he seems to have neglected.

But if finally even after long waiting our senses cannot learn the benefit received from prayer or perceive any fruit from it, still our faith will make us sure of what cannot be perceived by sense, that we have obtained what was expedient. And so he will cause us to possess abundance in poverty and comfort in affliction. For though all things fail us, yet God will never forsake us, who cannot disappoint the expectation and patience of his people. He alone will be for us in place of all things, since all good things are contained in him and he will one day fully reveal them to us.

26. *The Sacraments*

The sacraments were instituted in order that they might provide for us an exercise of our faith both before God and among men. And they indeed exercise our faith when they confirm it in God's truth. For because the Lord foresaw it to be expedient for the ignorance of our flesh, he set forth lofty and heavenly mysteries to be contemplated under physical elements. Not that such gifts have been endowed with the natures of the things set forth for us in the sacraments, but because they have by the Lord's Word been marked with this signification. For the promise always precedes, as contained in the Word; the symbol is added because it confirms and seals the promise itself and makes us more aware how the Lord provides appropriately for our slender capacity. For so scanty and weak is our faith that, unless it is propped on all sides and sustained by every means, it trembles, wavers, totters. Now it is exercised among men by the sacraments when it goes out into public confession and is aroused to render praise to God.

27. What a Sacrament Is

A sacrament is therefore an outward sign by which the Lord represents and attests to us his good will toward us in order to sustain the weakness of our faith. Or putting it more briefly and sharply: it is a testimony of God's grace, declared to us by an outward sign. The Christian Church uses only two sacraments.

28. Baptism

Baptism was given to us by God: first, to serve our faith before him; secondly, to serve our confession before men. Faith looks to the promise by which our merciful Father offers the communication of his Christ, that clothed with him we may share in all his benefits. Baptism especially represents two things: the cleansing which we get in Christ's blood; and the mortification of our flesh which we attain from his death. For the Lord commanded his own to be baptized for forgiveness of sins. And Paul teaches that the church has been sanctified by Christ her bridegroom and cleansed in the bath of water, in the Word of life. Again, he states that we have been baptized into Christ's death, buried together with him in his death, that we may walk in newness of life. These words do not signify that the cause or effective working of cleansing or regeneration inheres in the water, but only that the knowledge of such gifts is received in this sacrament when we are said to receive, obtain, get what we believe to have been given us by the Lord, whether at the time we first acknowledge it, or are more surely persuaded of it as previously acknowledged.

Thus it serves our confession among men. Indeed, it is a mark whereby we openly profess that we wish to be numbered among God's people in order to worship one God in the same religion along with all godly men. Since therefore the covenant of the Lord with us is principally ratified by baptism, we rightly baptize our infants, as sharers in the eternal covenant, by which the Lord promises he will be the God not only of us but also of our descendants.

29. The Lord's Supper

The promise added to it clearly asserts for what purpose the mystery of the Supper has been instituted and the goal to which it looks, namely, to confirm to us that the Lord's body was once for all so handed over to us, as now to be ours, and also forever to be so; that his blood was once for all poured out for us, as always to be ours. The symbols are bread and wine, under which the Lord exhibits the true communication of his body and blood—but a spiritual one which, obviously content with the bond of his Spirit, does not require an enclosed or circumscribed presence either of the flesh under the bread or of the blood under the cup. For although Christ, having ascended into heaven, ceases to reside on earth (on which we are as yet wayfarers) still no distance can prevent his power from feeding his believers on himself and bringing it about that they still enjoy ever-present communication with him, though he is absent from that place. In the Supper he furnishes us such a sure and clear proof of this matter that it should be established beyond doubt that Christ with all his riches is shown to us, just as if he, present, were set before our gaze and were touched by our hands. And this is so effective that it not only brings an undoubted assurance of eternal life to our minds, but also assures us of the immortality of our flesh. Indeed, it is now quickened by his immortality.

Accordingly, body and blood are represented under bread and wine, so that we may learn not only that they are ours, but that they are life and food for us. Thus, when we see bread consecrated in Christ's body, we must at once grasp this comparison. As bread nourishes, sustains, and keeps the life of our body, so Christ's body is the food and protection of our spiritual life. When wine is set forth as the symbol of blood, we must reflect on the benefits which wine imparts to the body, and so realize that the same are spiritually imparted to us by Christ's blood.

Now this mystery, as it is a proof of God's very great bounty toward us, ought at the same time to admonish us not to be ungrateful for such lavish kindness, but rather to proclaim it with fitting praises and to celebrate it with thanksgiving. Then we should embrace one another in that unity with which the members of this same body bound among themselves are connected. For there could be no sharper goad to arouse mutual love among us than when Christ, giving himself to us, not only invites us by his example to pledge and give ourselves to one another, but as he makes himself common to all, so also makes all one in himself.

30. The Pastors of the Church and Their Power

Since the Lord willed that both the Word and the sacraments be dispensed by human ministry, pastors had to be set over churches both to instruct the people publicly and privately in pure doctrine, to administer the sacraments and to teach them by the best example concerning holiness and purity of life. Those who reject this discipline and this order are slanderers not toward men but toward God, inasmuch as they factiously separate themselves from the society of the church, which without a ministry of this sort can in no wise stand.

Of no slight importance is the fact that the Lord testified once for all that when they are received, he is received; likewise when they are rejected, he is rejected. And in order that their ministry will not be contemptible they are equipped with a notable commandment of binding and loosing, with the promise added that whatever they have bound and loosed on earth will be bound and loosed in heaven. Christ himself elsewhere interprets "to bind" as "to retain sins"; "to loose" as to "to forgive sins." Now what the manner of loosing is the apostle explains when he teaches the gospel to be the power of God for the salvation of every believer. On the other hand, he states what the mode of binding is when he says the apostles have in their possession a ready penalty against all disobedience. Indeed, the sum of the gospel is that we slaves of sin and death are loosed and freed through the redemption which is in Christ Jesus; and those who do not receive him as Redeemer are constrained by the bonds of a new and heavier condemnation.

But let us recall that that power which is allotted to pastors in Scripture is wholly bounded by the ministry of the Word. For Christ did not explicitly give this power to men but to his Word, of which he made men ministers. Therefore, pastors may dare boldly do all things by God's Word, whose stewards they have been appointed to be. They may compel all worldly power, glory, wisdom, and loftiness to fall down and obey his majesty. Through it they are to command all from the highest even to the last. They are to build up Christ's household and cast down Satan's kingdom; to feed the sheep and slay the wolves; to teach and exhort the teachable; they are to accuse, rebuke, and subdue the rebellious and stubborn. But let them turn aside from this to their own dreams and figments of their own brains, then they are no longer to be considered to be pastors but rather as pestilential wolves to be driven out. For Christ does not command others to be heard than those who teach us what they have taken from his Word.

31. Human Traditions

We have Paul's general statement that in the churches all things are to be done decently and in order. Accordingly, civil observances, by which bonds as it were order and decorum are kept in the assembly of Christians, are by no means to be classed among human traditions, but are rather to be referred to that rule of the apostle, provided they are not believed to be necessary for salvation, or bind consciences by religion, or are related to the worship of God, or lodge piety in these things. But we are stoutly to resist those regulations which under the title of "spiritual laws" are in force to bind consciences as if necessary for the worship of God. For they not only overturn the freedom which Christ won for us but also obscure true religion and violate God's majesty, who alone wills to reign in our consciences through his Word. Let it therefore be an established principle that all things are ours, but we are Christ's. It is vain indeed to worship God where the doctrines and commandments of men are taught.

32. Excommunication

Excommunication is that act whereby open fornicators, adulterers, thieves, murderers, misers, greedy persons, wicked ones, quarrelers, gluttons, drunks, seditious ones, spendthrifts, after they have been admonished but still do not repent, are cast out according to the Lord's commandment. Not that the church casts them into everlasting ruin and despair, but condemns their life and conduct, and (unless they repent) makes them certain already of their condemnation. Now this discipline is necessary among believers for the reason that the church, since it is Christ's body, ought not to be polluted and befouled by unclean members who bring shame upon the head. Accordingly, let not the saints be corrupted by intercourse with wicked persons of this sort—a thing that commonly happens. Also it is profitable for them to be chastised for their wickedness because, if they were tolerated, they would only become more stubborn; now, confounded by shame, they learn to repent. If this is accomplished, the church kindly receives them into communion and into participation in that unity from which they had been excluded. In order that one may not obstinately reject the church's judgment or belittle the fact he has been condemned by the believers' judgment, the Lord testifies that such a judgment of the believers is nothing but the pronouncement of his own sentence, and that what they have done on earth is ratified in heaven. For they have the Word of God with which to condemn the perverse; they have the Word with which to receive the repentant one into grace.

33. Magistracy

The Lord has not only testified that the office of magistrate is approved and acceptable to him, but he also sets out its dignity with the most honorable titles and marvelously commends it to us. And indeed he affirms the work of his wisdom: "that kings reign, that counsellors decree what is just, that the judges of the earth are august." And elsewhere he calls them "gods," since they carry out his business. Also in another passage they are said to "exercise judgment for God not for man." And Paul names "ruling" among God's gifts. But when he undertakes a longer discussion of these matters, he very clearly teaches that their power is an ordination of God; further, that they are ministers of God—for those doing good, unto praise; for those doing evil, avengers unto wrath. Accordingly, it is the task of princes and magistrates to ponder who it is they are serving in their office and not to commit anything unworthy of God's ministers and vicars. Moreover, nearly all their care ought to be exerted to keep the public form of religion uncorrupted, to form the people's life by the best of laws, and publicly and privately to look after the welfare and tranquillity of their realm. But only by justice and judgment can these be obtained, two things most highly commended to them by the prophet. Justice, indeed, is to receive into safekeeping, to embrace, to protect, vindicate, and free the innocent. But judgment is to withstand the boldness of the ungodly, to repress their violence, to punish their misdeeds. In turn, the duty of subjects is not only to honor and revere their leaders, but also with their prayers to commend their safety and prosperity to the Lord, to subject themselves voluntarily to their authority, to obey willingly their edicts and constitutions; not to slip out from under the burdens imposed by them, whether these be taxes or tributes or civil duties, and anything else of this sort. Not only should we behave obediently toward those leaders who perform their office uprightly and faithfully as they ought, but also it is fitting to endure those who insolently abuse their power, until freed from their yoke by a lawful order. For as a good prince is a proof of divine beneficence for the preservation of human welfare, so a bad and wicked ruler is his whip to chastise the people's transgressions. Yet this we must hold as a universal truth: that power is given to each by God, nor can they be resisted without our resisting what God has ordained. But in obeying rulers we are always to make one exception, that such obedience is never to lead us away from obedience to him, to whose decrees the commands of all kings ought to yield.

The Lord, therefore, is the King of kings, who, when he has opened his sacred mouth, must alone be heard, before all and above all men. Next to him we are subject to those men who are in authority over us, but only in him. If they command anything against him, let it go unesteemed. But let us prefer this as our maxim: "We must obey God rather than men."

THE END

1

INTRODUCTION

I. HISTORICAL BACKGROUND

Soon after John Calvin first came to Geneva in August of 1536, he, along with Guillaume Farel who had initiated the reform movement in that city, set about to organize the church. This was Geneva's greatest need, for although Calvin's friend, Farel, and Pierre Robert, Pierre Viret, and other reformers had preached and witnessed there intermittently since 1531, the city had only formally opted for the Reformation three months earlier, in other words, in May of 1536.

Constitutionally, Geneva was now an evangelical city, and under the leadership of Farel residents were hearing fiery evangelical preaching. But the church was in a state of chaos and Farel himself recognized that he lacked the gifts to organize and direct the church. This is why, on learning of Calvin's stopover in Geneva one summer night in August, he urged Calvin to remain and become the leader of the new reformation in Geneva. In fact, he threatened the reluctant Calvin with the judgment of God if he dared decline this invitation. This is how the shy and timid young scholar from France (he was only twenty-seven years old) became "the" reformer of Geneva.

There were three things that Calvin felt were indispensable to a well-ordered church. The first was a confession of faith. It is not certain whether Calvin or Farel composed this—probably it was a joint effort—but in any case it was presented to the City Council in November of the same year (1536). It was not ratified without some difficulty, the biggest stumbling block being the insistence of the reformers that everyone sign it.

Early the next year—January 16 of 1537 to be exact—Calvin and Farel presented to the Council their "Articles Concerning the Organization of the Church and of Worship at Geneva." This encountered much more opposition, and Calvin had to compromise on several issues. One was his request for a weekly celebration of the Lord's Supper; the other was his desire to reserve ecclesiastical discipline for the church. (It was common in those days, whether in Lutheran centers of Germany or Reformed cities

39

such as Zurich and Basel, for the civil authorities to regard church discipline, including excommunication, as primarily their responsibility.)

One might think that with a confession and church constitution the task of organizing the church might be complete. For Calvin, however, a third thing was equally necessary for the faith and life of the church, and that was a brief compendium of the new evangelical faith. Calvin, like his heirs in the Reformed tradition, was convinced that faith must be undergirded and nourished by understanding, or else, after flowering briefly, it will wither and die. Calvin had already published his famous *Institutes of the Christian Religion* in Basel the previous year, but he realized that this was too long and difficult a work for most lay people and especially for youth. (This first edition of the *Institutes*, it should be kept in mind, was only a fraction of the size of the final 1559 edition that we have in English today. The first edition of 1536 had six chapters; the 1559 edition had 80!) Consequently, early in 1537 he also published his first Catechism in French under the title, *Instruction in Faith*. It was intended primarily for the instruction of the youth of Geneva.

The following year Calvin translated this Catechism into Latin so that it could reach a wider audience. He also had another purpose, namely, an ecumenical one. In his lifelong quest for the unity of the church his first approach was to share doctrinal statements—quite different from some ecumenical efforts which concentrate more on organizational unity than doctrinal unity.[1]

Calvin makes this plain in the subtitle and preface (*epistola*) to the Latin edition, which he now simply entitles *Catechism* and then adds,

> or *Institution of the Christian Religion,* accepted by the common approval of the Church of Geneva recently reborn in the gospel, and previously published in the vernacular [i.e., the French], but now also in Latin in order that the sincerity of that faith may be manifest also to other churches everywhere.[2]

Later, in his preface, he is even more explicit about the ecumenical motivation which prompted the Latin edition:

> Because we know it befits us especially that all churches embrace one another in mutual love, there is no better way to attain this than for all parties to work out an agreement and testify to it in the Lord. For there is no closer bond than this to keep minds in harmony. . . . Since we seemed to be able to attain this by no shortcut more readily than if some sure model of our doctrine—or rather catholic attestation thereof—were to stand forth publicly, we considered that this catechism . . . ought also to be published among other churches, and having been received as a guarantee, they may become more certain of our union with them.[3]

Fortunately, we now have in English translation both Battles's translation of the 1538 Latin edition and a translation of the 1537 French edition by the late Paul T. Fuhrmann, originally published by Westminster Press in 1949. The Fuhrmann translation of the French edition was out of print for about thirty years, and the Battles translation of the Latin version has never been available to the public. There was the danger that this little classic might suffer a fate similar to that of its ancient predecessor. For despite Calvin's own high estimate of its significance, soon after it was published it disappeared, and it was not rediscovered until 1877 when an original edition was found in Paris. Soon it was republished in Geneva and Germany, and later in Italy, in 1935, but for some inexplicable reason no English translation appeared until still later, more than 400 years after its original publication!

II. HISTORICAL AND
THEOLOGICAL SIGNIFICANCE

One of the reasons Calvin scholars and Reformed leaders of earlier generations may have thought it was unnecessary to bother with this first catechism was the fact that Calvin later produced another catechism (French edition 1541; Latin 1545).[4] This, the so-called Geneva Catechism, was written after Calvin's return to Geneva from his brief "exile" in Strasbourg. The reason, he indicates, is that his first Catechism was too difficult for children. Now he also uses the traditional question and answer form, whereas in his first attempt he uses a more topical approach.

Today, however, Calvin scholars are very appreciative of the first catechism and speak with great enthusiasm about its many virtues. The former dean of Calvin scholars, John T. McNeill, speaks of it as "a brilliant summation of the main teachings of the *Institutes*" (i.e., of the 1536 edition) and concludes: "The work remains a masterpiece of condensation and simplicity and is unsurpassed as a key to Calvin's teaching."[5]

Paul Fuhrmann, the translator of the French edition, is even more effusive in his praises.

> This *Instruction in Faith* is of the greatest help for the understanding of Calvin himself, for it offers the early, elemental, and positive core of his religion. With this key we now can open the early Reformed sanctuary and see its simple beauty and great power. . . . The reader will find, moreover, that the thought of this *Instruction* is clear and definite, qualities sadly needed in current Protestantism, so foggy and cold in comparison with that faith which was then an illumination of the mind and a warming of the heart.[6]

The special significance of this first Catechism for Ford Battles is its crucial place between the first (1536) and second (1539) editions of the more famous *Institutes*. The second edition represents a major breakthrough for Calvin, where he truly comes into his own as an independent theologian.

Lacking an English translation of that edition (nor is it available in the *Opera Selecta Calvini*), this is an invaluable clue to the development of the young Calvin's thought. We are most fortunate in having an annotated English translation of the 1536 edition of the *Institutes*, thanks to Ford Lewis Battles.[7]

All of this is of great interest to Calvin scholars and serious students. For lay people, however, as well as nonspecialists, this first catechism is peculiarly valuable because it provides, as Fuhrmann noted above, a brief, clear, and concise introduction to Calvin's thought for those who have neither the time nor the inclination to work through the whole of the *Institutes*. Here one does not lose sight of the forest for the trees.

Granted, something is lost in limiting oneself to such a radically reduced version of Calvin's thought. For example, here one misses such distinctive contributions as Calvin's teaching about the internal witness of the Spirit to the authority of the Word of God and his original treatment of the work of Christ as prophet, priest, and king. At the same time, one does not have to struggle through all of the polemical portions of the *Institutes*, many of which are not very edifying. In any case, the larger and more complete *Institutes* is always available (the McNeill-Battles edition is preferred) to supplement the gaps in the Catechism; and I have filled in, albeit briefly, many of those gaps in my commentary.

III. STRUCTURE AND CHARACTERISTICS

This first catechism, like the first edition of the *Institutes*, follows the basic plan of Luther's catechisms. Thus the treatment of faith (based on the Apostles' Creed) follows the section on the Law. (This order was reversed in all later editions of the *Institutes*.) Then follows a discussion of prayer and the two evangelical sacraments.

However, there are also significant differences. Calvin does not divide this catechism into five distinctive parts, as Luther did in his catechisms. More important, Calvin characteristically begins with a discussion of the knowledge of God and ends with a section on the civil magistrate. These are emphases peculiar to Calvin. It is also noteworthy that there are paragraphs devoted to such subjects as Christian hope (sec. 21), the ministry (sec. 30), and excommunication (sec. 32).

What is particularly interesting is the fact that in this earlier catechism there is a brief discussion of election and predestination (sec. 13), whereas in the later Geneva Catechism there is no explicit statement of this doctrine. The place of this treatment in the structure of the Catechism has theological significance as well, for it is not discussed theoretically in connection with the doctrine of God or creation, but is simply a discussion of the experiential fact in reference to the attitudes of believers and unbelievers.

Calvin is known particularly for two things: his systematic genius and his uncompromising, austere personality. But a careful examination of his writings, especially his commentaries, sermons, and letters, shows that this is only one side of the great reformer. He hated "frigid speculation," and always tried to show the relevance and "usefulness" of a doctrine. These key words do not occur often in the Catechism,[8] but the *Institutes* is rife with them. For example, referring to those people who in their vanity and pride seek to know God not in his self-revelation but according to "the yardstick of their own carnal stupidity," Calvin complains that it is "thus out of curiosity they fly off into empty speculations" (I.4.1). Moreover, it is not only unbelievers who are prone to do this, but the godly also. For "the rule of godliness prescribes that our readers may not, by speculating more deeply than is expedient, wander away from the simplicity of faith." The Spirit of God, on the other hand, teaches those things which edify and are profitable (I.14.3).[9]

Calvin was also a person of deep feeling and warm personal faith. He was a profoundly religious man whose piety (godliness) shines through these pages.[10] An illustration of this dynamic, personal faith is found in the closing sentence of section 1: "Hence the chief concern and care of our life ought to be to seek God, to aspire to him with our whole heart, and to rest nowhere else but in him." Or take his beautiful definition of faith in section 14: "Now we are to conceive the Christian faith as no bare knowledge of God or understanding of Scripture which rattles around the brain and does not affect the heart at all . . . but faith is firm and staunch confidence of the heart, by which we securely repose in God's mercy promised us through the gospel."[11] What these two quotations suggest—and what will become especially obvious in Calvin's discussion of faith—is that despite the Genevan reformer's obvious intellectual gifts, he was not so much a theologian of the head and the intellect as the heart and the affections. Hence it is quite fitting that the symbol of his faith was that of a burning heart.[12]

In this spirit let us read and study this little gem: not as an abstract book of doctrine but as a guide to the riches of the Christian faith. As Calvin himself put it, "The theologian's task is not to divert the ears with chatter, but to strengthen consciences by teaching things that are true, sure, and profitable" (*Inst.* I.14.4).

Thus, Calvin, the great theologian, wrote this book not to make us better theologians (although the person who really digests this little volume could qualify as a theologian!) but to deepen our understanding of the faith and thereby draw us closer to Christ, the object of our faith and the source of our salvation.[13]

2

TRUE RELIGION AND THE
KNOWLEDGE OF GOD

(Sections 1–3)

I. THE PURPOSE OF HUMAN EXISTENCE

Calvin begins his Catechism forthrightly with the fundamental question of human existence, namely, why am I here? What is the purpose of life? The answer is in the title of section 1: "All Men Have Been Born for Religion." (The title of the earlier French version reads: "All men are born in order to know *God*.") A few lines later he amplifies this thesis: "All of us have been created in order to acknowledge our Creator's majesty and to receive it and esteem it, once acknowledged, with all fear, love, and reverence" (sec. 1). This is almost repeated in the famous first question and answer of the *Westminster Larger Catechism* (1648): "What is the chief and highest end of man?" Answer: "Man's chief and highest end is to glorify God and fully to enjoy him forever."[1] Or, to return to Calvin, "The chief concern and care of our life ought to be to seek God, to aspire to him with our whole heart, and to rest nowhere else but in him" (sec. 1).[2] This, in short, is what life is all about. Apart from God life is meaningless. "For "without religion we live a most miserable life, not above the level of brute beasts" (sec. 2).

In contrast to the *Institutes,* which opens with the question of the knowledge of God and self, in the Catechism the initial focus is on the broader question of the goal of human existence, which includes not only the acknowledgment of the Creator's majesty and a life devoted to him, but also "a meditation on immortality."[3] For Calvin, this theme is inextricably bound up with the question of true religion. Recall the title of section 1, "All Men Have Been Born for Religion." Here we might well substitute the word "God" for "religion."

This leads naturally into the subject of section 2: "The difference between false and true religion." Calvin does not yet take up the matter of the knowledge of God, which is the opening theme of the *Institutes*, until section 3. In the *Institutes,* however, there is no chapter on religion, as such, but only scattered references to it.

The difference between true and false religion is "true godliness" (*pietas*) and worship of God on the one hand, and those who "untouched

44

by an earnest fear of God," adore "the dreams and ravings of their own heart," on the other (sec. 2).

Calvin takes it for granted that all people are religious in some sense, however ignorant or barbarous they may be. All people have a certain vague, confused notion of God and consciousness of his existence. For "no human being can be found, however barbarous or completely savage, untouched by some awareness (*sensu*) of religion . . ." (sec. 1).[4] Even those who reject God, "whether they want to or not, they are repeatedly brought up short by this thought, that there is a divinity (*divinitatem*) by whose decision they stand or fall." Nevertheless, "they lead a most depraved life . . . , display utter nonchalance in their contempt for God's judgment." Why? Because they measure God not by his infinite majesty but by the foolish and stupid vanity of their own nature (sec. 2). This subject is developed in chapters 3 and 4 of book I of the *Institutes*. There we read that God created humankind in his image (see Gen. 1:26, 27; James 3:9) and has planted "the seed of religion (*semen religionis*)" in all people,[5] but this image has been so mutilated and deformed by humanity's rebellion and fall that no true religion is found in the world (*Inst.* I.4.1). Nevertheless, the reason religions and idolatry flourish is because of this natural light in humanity which no one can completely extinguish (I.4.2).[6]

The difference, therefore, between true and false religion is that in false religion people seek to know God according to their own imagination and thus fashion "a dead and empty idol" (I.4.2). In true religion people "conceive him [God] just as he shows and declares himself to be" (sec. 2). That is, we must not measure God by the yardstick of our "own carnal stupidity," but rather as God offers himself to us in his Word (*Inst.* I.4.1).[7]

II. PIETY/GODLINESS:
THE BASIS OF TRUE RELIGION

Before proceeding to the next theme in the Catechism (which is the first theme in the *Institutes*, namely, the knowledge of God), it will be helpful to pay special attention to a key concept that characterizes Calvin's life of faith and permeates his whole theology, namely, *pietas*, which can be translated either as piety or godliness.[8] This word crops up in various contexts in these first two chapters. A careful reader of Calvin's writings will soon discover that "piety" and its corollaries occur again and again in a wide variety of contexts. "It could be said that *pietas* was his entire theological direction and goal, rather than merely one theme in his theology."[9]

We have hints of this already in the second section of the Catechism. It was noted above that the difference between true and false religion is that the former is characterized by genuine "piety and the worship of God," the latter by superstition and idolatry. I add "genuine" because Calvin acknowledges that all people have some form of piety and worship, but many do not truly fear (reverence) God and hence live self-centered, depraved lives.[10] To their idolatrous worship Calvin contrasts "true godliness" (or piety) which, he says,

> does not consist in a fear which willingly indeed flees God's judgment, but since it cannot escape is terrified. True godliness (*pietas*) consists rather in a sincere feeling which loves God as father as much as it fears and reverences him as Lord, embraces his righteousness, and dreads offending him worse than death (sec. 2).

In the next section on the knowledge of God he contrasts the ungodly and their "vain and empty speculations" with God's revelation "which begets, nourishes, and strengthens perfect godliness in us, that is, faith joined with fear" (sec. 3).

One more formal definition arises, this one from the *Institutes*. It comes in the context of "what it is to know God and to what purpose the knowledge of him tends" (title of chap. 2 of book I). Calvin first points out that, "properly speaking," God is not known "where there is no religion or piety" (I.2.1).[11] Then Calvin extols the majesty and mercy of God and concludes:

> For this sense of the powers of God (*virtutum Dei*) is for us a fit teacher of piety from which religion is born. I call "piety" that reverence joined with the love of God which the knowledge of his benefits induces (ibid.).[12]

From these definitions one can begin to see what Calvin means by piety/godliness. It is "reverence joined with love"; it is sometimes equated with the true worship of God; it is "a sincere feeling which loves God as Father" and "fears and reverences him as Lord"; it is the origin of and gives birth to true religion and the right knowledge of God. It is the opposite of empty and vain speculations about God and a confused knowledge of God.

But this is only the beginning; for as noted earlier, references to piety are found throughout the writings of Calvin, and they do not always fit into the above summary. On the one hand, it is something "instilled in the breasts of believers" (I.5.4). On the other, one can take "steps toward godliness," the first of which is to recognize that God is "our Father to watch over, govern, and nourish us" (II.6.1). Moreover, it is also one of the "fruits of repentance," that is, the lifelong growth in holiness. Here it is equated more with the first table of the law—the love of God—than the love of neighbor (III.3.16).[13]

However, in his discussion of the Decalogue Calvin says that "in the commandments of the law we have all the duties of piety and love." Here he refers specifically to both tables of the law—and to 1 Timothy 1:5: "The aim of the law is love from a pure conscience and an unfeigned faith"—and then concludes: "Here is true piety from which love is derived" (II.8.51).

Elsewhere piety can connote the faithful living out of pure doctrine in the context of the church (IV.1.6, 12). And in the final chapter of the *Institutes*, on civil government, piety is considered "the first concern of government," which means a concern for justice and righteousness (IV.20.9).[14] However, in other contexts Calvin can refer simply to "the doctrine of piety," as if this notion includes the whole of scriptural revelation (IV.1.5; IV.20.15).

This brief sampling of references to piety in the Catechism and the *Institutes* (and to commentaries in the notes) should give some idea of the richness and variety of Calvin's usage. At times it is the source of faith, love, reverence, and the true knowledge and worship of God. At other times, however, it is a synonym for any and all of the above. It is clearly a comprehensive term that points to something fundamental in the Christian life—so fundamental that Calvin can say, "Godliness is the beginning, middle, and end of Christian living, and where it is complete, there is nothing lacking."[15] This is probably why Calvin entitled the first Latin edition of 1536 and the first French edition of 1541 of the *Institutes* in the following way:

> Institutes of the Christian Religion
> Embracing almost the whole sum of piety and whatever is necessary to know of salvation. A work most worthy to be read by all persons zealous for piety.[16]

In the "Prefatory Address to King Francis I of France," which was appended to all the editions of the *Institutes,* Calvin states immediately why he wrote his classic: "My purpose was solely to transmit certain rudiments by which those who are touched with any zeal for religion might be shaped to true godliness (*formarentur ad veram pietatem*)."[17]

It should hardly be necessary to point out that Calvin's understanding and practice of piety has little to do with what is often unfortunately associated with "pietism." It is clearly no mystical inwardness—although there is that element in Calvin's understanding of faith—or private devotional life separated from the church and the world. "The Calvinist piety embraces all the day-by-day concerns of life, in family and neighborhood, education and culture, business and politics."[18] Thus, it is also a broader and more dynamic notion than the current understanding of "spirituality."[19] It is that—a life of devotion and communion with God—but it is obviously much more, for it is also a life of grateful service to the glory of God.[20]

III. THE KNOWLEDGE OF GOD

Calvin concludes his section in the Catechism on true religion with a sentence that forms a natural transition to section 3: "What We Must Know of God." For those who have been endowed with true godliness do not rashly fashion a god out of their own imaginations but rather "seek from him [God] the knowledge of the true God, and conceive him just as he shows and declares himself to be" (sec. 2).

A key verse for Calvin in this connection is John 4:23: "But the hour is coming and is now here, when the true worshipers will worship the Father in spirit and in truth, for the Father seeks such as these to worship him." Calvin comments: "This is a sentence worthy of being remembered, and teaches that we ought not to attempt anything in religion rashly or at random, because unless there be knowledge, it is not God we worship but a phantom or idol."[21]

There is thus for Calvin a logical and intimate linkage between authentic piety, true religion or worship, and a proper knowledge of God.

A. The mirror of God's glory in creation

What is curious about this brief section in the Catechism is that Calvin limits the knowledge of God here to the knowledge of God in the creation. He begins by asserting that since God's majesty "far outstrips the capacity of human understanding and cannot be comprehended by it at all, it is fitting for us to adore rather than to investigate its loftiness" (sec. 3). This might be taken as a call to give up on theology! And, in fact, Calvin here does not initially urge us to take up the Scriptures but rather to "search out and trace God in his works, which are called in the Scriptures 'the reflection of things invisible' [an allusion to Rom. 1:20], because they represent to us what we could otherwise not see of the Lord" (sec. 3).

Calvin is clearly thinking along the lines of the apostle Paul in Rom. 1:19–20, for he proceeds to enumerate the things we contemplate in the created order: God's immortality, power, wisdom, goodness, righteousness, and mercy;[22] although Calvin goes beyond Paul in suggesting that God's goodness, righteousness, and mercy are also revealed in the works of creation.

There is another difference between Paul's argument and Calvin's. The apostle is saying that God's "eternal power and deity" are revealed in creation and can be perceived even by those Gentiles who "by their wickedness suppress the truth" (Rom. 1:18b). The reformer, however, is saying that all the attributes of God would have been evident had it not been for the fall. For Calvin quickly adds, "From all this we *ought* abundantly to have been taught—as much as is sufficient for us—what God is like, *but for the fact* that our sluggishness was blinded by such great light" (emphasis mine). As a result of our spiritual blindness, God's good creation becomes a stone of stumbling. For "not only do we sin out of blindness alone, but such is our perversity that in reckoning God's works, there is nothing it does not interpret badly and wrongheadedly, and it turns completely upside down the whole heavenly wisdom which clearly shines in them" (sec. 3).

Calvin takes exactly the same tack in the *Institutes* but in a much more elaborate manner. What we have in section 3 of the Catechism is a description of God the Creator, which is the subject of book I of the *Institutes*.[23] There is no mention of Christ in section 3, even though its title is "What We Must Know of God." As we shall see later, Calvin will insist we cannot know God apart from Jesus Christ who is the heart, soul, purpose, and end of the Scriptures. So this is one of the oddities of Calvin's approach to the knowledge of God which, not surprisingly, has caused some consternation among Calvin interpreters.[24]

B. The failure of natural knowledge

In any case, in the *Institutes* as well, after extolling the glories of God's creation, which is "such a dazzling theater" (I.5.8)[25] and "spectacle of God's glory" (I.5.5), Calvin sadly concedes that because of the rashness, ignorance, and darkness of our fallen state, "scarcely a single person has ever been found who did not fashion for himself an idol or specter in place of God" (I.5.12). Why then bother to describe in such detail all the glories of God's creation? The answer, it appears, is that Calvin wants to remind us of the clarity and sufficiency of God's created order as a means of revelation, and the grateful response it should have evoked from the creature.[26] The source of the problem, therefore, is not on God's side but ours. God's revelation in creation was manifestly clear and sufficient for a true knowledge of the Creator. So the failure is ours, not God's.

But recall the "ought" in the crucial Catechism statement. From the revelation of God's power, goodness, righteousness, and so forth, in the creation "we ought abundantly to have been taught . . . " (sec. 3). Similarly, in an oft-quoted passage in the *Institutes*, Calvin points out that this knowledge of God the Creator is in fact only a hypothetical knowledge because of sin. Early on in the discussion he explains, "I speak only of the primal and simple knowledge to which the order of nature would have led us *if Adam had remained upright*" (I.2.1; emphasis mine).[27]

But that is precisely the problem! Adam did not remain upright, and therefore the goal of the revelation comes to nought. There is, however, a "benefit," if it may be called that, to be derived from this failed response to the revelation in creation. It renders us inexcusable. Here again Calvin is very Pauline in his thinking: "So they are without excuse" (Rom. 1:20b). "Although we lack the natural ability to mount up unto the pure and clear knowledge of God, all excuse is cut off because the fault of dullness is within us" (I.5.15).[28]

C. The spectacles of Scripture

Because of this failure to apprehend God's self-revelation in creation due to our blindness and perversity, a special remedy is required. "Therefore we must come to God's Word, where God is daily described to us from his works, while the works are not reckoned from the depravity of our judgment but the eternal rule of truth" (Catechism, sec. 3).

This is the only reference to the function of Scripture as such in the Catechism, although there are countless incidental allusions to the Word in various contexts. In the Catechism Calvin simply assumes the authority and inspiration of the Scriptures. In the *Institutes* he devotes three chapters to this subject and develops his thesis about the secret inner witness of the Spirit as the ultimate basis for believing the Scriptures are the very Word of God.[29] However, in the *Institutes* also the Scriptures are introduced at precisely the same point in the argument. That is, after spending five chapters detailing the glories of God's revelation in "the mirror of his works" (I.5.11), i.e., the creation, and humanity's failure to respond appropriately because of sin, Calvin begins the sixth chapter with the title: "Scripture Is Needed as Guide and Teacher for Anyone Who Would Come to God the Creator." [30]

Since the beauty and brightness of the created order do not bring a sinful humanity to acknowledge its Creator and Lord, "it is needful that another and better help be added to direct us to the Creator of the Universe" (I.6.1). That "better help" is God's revelation in Scripture, which Calvin likens to spectacles. In order to appreciate this analogy one must understand that Calvin's frequent references to the blindness caused by sin are not to be taken too literally. That is, we are not so blind "that we can plead ignorance," on the one hand, or that glasses (spectacles) cannot help us, on the other. Glasses are of no use to a blind person! The function, therefore, of the spectacles of Scripture is to sharpen our weak vision so that we can see what we should have seen all along, that is, God's power and majesty, goodness, and grace.

> Just as old or bleary-eyed men and those with weak vision, if you thrust before them a most beautiful volume, even if they recognize it to be some sort of writing, yet can scarcely construe two words, but with the aid of spectacles will begin to read distinctly; so Scripture, gathering up the otherwise confused knowledge of God in our minds, having dispersed our dullness, clearly shows us the true God. This, therefore, is a

special gift, where God, to instruct the church, not merely uses mute teachers but also opens his own most hallowed lips (I.6.1).[31]

Although Calvin elaborates his doctrine of Scripture in the next two chapters of the *Institutes* (I.7, 8), it is important to keep in mind that both here and in the Catechism, the initial purpose of Scripture is to assist us in seeing clearly the one true God in his creation, and to enable us to have a proper appreciation of that creation, including our original state. For now, instead of vain speculations which result in superstition and idolatry, we see what was "given at creation and how generously God continues his favor toward us, in order to know how great our natural excellence would be if only it had remained unblemished" (II.1.1).

But this is only the first step in coming to a true knowledge of God. For "even if all these things [God's righteousness, wisdom, power, etc.] appear most clearly in each part of heaven and earth, yet we at last comprehend their real goal, value, and true meaning for us only when we descend into ourselves and ponder in what ways the Lord reveals his life, wisdom, and power in us and exercises toward us his righteousness, goodness, and mercy" (Catechism, sec. 3).[32]

D. The knowledge of God and self

This last sentence in section 3 of the Catechism brings us to the famous opening sentence of the *Institutes*. This is one of the most quoted statements in all of theological literature.[33] "Nearly all the wisdom we possess, that is to say true and sound wisdom, consists of two parts: the knowledge of God and of ourselves" (I.1.1).[34]

For Calvin, this relationship is not a simple matter, for he immediately adds, "But while joined by many bonds, which one precedes and brings forth the other is not easy to discern" (ibid.) On the one hand, those who seriously examine themselves will inevitably think of God in whom we "live and move and have our being" (Acts 17:28). Calvin is also convinced that the "miserable ruin" into which we have fallen will "compel us to look upward." Hence "we cannot seriously aspire to God before we begin to become displeased with ourselves. . . . Accordingly, the knowledge of ourselves not only arouses us to seek God, but also, as it were, leads us by the hand to find him" (ibid.)

Thus far it appears that the knowledge of self precedes the knowledge of God. However, Calvin immediately turns around, so to speak, and affirms just the opposite. "It is certain that man never achieves a clear knowledge of himself unless he has first looked upon God's face and then descends from contemplating him to scrutinize himself" (I.1.2). In practice it appears that the relationship is circular, but logically the knowledge of God comes first. "However the knowledge of God and of ourselves may be mutually connected, the order of right teaching requires that we discuss the former first, then proceed afterward to treat the latter" (I.1.3).

The more important questions are what we need to know about ourselves and how this self-knowledge is acquired. Recall that in the last sentence of section 3 of the Catechism quoted above Calvin said that in order to understand the "true meaning" of God's revelation in creation we not only need the Word of God but also must "descend into ourselves and ponder" the ways in which the Lord reveals himself in us. This is repeated several times in the *Institutes* and elsewhere.[35] Generally, Calvin uses this phrase to suggest "the intense self-examination in which we are confronted by God and, at the same time, by our sinfulness."[36] It can also simply imply a more general introspection. "Nothing is better for us, when God rebukes us, than to descend into our consciences."[37]

But the conscience is not always a reliable guide; hence a more objective norm, the Word, is required if this self-examination is to be fruitful. More particularly, this self-examination must be conducted in the light of God's law; "mere comparison of ourselves with other human beings is useless, 'since a one-eyed man among the blind appears to see well, and a swarthy man among blacks considers himself white.'"[38] So the law is like a mirror in which we can see ourselves as God sees us. The result should not be despair but rather a godly humility (*Inst.* I.1.1). For "whoever is utterly cast down and overwhelmed by the awareness of his calamity, poverty, nakedness, and disgrace has thus advanced farthest in himself" (II.2.10).

Such self-knowledge is largely negative. However, for a true knowledge of God, as we saw earlier, there must be a genuine piety which includes, among other things, reverence, faith, and love (*Inst.* I.2.1). We are not called to a knowledge of God "which, content with empty speculation, merely flits on the brain, but that which will be sound and fruitful if we duly perceive it, and if it takes root in the heart" (I.5.9). Note here the contrast between the brain and the heart. This is crucial for understanding both Calvin's view of knowledge in general and above all his view of the knowledge of faith. As we shall see in more detail later,[39] though Calvin defines faith as knowledge, it is more a knowledge of the heart than the head, more of the affections than the understanding (*Inst.* III.2.8). Thus the true knowledge of God, though informed by the Word, is a personal, existential knowledge,[40] rather than an intellectual knowledge.[41]

Calvin also contrasts "the knowledge of faith which is received from the Word alone and the knowledge of experience, as we say, which depends on its effect." In this case the prophet Joel recognizes that the Israelites knew that Yahweh was their God (by the Word) but they did not really experience him as such. Hence the prophet says, "So you shall know that I am the Lord your God" (Joel 3:17a). Calvin concludes:

They certainly do not by effect feel God to be their Father. Therefore, the prophet now speaks of real knowledge [*notitia*] when he says that they shall know that they have a God. How are they to know this? Of course, by experience.[42]

One thing is still missing, however, for a complete understanding of Calvin's concept of the knowledge of God, and for this we must turn again to the *Institutes*. In I.6.2 there is a statement that particularly impressed Karl Barth,[43] namely, "All right knowledge of God is born of obedience." We cannot really know God unless we are willing to seek to do his will. "The basis of true religion," Calvin says elsewhere, "is obedience . . . God cannot be truly served unless we obey his voice."[44] The test of the reality of our knowledge of God is not how much we know *about* him, but whether we love him, for those who love him walk in his ways and keep his commandments (1 John 2:3–6). In the last analysis, "godliness (piety) and holiness of life distinguish true faith from a fictitious and dead knowledge of God."[45]

In all of this, except for references to the knowledge of faith, it should be kept in mind that in both the Catechism and the *Institutes* Calvin is deliberately limiting himself to the knowledge of God the Creator. In a sense, this is simply a formal device, for there can be no true knowledge of God apart from Jesus Christ. For "all knowledge of God without Christ is a vast abyss which immediately swallows up all our thoughts."[46] Hence a more natural and better balanced approach to the twofold knowledge of God as Creator and Redeemer is found in Calvin's famous "Argument" to his Genesis Commentary.[47] Here Calvin outdoes himself in a rhapsodical description of the glories of creation, but at the same time he maintains that we can only "contemplate the true and only God in his image," namely, Jesus Christ.[48]

3
EXCURSUS:
THE AUTHORITY OF SCRIPTURE—
THE INNER WITNESS OF THE SPIRIT

I. CONCERNING THE OMISSION IN THE CATECHISM

For some inexplicable reason Calvin does not have a separate treatment of Scripture, either in his first Catechism or in the later Geneva Catechism. This is strange, since Calvin (and the Reformed Confessions) emphasized the authority of the Bible even more than Luther (and the Lutheran Confessions). One reason may be that he assumes his readers will also read the Geneva Confession, which was written before this catechism and was appended to some editions of it. The first article of the Confession is entitled: "The Lord's Word." Then follows a simple one-sentence definition of the authority of that Word:

> First, we declare we wish to follow Scripture alone as the rule of our faith and religion, and we do not allow anything to be mixed with it conceived by human sense apart from God's Word, nor do we embrace any other doctrine for our spiritual government than what has been taken from that Word, so that nothing is to be added or taken away, as we are taught by God's prohibition.[1]

However, even if this is a valid assumption, it is still strange that Calvin does not seem to think it is necessary to state more explicitly the Reformation doctrine of *sola scriptura*. He certainly believed it and regarded it as very important. The same is true of the doctrine of predestination, which is also not treated in the Geneva Catechism. In that case, he may have felt that this doctrine was too difficult for children; but that would not be the case with the authority of Scripture.

The best explanation for this omission is probably Calvin's concern for brevity and simplicity. For his approach in the Catechism is similar to that of the *Institutes*; only in the Catechism he says in one sentence what he takes four chapters to say in the *Institutes*!

In section 3 ("What We Must Know of God") of the Catechism, Calvin begins by pointing to God's revelation in creation. In the universe we have abundant evidence of God's power, wisdom, goodness, righteousness, and mercy. All of this *should* be adequate to teach us what God is like, but because of our spiritual blindness and perversity we "turn completely upside down the whole heavenly wisdom that shines" in God's works. (Thus far the argument is the same as in the *Institutes* I.5.) At this point Calvin interjects the one statement in the Catechism that concerns the necessity of Scripture: "Therefore we must come to God's Word, where God is duly described to us from his works, while the works themselves are reckoned not from depravity of our judgment, but by the eternal rule [*regula*] of truth."[2]

This statement is amplified in chapter six (book I) of the *Institutes*, which has the title: "Scripture Is Needed as a Guide and a Teacher for Anyone Who Would Come to God the Creator." (The same would be even more true of knowing God the Redeemer!) Here, as elsewhere, Calvin shows his practical concern, that is, that we should not wander around on our own, seeking to know God by our own wisdom. Our human tendency is to want to go beyond the limits God has set for us. Hence God must "fence" us in "lest we seek some uncertain deity by devious paths" (I.6.1). For "there are very few who . . . contain themselves within bounds [and] apply themselves teachably to God's Word . . ." (I.6.2).[3]

Calvin's concern continues to be a timely one in view of the new theologies which are loath to confine themselves to the revelation of God in his Word. The history of theology is the history of ways in which theologians go beyond the bounds of the Word in seeking to be "creative" and relevant.[4] The history of religions also illustrates this truth. The rash of new sects and cults in both Japan and the United States only confirms Calvin's observation about "how great the lust [is] to fashion constantly new and artificial religions" (I.6.3).

The remedy is to "strive onward" by the "straight path" of the Word (I.6.3). Or, to change the metaphor, in order to avoid stumbling about half-blindly, we need the help of the "spectacles" of Scripture (I.6.1). "For just as eyes when dimmed with age or weakness or by some other defect, unless aided by spectacles, discern nothing distinctly; so, such is our feebleness, unless Scripture guides us in seeking God, we are immediately confused" (I.14.1).

One more point must be made before proceeding to Calvin's view of Scripture as such. That is the important notion of accommodation. God, of necessity, must communicate to us in human words, and "mean and lowly words" at that. For "if they had been adorned with more shining eloquence, the impious would scoffingly have claimed that its power is in the realm of eloquence alone" (*Inst.* I.8.1). Rather than finding this offensive or a stumbling block, Calvin sees in this humble form of Scripture its "uncultivated and almost rude simplicity," a testimony to the inherent power of the Word. As Paul reminded the Corinthians, their faith was founded "upon God's power, not upon human wisdom" and "not in persuasive words of human wisdom but in demonstration of the Spirit and of might" (1 Cor. 2:4–5). Likewise with the Scriptures, says Calvin: they derive their power and authority not from polished human eloquence but from their subject matter, which "serves as its own support" (I.8.1).

The *locus classicus* of God's accommodating himself to our capacity, as far as Scripture is concerned, is found in the *Institutes* I.13.1. Here Calvin warns against trying to "measure" God's essence and infinity "by our own senses." Since our "slow minds sink down upon earth," it is necessary for God to use anthropomorphisms, for example, for Scripture to speak of God as having a mouth, ears, eyes, and hands. But this should not lead us to think of God as having a body:

> For who even of slight intelligence does not understand that, as nurses commonly do with infants, God is wont in measure to "lisp" [*babultire*] in speaking to us? Thus such forms of speaking do not so much express clearly what God is like as accommodate the knowledge of God to our slight capacity. To do this he must descend far beneath his loftiness.

This notion of accommodation is used widely by Calvin in a variety of contexts,[5] but this one illustration should suffice to show how Calvin uses this important hermeneutical principle.[6] For Calvin, the whole history of salvation, climaxing in the incarnation, is an illustration of how the creator of heaven and earth continually condescends to accommodate himself to our limited human capacity in order that we might be redeemed and might enjoy fellowship with our Creator and Lord.

II. CALVIN'S HIGH VIEW OF SCRIPTURE

Although Calvin has no formal doctrine of the inspiration of Scripture, there is no doubt that he regarded it as the very Word of God.[7] He acknowledged the humanity of Scripture, and in his commentaries even concedes that there are minor discrepancies between writers.[8] However, at the same time he could speak of the words of Scripture as "those of God and not of men."[9] The Word of God "is absolute truth and his own living image."[10]

The authors of the Bible were "organs of the Holy Spirit."[11] The apostles "were sure and genuine scribes of the Holy Spirit" (*Inst.* IV.8.9). Hence we have in the Scriptures "heavenly doctrine" (*Inst.* I.6.2, 3), which will only have "full authority" among us when we "regard them as having sprung from heaven, as if there the living words of God were heard" (*Inst.* I.7.1). It would be difficult to find a higher view of Scripture than this unless one believed that the authors of Scripture were totally passive and simply wrote down what God dictated to them.

Calvin's main interest here again is a practical one—the concern for certainty. In order that we may have a firm, solid basis for our faith we need a "certainty, higher and stronger than any human judgment . . . " (*Inst.* I.8.1). This is why "God by his Word, rendered faith forever impervious to doubt, a faith that should be superior to all opinion" (I.6.2).

For this kind of certainty, however, not even the many inherent virtues of Scripture will suffice. "So far as human reason goes, sufficiently firm proofs are at hand to establish the credibility of Scripture" (title of book I, chap. 8), such as its antiquity, confirmed prophecies, the miracles performed by God's servants, the preservation of these ancient writings, and "the heavenly majesty" of the message of the gospel and epistles.[12] All of these qualities are important, "useful aids."[13] They provide a "wonderful confirmation" of the authority of the Bible; but note well: in and of themselves they are "not strong enough to engraft and fix the certainty of the Scripture in our minds" (*Inst.* I.8.1).

III. THE INTERNAL WITNESS OF THE SPIRIT[14]

This absolute and necessary certainty can only come directly from God himself. Consequently, *prior* to presenting all of the confirmatory arguments and "proofs" of the divine origin and authority of Scripture in chapter 8, Calvin devotes a chapter to the ultimate source of authority which will "banish all doubt" (I.7.1), namely, "the secret testimony of the Holy Spirit" (I.7.4). For "Scripture will ultimately suffice for a saving knowledge of God only when its certainty is founded upon the inward persuasion of the Holy Spirit" (I.8.13).

Thus Scripture is self-authenticating (*autopistos*). "The objective basis for the certainty of Scripture [*Schriftgewissheit*] lies in the Scripture itself, not in the judgment of an external court."[15] No amount of argumentation will ever finally convince anyone that the Bible is the Word of God. "They who strive to build up firm faith in Scripture through disputation are doing things backward" (I.7.4). Nothing less than the Spirit witnessing to our spirits can give this certainty which the Scripture deserves. For "the testimony of the Spirit is more excellent than all reason. For as God alone is a fit witness of himself in his Word, so also the Word will not find acceptance in men's hearts before it is sealed by the inward testimony of the Spirit" (I.7.4).

In view of the older portrayal—and common misunderstanding—of Calvin as simply a legal mind which excelled in argumentation, this is a surprising conclusion. One would expect far more reliance on rational proofs, which is more typical of seventeenth-century scholasticism and some contemporary conservative evangelical apologetics. Instead Calvin appeals to experience, to what today we might call existential certainty. Nowhere is this clearer than in his classic lines from I.7.5 of the *Institutes:*

Let this point therefore stand: that those whom the Holy Spirit has inwardly taught truly rest upon Scripture, and that Scripture indeed is self-authenticated; hence, it is not right to subject it to proof and reasoning. And the certainty it deserves with us, it attains by the testimony of the Spirit. For even if it wins reverence for itself by its own majesty, it seriously affects us only when it is sealed upon our hearts through the Spirit. Therefore, illumined by his power, we believe neither by our own nor by anyone else's judgment that Scripture is from God; but above human judgment we affirm with utter certainty (just as if we were gazing upon the majesty of God himself) that it has flowed to us from the very mouth of God by the ministry of men. We seek no proofs, no marks of genuineness upon which our judgment may lean; but we subject our judgment and wit to it as to a thing far beyond any guesswork! This we do, not as persons accustomed to seize upon some unknown thing, which, under closer scrutiny, displeases them, but fully conscious that we hold the unassailable truth! Nor do we do this as those miserable men who habitually bind over their minds to the thralldom of superstition; but we feel that the undoubted power of his divine majesty lives and breathes there. By this power we are drawn and inflamed, knowingly and willingly, to obey him, yet also more vitally and more effectively than by mere human willing or knowing!

IV. THE CIRCULAR ARGUMENT

Not surprisingly, questions have been raised about this approach. Those of a more rational bent, both to the right and to the left, regard this argumentation as too subjective. Those to the right of Calvin, the orthodox, do not dare to challenge the revered "father" directly; instead they subtly shift the accent in his argument. The seventeenth-century authors of the Westminster Catechism, for example, reverse Calvin's order. *First* they list the "incomprehensible excellencies of the Word whereby the Bible doth abundantly evidence itself to be the Word of God"; *then* they add at the end that "our full persuasion and assurance of the infallible truth and divine authority" of the Scripture comes from "the inward work of the Holy Spirit" (I.5).

This approach, which has been followed by some conservative Reformed theologians,[16] is a variation of Aquinas's nature and grace scheme. That is, one begins with rational arguments and appeals to the testimony of the Spirit only as a last resort. However, the opposite approach is also to be avoided if one follows Calvin, in other words, to deny any value to the so-called *motiva credibilitas* (grounds for belief) in the Scriptures. We have already seen that Niesel does this. Here—as so often—he is only following Barth, who feels it is "unfortunate" that Calvin also added these secondary arguments for the divine nature of the Bible in chapter 8 of the *Institutes*.[17]

From a liberal perspective, this appeal to the internal witness of the Holy Spirit as the ultimate ground of the authority of Scripture is the "Achilles' heel of the Protestant system" (David Friedrich Strauss). For admittedly there is no rational "objective" basis for belief in the Bible as the Word of God when one appeals to God himself, although this does not mean that by appealing to the testimony of the Spirit Calvin is thereby taking refuge in an *asylum ignorantiae* (an asylum of ignorance).[18] The argument is obviously circular: Why do we believe the Bible is the Word of God? Because God by his Spirit assures us of this truth. How does God do this? Through the Bible.

Can we avoid such circular reasoning? Not only Calvin but some of the best theological minds of our time (e.g., Herman Bavinck, Karl Barth, and Otto Weber) say "no." The only alternative is to appeal to some external authority. But to do so would leave the Bible vulnerable to all kinds of skeptical, rationalistic criticism. Here Barth agrees with Calvin: The doctrine of the internal witness of the Spirit, "at its weakest point, where it can only acknowledge and confess, has all its indestructible strength."[19]

Moreover, this approach is the one followed by Scripture itself (see John 8:13ff. and 1 John 5:6–7; cf. 1 Cor. 2:11; Rom. 8:16). "Nowhere does the Bible appeal to any external authority in order to vindicate its own authority; but it appeals directly to God himself and presents itself as the Word of God. . . . If the Bible is the Word of God it can only provide its own proof."[20]

The argument is indeed circular but it is a "logical circle."[21] Thereby we are not left to an existential subjectivism or psychological mysticism. The appeal to the Spirit cannot be separated from the Word, as Calvin takes great pains to point out in chapter 9 of the *Institutes*. "For by a kind of mutual bond the Lord has joined together the certainty [Note the key word again!] of his Word and of his Spirit so that the perfect religion of the Word may abide in our minds where the Spirit, who causes us to contemplate God's face, shines; and that we in turn may embrace the Spirit with no fear of being deceived when we embrace him in his own image, namely, in the Word" (I.9.3).[22]

Thus the subjective and objective coalesce. As Otto Weber points out, what appears to be "objective" (the Bible), is "by its very essence also 'subjective'" (the persuasion of its divine origin). The testimony of the Spirit encounters us in the testimony of the biblical witnesses and thereby the "polarity of object and subject is overcome."[23] The result is (now in Calvin's words) "a conviction that requires no reasons, a knowledge with which the best reason agrees—in which the mind truly reposes more securely and constantly than in any reasons . . ." (*Inst.* I.7.5). Thus this doctrine of the internal testimony of the Spirit

> announces the discovery that the authority of Scripture can be secured neither objectively (in the sense of the classical doctrine of inspiration) nor subjectively (in the sense of our own experience), but rather that we will only be persuaded of it when God the Holy Spirit, God in his freedom as the One who effects both our freedom and our bondage, reaches out to us through the scriptural Word. The *theopneustia* of Scripture is not a passive characteristic of Scripture but rather a vital saving activity.[24]

This should not be taken to mean that Scripture does not possess an intrinsic authority apart from the witness of the Spirit to the believer. That is, the Spirit does not impart authority to the Scripture but rather confirms in our hearts the authority that it already possesses.

> The *testimonium* is not the proof of the divinity of Scripture. It is not the *ground* of the authority of Scripture. The Scriptures are *autopistic*, that is, they are in themselves the Word of God. . . . The *testimonium* enlightens the eyes of the mind to see this divinity. . . .[25]

The point of Calvin's argument in the *Institutes* is "not only to prepare our hearts to receive it [the authority of Scripture] with reverence but to remove every doubt" (I.7.1). The role of the Spirit in this process is to seal on our hearts the truth of God as revealed in the Scriptures.[26] That truth is objectively there, but "it remains mute in its witness . . . without the internal testimony of the Spirit."[27] Hence the cruciality of this important notion of the internal witness of the Spirit as developed by Calvin.

4
OUR PLIGHT APART FROM GOD
(Sections 4–7)

I. THE EFFECTS OF THE FALL

Calvin is famous for his pessimistic view of human nature and its possibilities. However, the doctrine of total depravity, as such, is not so characteristic of Calvin as of later Calvinism.[1] (This doctrine is one of the so-called five points of Calvinism which were enunciated at the Synod of Dordt in the Netherlands in 1619.) Calvin in some ways was not as negative about human nature as Luther, for example, in his attitude toward reason.[2] This is partially due to Calvin's humanist background, for Calvin had read widely in writers such as Cicero and Seneca as well as the Greek philosophers.[3]

In the Catechism, however, the impact of humanism is not apparent. Here the portrayal of fallen humanity is pretty bleak. In section 4 ("Man") Calvin exhibits a very negative attitude about natural capabilities in the spiritual realm. As a result of their sin and rebellion, humans have been "stripped of all of God's gifts"[4] and "savor nothing but flesh" (sec. 4).[5] This affects not only their intellect and will but also their physical strength, which is vitiated and corrupted. "Consequently, whatever way we turn our eyes, we can see nothing but what is impure, profane, and abominable to God" (ibid.). To use scriptural terminology, by nature we are "slaves of sin" and under its dominion (Rom. 6:12–22).[6] Thus, the human heart, "deeply steeped in sin's poison can bring forth nothing but the fruits of sin" (sec. 5).[7]

II. A BASIC DISTINCTION

In the Catechism Calvin stops at this point and does not take up a discussion of human capabilities in the realm of the arts and sciences. In the *Institutes*, however, Calvin distinguishes between human knowledge and achievements in the realm of "earthly things" in contrast to human ability in the realm of "heavenly things" (II.2.13).[8] In the latter realm, unaided human capabilities are nil. As far as spiritual insight is concerned, even the "greatest geniuses are blinder than moles!" (II.2.18). Without the help of God's Spirit we are "utterly blind and stupid in divine matters" (II.2.19).[9] But this is only one side of the picture. Calvin takes a much more positive view of natural capabilities in what we today would call the cultural or secular realms. Despite the fall, human beings still possess a degree of conscience, common sense, natural instinct, reason, sense of justice, equity, and political order as well as general ability in government, household management, mechanical skills, and the liberal arts (II.2.13).[10] The fact that "some seed of political order has been implanted in all men . . . is ample proof that in the arrangement [constitutione] of this life no man is without the light of reason" (ibid.). This is what later Dutch Calvinists were to call the realm of common grace.[11] Therefore, it is quite false to assert that Calvin "completely rejected the humanist concern with earthly excellence. . . ."[12]

Calvin's aim, however, in recognizing sinful humanity's accomplishments and abilities is not to give them any ground for pride or self-confidence. In this respect he differs from the spirit of the Renaissance and most humanists, who felt that people are capable of raising themselves by their own bootstraps. Calvin, rather, wishes to give God the glory for his infinite mercy and kindness in allowing fallen humanity to retain this remnant of the gifts that God originally bestowed on Adam and Eve. Our attitude, therefore, should not be one of pride but of humble gratitude (II.2.15).[13] Were it not for the grace of God, we, by our rebellion and fall, would have been no better than brute animals (II.2.17).

Calvin, on the other hand, warns against what is popularly regarded as a Puritan or pietistic rejection of the world, its wisdom, and its accomplishments.[14] The achievements of pagan or secular philosophers, poets, and artists show us that "the mind of man, though fallen and perverted from its wholeness, is nevertheless clothed and ornamented with God's excellent gifts. If we regard the Spirit of God as the sole fountain of truth, we shall neither reject the truth itself, nor despise it wherever it shall appear, unless we wish to dishonor the Spirit of God" (II.2.15). This is a most remarkable statement, revealing an openness and breadth of spirit which has been ignored by many later Calvinists[15] and is not familiar to most of Calvin's detractors.

III. THE IMAGE OF GOD LOST?[16]

One statement in section 4 of the Catechism could leave a mistaken impression, namely, that the image of God in fallen humanity is totally lost. Calvin begins the section with a reference to "God's image and likeness," which for him are basically the same.[17] "Man was first formed to God's image and likeness, that in his adornments, with which he had been re-splendently clothed by God, he might look up to their Author and might worship him with fitting gratitude" (sec. 4). Here Calvin does not elaborate concerning those "adornments" with which we were "clothed by God." But he discusses this question at some length in the *Institutes*. In short, despite certain distinctive "outward marks" (*externis notis*), the image of God is basically spiritual. "For although God's glory shines forth in the outer man, yet there is no doubt that the proper seat of his image is in the soul" (*Inst.* I.15.3).[18]

The nature of that image or likeness of God

> extends to the whole excellence by which man's nature towers over all the kinds of living creatures. Accordingly, the integrity with which Adam was endowed is expressed by this word, when he had full possession of right understanding, when he had his affections kept within the bounds of reason, all his senses tempered in right order, and he truly referred his excellence to exceptional gifts bestowed upon him by his maker (ibid.).

This is a rather flowery, sophisticated description of the original image. Elsewhere, in reference to Ephesians 4:24, Calvin can simply say that "Adam was at first created in the image of God so that he might reflect, as in a mirror, the righteousness of God."[19] As a result of differing descriptions of the image, Calvin scholars debate about whether the image consists in reason and will, which are natural gifts, or true worship and piety, which are supernatural gifts.[20] It would appear that it consists of both.

In any case, in the Catechism Calvin gives the impression that the image is totally lost. Without any qualifications he simply says, "God's likeness is wiped out" (sec. 4).[21] In other places Calvin gives the same impression, although one must note in each case the context and precise wording. Is Calvin speaking of the "supernatural gifts"—faith, love, and righteousness—or the more natural gifts of reason, the will, and understanding—which are essential characteristics of being human, whether sinful or not? On the negative side of the ledger, note the following: Due to the fall, "the heavenly image was obliterated [*obliterata*] in him [man]" (*Inst.* II.1.5). After Adam's fall and the loss of our "primal worthiness," the virtues of humility and a zeal for meditation on the future life, which are characteristics of the image of God, are "utterly and completely lost" (*Inst.* II.1.1). Adam, "by falling from the Lord, in himself he corrupted, vitiated, depraved, and ruined our nature—having lost the image of God [*abdicatus a Dei similitudine*]."[22] The image of God, "*having been wiped out by sin*, must now be restored in Christ" (emphasis added).[23]

All of this seems to point to one conclusion: because of sin the image of God has been effaced, obliterated, wiped out, and completely lost. But there are other places where Calvin moderates such extreme statements—and sometimes in the same context. In the *Institutes*, for example, in his principal discussion of the image (I.15.3–4), he uses a "more discreet formula."[24]

> Even though we grant that God's image was *not totally annihilated and destroyed* in him [Adam], yet it was so corrupted that whatever remains is frightful deformity. . . . Now God's image is the perfect excellence of human nature which shone in Adam before his defection, but was subsequently so *vitiated and almost blotted out* that nothing remains after the ruin except what is confused, mutilated, and disease-ridden (I.15.4, emphasis added).

Similar distinctions and qualifications are found in other writings of Calvin's. In his commentary on Daniel 2:22, for example, he writes:

> God's goodness is conspicuous, not only in the ordinary prudence of mankind—for no one is so made as to be unable to discern between justice and injustice, and to form some plan for regulating his life—but in prophets there is something extraordinary, which render God's wisdom more surprising.

Moreover, we are gifted with "a small portion of common sense"; otherwise "we should be like stocks or stones." We are also "adorned with ordinary foresight, enabling us to discern between good and evil." This is true even "at the ordinary level of human nature [*communem naturam*]." However, believers are additionally "so enlightened that we can understand things far exceeding our [natural] capacities."[25]

An especially illuminating passage is found in Calvin's treatise against the Libertines. Here the particular subject is the soul, but Calvin's comments speak directly to the issue of whether the image of God is lost, and if not, in what sense it remains despite the fall.

> As for man, the Scripture clearly teaches us that from the time he turned away from God his soul has been full of ignorance and vanity, full of perversity and rebellion against God, given over to evil, oppressed and vanquished by weakness. Nevertheless it continues to call him a creature of God, possessing in himself those natural conditions which God placed in him, unless all of it is corrupted and depraved by sin.

> Consequently, according to Scripture, man's soul is a spiritual substance endowed with sense and reason, in order to understand and pass judgments, and endowed also with will, in order to choose and desire those things that his life wants.[26]

> True, the Scripture immediately admonishes us that our intelligence is perverted because of sin—so much so that we are blind and that our will is corrupt, even to such an extent that only iniquity flows out of it. Nev-

ertheless the soul continues to exist in its essence and to retain the inseparable qualities of its nature, according to the order that God has established.[27]

The loss is thus not total, although the image in fallen humanity is so vitiated and corrupted that not much good remains. However, recall that key distinction discussed earlier between "natural man's" abilities in the realm of "earthly things" as over against the realm of "heavenly things" (*Inst.* II.2.13). In the latter realm "the greatest geniuses are blinder than moles" (II.2.18), for "man's keenness of mind is mere blindness as far as the knowledge of God is concerned" (II.2.19). But in the realm of "earthly things," there remain in all people, despite the fall, "some remaining traces of the image of God, which distinguish the entire human race from other creatures" (II.2.17). These "traces" are not insignificant, for they include "a universal apprehension of reason and understanding" that are "by nature implanted in men," along with other gifts and abilities in the realm of the arts and sciences.[28]

Moreover, despite Calvin's frequent negative references to philosophers, in this context—the discussion of sin!—along with the pagan poets and classical writers such as Cicero, the reformer readily concedes that these "natural men" (see 1 Cor. 2:14) "were indeed sharp and penetrating in their investigation of inferior things. Let us accordingly"—Calvin immediately adds—"learn by their example how many gifts the Lord left to human nature even after it was despoiled of human good" (II.2.15).

Although some Calvin scholars, notably Richard Stauffer, maintain that it is impossible to resolve these apparent contradictions because of their incoherence,[29] it is possible to make some sense of the apparently conflicting statements cited above. Calvin himself provides several clues. One is his distinction between natural and supernatural gifts. He quotes with approval a medieval saying: "The natural gifts in man were corrupted, but the supernatural taken away" (*Inst.* II.2.4).[30] One can go further, for quite apart from the various gifts with which humankind has been endowed, whether natural or supernatural, there is also something inherent in being a human being created in the image of God that makes each person worthy of respect. For example, various callings and abilities of people are signs of their being created in God's image. So "we see in this diversity some remaining traces of the image of God, which distinguish the entire human race from other creatures" (*Inst.* II.2.17). Moreover, although the soul is the peculiar seat of the various gifts that make human beings special, their physical form also reflects in some sense the image and likeness of God.[31] Here Reinhold Niebuhr is more perceptive than some Calvin specialists, for he sees that "Calvin defines the image of God in terms of both a unique structure of human nature and of an original and now lost perfection of character."[32] What is missing here, however, is that the true nature of the image cannot be understood apart from its restoration in Christ, a point we shall make shortly.

That the image of God is an indelible feature in all of humanity is confirmed in Calvin's interpretation of the command to love one's neighbor. Here he shows a remarkable breadth of outlook. In discussing the second great commandment—"love your neighbor as yourself"—Calvin concedes that the greater part of humanity "are most unworthy if they be judged by their own merit." However, Calvin believes that "Scripture teaches us that we are not to consider what men merit of themselves but to look upon the image of God in all men, to which we owe all honor and love" (*Inst.* III.7.6). Granted, this image is "more carefully to be noted among members of the household of faith (Gal. 6:10) insofar as it has been renewed and restored through the Spirit of Christ," but that does not warrant thinking of anyone, "He is a stranger," or that "he is contemptible and worthless," for "the Lord shows him to be one to whom he has deigned to give the beauty of his image" (ibid.).

Then Calvin concludes this section with a similar sentiment expressed even more eloquently:

> Assuredly there is but one way in which to achieve what is not merely difficult but utterly against human nature: to love those who hate us, to repay their evil deeds with benefits, to return blessings for reproaches [Matt. 5:44]. It is that we remember not to consider men's evil intention but to look upon the image of God in them, which cancels and effaces their transgressions, and with its beauty and dignity allures us to love and embrace them.

In his commentary on Genesis 9:6 Calvin makes a similar comment, but with a crucial qualification that provides us with a valuable clue for resolving Calvin's apparently contradictory views regarding the image of God.

> Men are indeed unworthy of God's care, if respect be had only to themselves; but since they bear the image of God engraven on them, he deems himself violated in their person. Thus, although they have nothing of their own by which they obtain the favour of God, he looks upon his own gifts in them, and is thereby excited to love and to care for them. This doctrine, however, is to be carefully observed, that no one can be injurious to his brother without wounding God himself. . . . *Should any one object, that this divine image has been obliterated, the solution is easy; first, there yet exists some remnant of it, so that man is possessed of no small dignity; and secondly, the Celestial Creator himself, however corrupted man may be, still keeps in view the end of his original creation;* and according to his example, we ought to consider for what end he created men, and what excellence he has bestowed upon them above the rest of living beings (emphasis added).[33]

In addition to the remark that even in sinful humanity, there still "exists some remnant of it," there is a critical contrast between sinful human beings "if respect be had only to themselves," and the fact that despite our corruption, God "still keeps in view the end of his original creation." This contrast suggests a way out of the dilemma. On the one hand, in and of ourselves we are totally corrupt, totally alienated from God, and therefore totally deprived of the image of God. From this standpoint it is appropriate to speak of the image being obliterated and lost. It is not merely defaced and despoiled, despite the remnants of the image which remain.

However, in view of the original purpose of our creation and our very humanity which distinguishes us from all other creatures, we should view all human beings, whatever their condition, as created in the image of God.[34] People are not sticks and stones, nor are they beasts,[35] for they possess immortal souls which give them their preeminent place in the created order.[36] However, the essence of the image is not so much substantial as relational,[37] for "Calvin is intent on following the biblical story and vocabulary by portraying created man as 'in communion with God' and fallen man as 'alienated from God.'"[38] But even in our alienation and fallenness we still bear not only the imprint of our origin and the potential of our future but also the fact that we are still uniquely related to God and have a "dignity" and an "excellence" which distinguishes us from all the rest of creation. To be human is to bear the image of God, even though in one sense it can be said to be defaced and obliterated.[39]

No discussion of the *imago dei* is complete, however, without noting that the true image of God is seen not in Adam and Eve prior to their fall but in Jesus Christ; for God "cannot be known except in Christ, his lively image."[40]Even in commenting on Genesis 1:26—"in our image and in our likeness"—Calvin acknowledges the truth of the saying that "the image of God was only shadowed forth in man until he should arrive at his perfection," although he does not believe that "anything of the kind entered the mind of Moses." He also concedes that "it is also truly said that Christ is the only image of the Father," but again Calvin adds that this should not be read into this Genesis text.[41]

However, Calvin does not hesitate to see this truth in Ephesians 4:24: "and put on the new nature created after the likeness of God in true righteousness and holiness" (RSV).

> Adam was at first created in the image of God, so that he might reflect, as in a mirror[42] the righteousness of God. But that image, having been wiped out by sin, must now be restored in Christ. The regeneration of the godly is indeed, as is said in 2 Corinthians 3:18, nothing else than the reformation of the image of God in them. But there is a far more rich and powerful grace of God in this second creation than the first.[43]

This is similar to what Calvin says in the *Institutes* I.15.4, although here he grants that "God's image was not totally destroyed in him [Adam]." Nevertheless, "the beginning of our recovery of salvation is in that restoration which we obtain through Christ. . . ." Also here, as in his commentary, Calvin sees a "richer measure of grace in regeneration" than in our original creation, the end of which is "that Christ should reform us to God's image."

The true image, therefore, is more clearly seen in Christ than in Adam, even in his pristine state. Believers as well are only in the process of having that original image restored, which ultimately will be not only a restoration but also an enhancement of that original image. For "whatever excellence was engraved upon Adam derived from the fact that he approached the glory of his Creator through the only-begotten Son." "Even then," that is, in the very beginning, "Christ was the image of God" (*Inst.* II.12.6).

> And all of us, with unveiled faces, seeing the glory of the Lord as though reflected in a mirror, are being transformed into the same image from one degree of glory to another; for this comes from the Lord, the Spirit (2 Cor. 3:18).[44]

IV. THE WILL, BOUND OR FREE?

The next section (sec. 5), entitled "Free Will," is the shortest in the whole Catechism. Yet it deals with one of the most debated questions in the history of theology.[45] Even the young Calvin was no doubt aware of two famous controversies concerning the bondage/freedom of the will prior to his time, the one between Augustine and Pelagius and his followers at the turn of the fourth century,[46] the other between Luther and Erasmus.[47]

Although there are differences in the way Augustine, Luther, and Calvin deal with this issue, all agree on one fundamental issue: the sinful will is an enslaved will and is free only to choose evil until assisted by the grace of God. Calvin leaves no doubt that this will be his conclusion (despite his title, "Free Will") in his opening sentences, which portray sinful existence in the darkest of colors:

> That man is enslaved to sin the Scriptures repeatedly testify. This means that his nature is so estranged from God's righteousness, that he conceives, desires, and strives after nothing that is not impious, distorted, evil, or impure. For a heart deeply steeped in sin's poison can bring forth nothing but the fruits of sin.

The conclusion, as I have suggested, is quite predictable. Sinful humanity is not "endowed with the free capacity to choose good and evil which men call 'free will'" (ibid.). However, note that between his opening statements which set the stage for this conclusion and the last line where free will is simply denied, Calvin makes a crucial distinction. Even though all human beings are enmeshed in sin since the fall, it should not be concluded that they therefore sin out of necessity and hence cannot be held accountable for their sinful acts. Despite the fact that by nature we are so "deeply steeped in sin's poison" that our hearts "can bring forth nothing but the fruits of sin," Calvin quickly adds, "we are not to suppose for that reason that man has been driven by violent necessity to sin." Rather, "he transgresses out of a will utterly prone to sin" (ibid.).

This may appear to be a subtle scholastic distinction of little practical significance, but for Calvin—and all those who hold to the view of the bondage of the will, from Augustine to Jonathan Edwards and beyond—this is extremely important. For to be human is to be responsible, to be free and not driven by external forces over which one has no control. Hence this issue of necessity is so crucial to the whole debate.

Earlier a passage was quoted in which Calvin referred to this issue in passing. Here he clarifies, to some extent, his statement in the Catechism that we are *not* "driven by violent necessity [*violenta necessitate coactu*] to sin." In reference to Romans 7:14 ("I am carnal, sold under sin")[48] Calvin comments:

> We are so completely driven by the power of sin, that our whole mind, our whole heart, and all our actions are inclined to sin. Compulsion I always exclude, for we sin of our own free will. It would not be sin if it were not voluntary. We are, however, so addicted to sin, that we can do nothing of our own accord but sin. The wickedness which holds sway within us drives us to it. This comparison does not therefore mean, as is said, a forced restraint, but a voluntary obedience, to which an inborn bondage inclines us.[49]

On the one hand, we are "so addicted to sin that we can do nothing of our own accord but sin." On the other hand, we are not compelled to sin, for "we sin of our own free will." In reference to Romans 7:15 ("I do not do what I want, but I do the very thing I hate"), Calvin puts the matter a little differently. "Since carnal man rushes into the lust of sinning with the whole inclination of his mind, he appears to be sinning with as free a choice as if it were in his power to govern himself." And a little later in the same commentary: "It has, therefore, been well said that the carnal man plunges into sin with the consent and concurrence of whole soul. . . ."[50]

How can such statements be reconciled? For this we must turn to the *Institutes*, although there are no simple answers to this complex question. The title of book II, chapter 2, however, leaves no doubt as to Calvin's fundamental position: "Man Has Now Been Deprived of Freedom of Choice and Bound Over to Miserable Servitude." He begins his discussion by affirming that "man" was originally endowed with freedom to choose the good. For "God provided man's soul with a mind by which to distinguish good from evil, right from wrong; and, with the light of reason as a guide, to distinguish what should be followed from what should be avoided" (I.15.8). Thus in his original integrity, "man by free will had the power, if he so willed, to attain eternal life." Adam, accordingly, "could have stood if he wished, seeing that he fell solely by his own will" (ibid.).

The rest, as they say, is history. Adam lacked "the constancy to persevere" and "fell so easily" (I.15.8). As a result, the will is free only to choose evil. At this juncture Calvin bemoans the fact that not only the philosophers but also the early church fathers did not see clearly the impact of the fall on the will. Later medieval theologians and scholastics professed allegiance to Augustine in this regard, but they too went astray.[51] However, Calvin does accept a scholastic distinction concerning three kinds of freedom: freedom from necessity, freedom from sin, and freedom from misery. The first "so inheres in man by nature that it cannot be taken away, but the other two have been lost through sin." But here, again, Calvin makes the distinction he had made in the Catechism. He adds, "I willingly accept this distinction except insofar as necessity is confused with compulsion" (II.2.5).

Here Calvin is thinking particularly of Peter Lombard (d. 1160), whose *Sentences* were still the standard textbook for Roman Catholic theology. Lombard believed that we have free will, although he conceded that we are not equally capable of choosing good or evil. But our will is free, according to Lombard, insofar as we are freed from compulsion.[52] Calvin agrees with the point that we do not sin by compulsion, but he objects to Lombard's failure to see that by nature we inevitably will to sin and do so by necessity. Worse, Lombard still insists that our will is free. To this Calvin scornfully retorts: "Well put indeed, but what purpose is served by labeling with a proud name such a slight thing? A noble freedom, indeed—for man not to be forced to sin, yet to be such a willing slave that his will is bound by the fetters of sin!" (II.2.7).[53]

Obviously, for Calvin, "free will" is a dirty word. He will countenance no compromises on this score. At the same time, he is sensitive to the charge that to deny human freedom implies a determinism that undercuts moral responsibility. One person in particular who challenged Calvin on this issue was the Dutch Catholic theologian Albert Pighius (d. 1542). In response to Pighius's attack that he (Calvin) was irrational, among other things, Calvin is willing to allow for the term free will, *if properly understood:*

> If one speaks of liberty in opposition to coercion [*coactio*], I confess and constantly affirm that the will is free and regard as a heretic anyone who

thinks otherwise. If, I repeat, one calls it free in the sense that the will is not coerced [*coagatur*] or drawn violently by some external motion, but acts of its own accord [*sponte agatur sua*], I have no objection.[54]

But Pighius went beyond Lombard and took a basically Pelagian position that "man has good and evil in his own power, such that of his own capacity [*virtus*] he can choose the one or the other."[55] As a result, Calvin preferred to drop the term.

The key distinction is between necessity and compulsion, a distinction he also makes in the *Institutes* (II.3.5).[56] Those who cannot distinguish between the two are bound to misunderstand his position, avers Calvin.

> The chief point of this distinction, then, must be that man, as he was corrupted by the Fall, sinned willingly, not unwillingly or by compulsion; by the most eager inclination of his heart, not by forced compulsion; by the prompting of his own lust, not by compulsion from without. Yet so depraved is his nature that he can be moved or impelled only to evil. But if this is true, then it is clearly expressed that man is surely subject to the necessity of sinning (II.3.5).

In short, "man sins with his will, not against his will; through inclination, not compulsion; through desire, not through external compulsion."[57] Or, in the words of Reinhold Niebuhr, the sinful self sins inevitably but bears responsibility.[58] Niebuhr's view of original sin is not the same as Calvin's; nor is Calvin's approach as dialectical as Niebuhr's, but there is a certain affinity in their views. The following is an illustration of this:

> The Christian doctrine of original sin with its seemingly contradictory assertions about the inevitability of sin and man's responsibility for sin is a dialectical truth which does justice to the fact that man's self-love and self-centredness is inevitable, but not in such a way as to fit into the category of natural necessity. It is within and by his freedom that man sins. The final paradox is that the discovery of the inevitability of sin is man's highest assertion of freedom.[59]

In the last analysis, did Calvin allow for the freedom of the will in any meaningful sense? The answer depends on how one defines the term. As we have seen, Calvin rejects the term if it is used to suggest that we are free to do good or evil in the moral realm. When it comes to the decisions of daily life, however, Calvin had no hesitation about affirming our freedom. There is no trace of fatalism or determinism in any of his writings.

In more recent discussions of this question, a distinction is sometimes made between psychological and moral freedom. It is clear that Calvin rejects the latter, but it might be said that he affirms the former, at least in the realm of general activities. Berkouwer, however, is convinced that Calvin's sharp rejection of Lombard's position rules that out. At the same time, Berkouwer maintains that for Calvin (and the New Testament) it is proper to speak of true human freedom, but only as it is restored in Christ—and then not perfectly in this life.

Hendrikus Berkhof distinguishes between "psychological observation," where he says it is proper to "stress man's free will and responsibility," and "personal confession," which is the way the Reformers handled this question. "For them the philosophical conception of free will was self-evident, but they considered it a minor truth. Confronted with God, man does not confess his free will, but his complete abuse of it."[60]

John Leith makes a distinction similar to that made by Calvin concerning the ability of fallen humanity in regard to the realm of heavenly things as over against the realm of "earthly things" (*Inst.* II.2.13). That is, when Calvin speaks of the loss of the freedom of the will, "a close reading indicates that he only denies freedom of the will as the power of choice in certain particular situations in which the self is deeply involved and in particular with the self's relationship to God." However, as we saw earlier, in the realm of the arts, social, and political life "Calvin is enthusiastic about the accomplishments of fallen man. . . ."[61]

The British Calvin scholar Tony Lane concludes one portion of his essay "Did Calvin Believe in Freewill?" in the following way:

> To answer the question is to presuppose that the term has a clearly agreed meaning. This is not so. The answer must be that Calvin did believe in freewill in one sense (which he clearly defined) and did not believe in it in another sense (which he equally clearly defined). It is for the reader to decide for himself whether or not this accords with his own understanding of "freewill."[62]

However one answers this question, it is important to keep in mind that this issue, along with closely related ones such as original sin and predestination, is ultimately about the grace and glory of God. If that grace is undercut by some form of cooperation (synergism) between a semiautonomous "free" human being and the sovereign Lord, the glory of God is compromised, as far as Calvin is concerned.[63] This, for him, was one of the fundamental differences between the sixteenth-century Reformation and late medieval Roman Catholicism. Hence he calls Roman compromises here "evasions with which Satan has attempted to obscure God's grace." Calvin grants that "they hold with us that human beings, as corrupt, cannot move even a finger to perform some duty for God," but then they err in two respects. They hold that both the mind and the will have some wholeness even in regard to God, and they teach that "the grace of the Holy Spirit is not effective without the agreement or cooperation of our free choice." The result: "they leave people suspended in midair when they deal with the grace of the Holy Spirit."[64]

Today this "question of the ages" is no longer a major issue between

Protestants and Catholics, although on a confessional level certain sticky points remain. Rather, it is a universal problem that divides Protestants among themselves as much as or more than Protestants and Catholics. Today we might want to state the issue in different terms, for we have learned much about human behavior and have gained new biblical insights since the sixteenth century. Still the basic issue remains: Wherein lies the beginning and end of our salvation, and who deserves the glory? Calvin's answer will find acceptance in many Christian circles, that is, God.

V. THE KNOWLEDGE
THAT LEADS TO SALVATION

The next two sections[65] can be dealt with more briefly. They appear to be only indirectly related, for section 6 is on "Sin and Death," and section 7 is entitled, "How We Are Restored to Salvation and Life." What they have in common, however, is that in both cases it is a knowledge of our sin and our desperate plight which prepare us for the reception of God's grace and mercy revealed in Jesus Christ.

Because of the corruption of human nature, apart from God's grace in Christ and the aid of the Spirit, we continually "heap upon ourselves a heavier judgment." Each day brings us closer to death, which means the end of all human dreams and aspirations (sec. 6). In the words of Heidegger, there is always a cloud over human existence because it is "an existence unto death" (*Sein zum Tode*). Or, to use Kierkegaard's terminology, we suffer from a "sickness unto death."

But we will never come to this realization by ourselves. As Calvin points out again and again, true knowledge of self is impossible apart from knowledge of God. Calvin focuses, however, in these two sections on the first part of that equation. We must be aware not only of our mortality, which is the end result of our sinfulness, but must also be conscious of God's wrath against our sins to the extent that we feel "pressed down under a huge weight of sins" (sec. 7).

> This knowledge, though it strikes man with terror and overwhelms him with despair, is nevertheless necessary for us in order that stripped of our own righteousness, cast down from confidence in our own power, deprived of all expectation of life, we may learn through the knowledge of our own poverty, misery, and disgrace to prostrate ourselves before the Lord, and by the awareness of our own wickedness, powerlessness, and ruin may give all credit for holiness, power, and salvation to him (sec. 6).

Calvin has made his point! Knowledge of self should produce a profound consciousness of sin and unworthiness. But this is all prolegomena, in a sense, to set the stage for the real point Calvin wants to make, that is, that such knowledge is a preparation for bringing us to a knowledge of God. "From this knowledge of ourselves, which shows us our nothing-ness, if it seriously lodges in our hearts, provides ready access also to a truer knowledge of God" (sec. 7).[66]

In the Catechism, however, Calvin does not specify how we obtain this knowledge. Nor does he explain how it is that this self-knowledge does not simply leave us in despair. He only adds the qualification, "if it [this knowledge] seriously lodges in our hearts."[67] Elsewhere, however, he ob-serves that an awareness of "the wretched condition of our nature" can "produce a double state of mind." On the one hand, it "can produce noth-ing but dread, weariness, anxiety, and despair." On the other hand, "it is truly to our advantage that we should be completely laid low and bruised that we may at last cry to him [God]." For "this dread, which is conceived from self-examination, does not prevent our minds from relying on his goodness."[68]

Calvin makes similar statements in the *Institutes*,[69] but here too he seems to assume that this knowledge of our misery will vanquish our pride and thereby move us to seek help from God. As we shall see shortly, such knowledge of self and of God is possible only through a knowledge of the Word and the assistance of the Holy Spirit. But in most of Calvin's writings he seems to take these factors for granted. In any case, this knowl-edge of self which leads to "a truer knowledge of God" opens "the first door into his [God's] kingdom, when it has overcome those two most harmful plagues of all, carefree disregard of his vengeance and false con-fidence in our own capacity" (sec. 7).

Note that this knowledge is only "the *first* door."[70] Calvin also speaks of "steps" by which the Lord "extricates us from our weakness, and calls us back from error to the straight path, from death to life, from disaster to safety, from the devil's sway into his own kingdom." But whereas "the first step (*primum gradum*) for all those whom he [the Lord] deigns to re-store into the inheritance of heavenly life" is to be "exercised" in the knowledge of the law (sec. 7), the "first door" in that process is a proper humility. In the Catechism Calvin speaks of the barriers ("two most harm-ful plagues") to our being restored to God as disregard of God's ven-geance and a false self-confidence; but in the *Institutes* and elsewhere he combines these two barriers in one positive virtue: humility.

"A saying of Chrysostom's has always pleased me very much," writes Calvin, namely, "that the foundation of our philosophy is humility." Then, creating a variation on a statement of Augustine's, he adds: "If you ask me concerning the precepts of the Christian religion, first, second, third, and always I would answer, 'humility'" (*Inst.* II.2.11). For humility is "the sovereign virtue . . . , the root and mother of all virtue."[71] And this virtue of humility is inseparably related to a true knowledge of self. From an awareness of our poverty and misery "we shall learn humility" and at the same time be compelled "to look upward," that is, look to God for help.[72] An awareness of "our own ills" should prompt us "to contemplate the good things of God"; but "we cannot seriously aspire to him before we begin to become displeased with ourselves" (*Inst.* I.1.1). At that point in our self-discovery, however, we will "then lift our eyes, formerly glued to earth, heavenward; and we who were resting secure in ourselves now long for the Lord" (Catechism, sec. 7).

Yet we will never come to this realization or longing by ourselves. As Calvin characteristically stresses, true knowledge of self is impossible apart from God. And God cannot be known apart from special revelation and the grace of the Spirit.[73] Only those people "who scrutinize and examine themselves according to the standard of divine judgment" will come to this knowledge of self and of God's will (*Inst.* II.1.3). The whole of Scripture serves this purpose, but it is "the standard (*norma*) of the written law" which plays a special role in this connection.[74] Confronted by the mirror of God's law, we learn not only "how far we are from conforming to God's will," but also that we are totally unable to fulfill the demands of the law (*Inst.* II.8.3).

> Thus it finally comes to pass that man, thoroughly frightened by the awareness of eternal death, which he sees as justly threatening him because of his own unrighteousness, betakes himself to God's mercy alone, as the only haven of safety. Thus, realizing that he does not possess the ability to pay to the law what he owes, and despairing in himself, he is moved to seek and await help from another quarter (ibid.).[75]

That "quarter" is the Father of mercy, "who does not deal with us as we deserve," but "on account of his inexpressible kindness . . . offers himself to us thus afflicted and stricken" (Catechism, sec. 7).

5

THE LAW OF GOD
AND THE SHAPE OF THE CHRISTIAN LIFE
(Sections 8–11, 17)

The law is peculiarly suited to perform this function because in it we are confronted with "the most perfect rule [*regula*] of all righteousness, which is for the best of reasons to be called the Lord's everlasting will" (sec. 8). Calvin's high regard for the law is demonstrated in a later section (sec. 10) when he describes it as "the true pattern [*exemplar*] of a righteous and holy life, and even the most perfect image of righteousness itself." The law of God is not only a divinely given rule or standard by which to measure our lives; it also "shows the way of life" and true righteousness. But alas! due to our sin none of us can fulfill the demands of the law. Hence, at this stage, the law performs primarily a negative role. It "unmasks our iniquity," catches us in "greater transgression," and thus judges us deserving of a "heavier judgment" from God (sec. 10). All that remains is a curse and death.[1]

I. THE USES OF THE LAW[2]

Thus it happens that God's good law which is holy, just, and spiritual becomes the occasion for our death (see Romans 7:5–14).[3] However, this negative function is only a means by which the Lord, "having warned us through the law both of our weakness and impurity," consoles us "with the faithfulness of his power and mercy" (sec. 11; this section is repeated almost verbatim in the *Institutes* II.7.8). Paradoxical though it may seem, by means of the punitive function of the law God is able to perform his saving work in us. For nothing less than the demands of the law will help us realize the futility of satisfying God with our own righteousness. We must be stripped of every defense, every excuse. Only then will we, "naked and empty-handed, flee to his mercy, repose entirely in it, hide deep within it, and seize upon it alone for righteousness and merit" (*Inst.* II.7.8). Calvin quotes Augustine to the same effect: "The law was given for this purpose: to make you, being great, little; to show that you do not have in yourself the strength to attain righteousness, and for you, thus helpless, unworthy and destitute, to flee to grace" (II.7.9).

Here the law only indirectly works to our benefit. For those who refuse to repent and seek God's mercy in faith, the law continues to play an accusing, condemning role. For the Christian, however, who is freed from the curse of the law (see Rom. 6:14; 7:4; and Gal. 3:13), the law is still relevant. For it proves useful in two ways: (1) it continues to instruct us concerning God's will for our lives, and (2) it serves as an instrument of exhortation that spurs us on to obey God and forsake evil. Calvin calls this "the third and principal use which pertains more closely to the proper use of the law" (*Inst.* II.7.12). In the Catechism Calvin does not teach the so-called threefold use or function of the law. The first use—to make us aware of our sinfulness and need of a savior—is described above and in the *Institutes* II.7.6–9. The second function is called the political or civil use and is also described in the *Institutes* II.7.10, 11. Even in the Catechism, however, Calvin approaches the third use of the law when he writes just before his exposition of the Ten Commandments, "Let us therefore hear it [the Law], and afterward we shall see what sort of teaching we are to grasp from it as well as what fruits we are to gather" (sec. 8).

II. THE TEN COMMANDMENTS

But how, concretely, can we know what the will of God is? Both the Old and New Testaments are full of commandments and prohibitions, exhortations and warnings. How then can we say simply: "This is God's will for my life; this is the divine standard"? The answer for Calvin—and also Luther—is that fortunately God has given us an orderly summary of the law in the Ten Commandments. Moreover, the Ten Commandments can be further divided into two tables, namely, the requirements to love God (commandments 1–4) and to love our neighbor (commandments 5–10).[4] This division of the law into two parts is based on the traditional identification of the two "tables of stone" (Ex. 24:12; 2 Cor. 3:3) with the two great commandments to love God and neighbor (Matt. 22:35–40; Jesus here is simply quoting Deut. 6:5 and Lev. 19:18). These two great commandments, Calvin adds, point out "the direction in which all the commandments of the law tend" (Catechism, sec. 9). "First our soul should be entirely filled with the love of God. From this will flow directly the love of neighbor" (*Inst.* II.8.51).[5]

It is extremely interesting that although Luther usually equated the law with works-righteousness as opposed to the righteousness of faith and hence had a basically negative view of the law, his esteem for the Decalogue (Ten Commandments) was at least as high as Calvin's. He devotes much space to it in his Catechisms and often preached on it. In the preface to his Large Catechism he tells us that "Every morning and whenever else I have time, I read and recite word for word the Lord's Prayer, the Ten Commandments, the Creed, the Psalms, etc." Again, later in the same preface, "This much is certain: anyone who knows the Ten Commandments perfectly knows the entire Scriptures. . . . What is the whole Psalter but meditations based on the First Commandment?" Then, at the conclusion of his exposition of the individual commandments he writes,

> Here, then, we have the Ten Commandments, a summary of divine teaching on what we are to do to make our whole life pleasing to God. They are the true fountain from which all good works must spring, the true channel through which all good works must flow. Apart from these Ten Commandments no deed, no conduct, can be good or pleasing to God, no matter how great or precious it may be in the eyes of the world.[6]

I quote these passages at length for two reasons: First, because the difference between Calvin and Luther regarding their view of the relation of law and gospel has been greatly overstated by certain Lutheran scholars who insist that Luther did not teach the third use of the law. There is a significant difference in their overall approach, but it has been magnified by many Lutheran theologians.[7] Second, this respect for God's law as expressed in the Ten Commandments is conspicuously absent in most churches in the United States. In Europe, however, most children are taught the Ten Commandments, and sermons are often preached on them.

The reasons for this neglect are not hard to find: the fear of legalism, the influence of certain types of fundamentalism and liberalism, a superficial understanding of the apostle Paul's negative remarks about the law, the failure to see the Decalogue in the context of the covenant of grace, and so on. But note well! Neither Calvin nor Luther would have us interpret the Ten Commandments literally and legalistically. In order to understand Calvin's treatment of the law in his Catechism (sec. 8), it is necessary to examine the three rules of interpretation that he sets forth in the *Institutes* II.8.6–11.

First, the law is spiritual (Rom. 7:14); therefore, its commands must be spiritually understood and interpreted. That is, the commandments require not so much external behavior as "inward and spiritual righteousness." God is a "spiritual lawgiver" and is therefore "concerned not so much with outward appearance as with purity of heart" (II.8.6). Here Calvin maintains he is only following the example of Christ who is the law's "best interpreter" (II.8.7).

Second, the commandments are largely negative and of necessity limited in their expression of God's will. Therefore, we must try to discover God's intention in each commandment and then interpret it positively. The implications and consequences of this affirmation are extremely significant. For Calvin interprets the various commandments in the light of the New Testament. Accordingly, he eschews a literalistic interpretation of the commandments—"He who would confine his understanding of the law within the narrowness of the words deserves to be laughed at" (II.8.8)—and looks for the positive implications of each of the negative commands. This is what Karl Barth does in his treatment of the commandments in the *Church Dogmatics*.[8] The command "Thou shalt not kill," for example, is treated under the headings "Respect for Life" and "The Protection of Life" (cf. the *Institutes* II.8.9).

Third, the Ten Commandments are to be considered from the perspective of the two great commandments, which direct us to the honor and fear and love of God on the one hand, and to love and service to our neighbor on the other. In short, the law thus comprehends the whole of life, both in our vertical and horizontal relationships (II.8.11, 12). Note that what Calvin is doing here in each of these three rules of interpretation is to see the Decalogue through the eyes of Jesus Christ. Not only does he conclude his exposition of the Decalogue with a discussion of the principles of the law in the light of Christ's teaching (both in his *Commentary on the Last Four Books of Moses* and in the *Institutes* II.8.51–59), but his whole treatment of the Decalogue is suffused with the spirit of the Sermon on the Mount. Hence this is not, as is often alleged, an "Old Testament religion," a legalistic approach to the Scripture, but just the opposite. As Calvin emphasizes over and over again, Christ is the heart and soul, the life and spirit, the purpose, end, and fulfillment of the law.[9] Therefore, if the law—and the Bible as a whole—is interpreted in isolation from Christ, it is grossly misunderstood and perverted (II.7.1, 2).

Hence, although there is no separate treatment of the Sermon on the Mount (nor is there in most contemporary dogmatics), chapter 8 (the exposition of the Ten Commandments) is in effect a treatment of many of the themes in the Sermon on the Mount. (There are, in fact, numerous references to Matthew 5 in particular in this chapter of the *Institutes*. See especially II.8.7, 26, 57, 59.) Thus it is quite unjust to declare that "Unlike Jesus, he [Calvin] conceived of the will of God in terms of biblical literalism and set up a legalistic moral code."[10] And it is equally far off the mark to assert that his "whole outlook on life is tinctured with the spirit of Moses rather than Christ...."[11] It would be far more fitting to make the opposite complaint, namely, that Calvin has so Christianized the law[12] that the norm of the Christian life is not so much the Ten Commandments as the teaching of Jesus! Calvin, in any case, would acknowledge no such polarization as law over against Christ, or the Ten Commandments over against the Sermon on the Mount. As Paul Lehmann observes, "Indeed, on the basis of an inner meaning of the law, the Reformers were right in seeing an intrinsic parallelism between the Sermon on the Mount and the Decalogue."[13]

It is not possible here to discuss Calvin's interpretation of all of the commandments. A fuller discussion is given by Calvin himself—in the Geneva Catechism, Questions 136–216, and in the *Institutes* II.8.13–50. But three points deserve special mention. Note, for example, the importance for Calvin of the preface to the Ten Commandments in Exodus 20:2, 3 (Catechism, sec. 8). The significance of this is that the law must be interpreted in the light of God's great redemptive act (the deliverance from Egypt) which preceded its promulgation. Thus, the phrase "I am the Lord your God who brought you out of the land of Egypt, out of the house of bondage" (Ex. 20:2) is "a sort of preface to the whole law." Calvin sees here a twofold basis for obeying these commandments; first, because God is the Lord who has the right to give commandments and require our obedience; but more importantly, because he is also a gracious Father who has redeemed his people and thus deserves their gratitude. "For by that kindness he once set the Jewish people free from Jewish bondage; by the same kindness he also frees all his servants from the everlasting 'Egypt' of believers, that is, from the power of sin" (ibid.).[14]

Law and grace are not antithetical. Just the opposite, for the law is not first of all a demand but a gift of grace! Abstract the law, however, from its proper context of the covenant of grace, and it withers into bare, moralistic precepts.

Calvin's interpretation of the Sabbath commandment is particularly interesting. In the Reformed tradition this commandment has often been legalistically applied to Sunday behavior with some unfortunate consequences. This is not Calvin's fault, however. For him even more important than having a special day for rest and worship is the spiritual, symbolic significance of the sabbath idea. Its primary purpose is that we "might throughout life meditate on an everlasting Sabbath from our works that the Lord may work in us through his Spirit" (ibid.).[15]

Finally, note the two references in the exposition of the tenth commandment to "the rule of love" and "the law of love" (cf. *Inst.* III.7.5, 7). This, ultimately, is what the law is about—love. This is brought out with special force in Calvin's *Commentary on the Last Four Books of Moses.* There, just as in the Catechism, after completing his exposition of the various commandments, he deals with the sum of the law. (Here, in addition to citing Deut. 6:5; Lev. 19:18; and Matt. 27:37; he also quotes such passages as Deuteronomy 12, 13 and 1 Tim. 1:5; Rom. 13:8; Col. 3:14; and Gal. 5:14.) Love, however, must not be misconstrued as mere sentiment or emotion; for Calvin, too, it is "a wonderful affection" and "a surpassing ardor" (Catechism, sec. 8), but one that produces fear and reverence toward God and a selfless concern for one's neighbor. In short, love is but another way of describing the obedience of faith, which is a grateful response to God's grace manifest in Jesus Christ (*Inst.* II.8.49–55).

III. THE SHAPE OF THE
CHRISTIAN LIFE ACCORDING TO CALVIN

We have seen how Calvin in various connections either speaks of the law as an expression of the will of God or simply directs all of our activity to the will of God as the ultimate and most comprehensive norm of the Christian life. The following statement is typical: "He alone has truly denied himself who has so totally resigned himself to the Lord that he permits every part of his life to be governed by God's will" (*Inst.* III.7.10).

This much is almost self-evident and would hardly be a point of controversy. For it is generally agreed that the Christian life is to be lived, insofar as possible, in accordance with God's will. The matter becomes more complicated and problematic, however, when we try to determine how and where God's will is to be known—especially when facing difficult and often ambiguous ethical decisions. Yet for Calvin it would seem as if the answer were relatively simple, for he merely affirms that "the precepts of the law . . . comprehend the will of God" (*Inst.* I.17.2). "God has revealed his will in the law" (*Inst.* II.8.59). In the law God has delineated his own character (*Inst.* II.8.51); here his will, so to speak, is placed before our eyes.[16] Moreover, not only does God reveal in the law what kind of God he is, but there also "lays down what he demands from us, and in short, everything necessary to be known."[17]

In some of the above references the word "law" may refer to the Mosaic revelation or the Pentateuch. Nevertheless, Calvin does not hesitate to speak in the same way about the moral law as comprehended in the Decalogue.[18] Since it contains "a perfect pattern of righteousness," it is the "one everlasting and unchangeable rule to live by" (*Inst.* II.7.13).

It is at this point that Calvin, as well as the other reformers, are often criticized; for in their catechisms in particular they give the impression that the only norm for the Christian life is the Decalogue. This apparent "reduction" of the will of God to the Decalogue without any consideration of the Sermon on the Mount, the apostolic exhortations and injunctions, and so forth, is held to be an unfortunate hangover from the earlier Catholic tradition. Moreover, it is alleged that this approach is also unbiblical, since the Old Testament law rather than Jesus Christ is declared to be the sole source and norm of the Christian life. These criticisms can be found in a published doctoral dissertation that is critical of the whole tradition of giving a central place to an exposition of the Decalogue in catechetical instruction: *Kirche am Sinai—Die Zehn Gebote in der christlichen Unterweisung,* by Hugo Rothlisberger.[19] In regard to Calvin, however, Rothlisberger points to a different approach in the *Institutes,* where he finds *two* norms for the Christian life, that is, the law and Christ.[20] That this is not an adequate understanding of Calvin's approach will be shown below. Emil Brunner also chides the reformers for having overlooked the fact that in the New Testament the Decalogue scarcely appears to be the norm for the Christian church.[21] He also declares that "the New Testament knows nothing of a third use of the law."[22]

The question then is whether Calvin limits the knowledge of the will of God to the law, and further, whether he unconsciously operates with two norms (the law and Christ). A related question is whether Calvin in practice overlooks Christ and the new insights of the gospel in his treatment of the third use of the law. In sum, what is the concrete content of the will of God? There is no simple answer to these questions, but if we recall Calvin's interpretation of the Decalogue as outlined in the previous section, together with an examination of what is normative in his exposition of the Christian life in book III of the *Institutes*, it should be possible to give at least a provisional answer to these questions.

IV. A MORE PRECISE PRINCIPLE[23]

The three uses of the law, as we have seen, are discussed briefly in book II of the *Institutes*, but whereas the civil or political use is taken up again in chapter 20 of book IV ("Civil Government"), it appears that the third and "principal use" is dropped after the brief treatment in sections 12 and 13. (There is also an allusion to this function of the law in III.19.2.) This, however, is not actually the case, for Calvin takes up the third use of the law again in his discussion of the Christian life in book III, particularly chapters 6 and 7. One finds no explicit reference to the third use of the law in either of these chapters, but rather incidental references to the law at the beginning of both chapters which indicate that Calvin is presupposing the discussion of the law in book 2, chapter 7. As Paul Jacobs has pointed out, "The treatment of the doctrine of sanctification, the so-called ethic of Calvin's, is an unfolding of the doctrine of the *tertius usus legis*" (the third use of the law).[24]

In chapter 6, where Calvin collects various scriptural data relevant to the Christian life, after noting the object of regeneration he states: "The law of God contains in itself that newness by which his image can be restored in us" (III.6.1). But that is the last reference to the law in this chapter! He continues: "But because our slowness needs many goads and helps, it will be profitable to assemble from various passages of Scripture a plan for the regulation of our life [*rationem vitae formandae*] in order that those who heartily repent may not err in their zeal" (ibid.).

Calvin concedes the impossibility of doing justice to this subject in one short chapter, so he tries to find some "universal rule [*regulam*]" which aids the believer in living a "rightly ordered life" (ibid.). Since we have been adopted as children by God in order to live in harmony with him, the first principle must be a love of righteousness or holiness on our part. The goal of our calling is that we should be holy because our God is holy (Lev. 19:2; 1 Peter 1:15, 16; *Inst.* III.6.2). "The beginning of living rightly is spiritual, where the inner feeling of the mind is unfeignedly dedicated to God for the cultivation of holiness and righteousness" (III.6.5).

But Calvin proceeds to make another significant qualification in this chapter. It is true, he points out, that in many places in Scripture we are exhorted to live righteously, but he finds a stronger motive for holy living in the redemptive work of Christ. Consequently, "to wake us more effectively, Scripture shows that God the Father, as he has reconciled us to himself in his Christ, has in him stamped for us the likeness to which he would have us conform" (III.6.3). Later, in refuting the charge that the doctrine of justification by faith stifles zeal for good works, Calvin lists more than ten scriptural motives (or "spurs") for arousing us to fulfill our calling. The first is one of gratitude to "reciprocate the love of him 'who first loved us'" (1 John 4:19; *Inst.* III.16.2). For no one will truly pursue holiness unless he has first "imbibed" the doctrine that we are justified by Christ's merit alone (III.16.3).

The prime motive for the Christian life is thus the grace and forgiveness we have received in Jesus Christ. He is also the model of the Christian life. For Christ "has been set before us as an example [*exemplar*] whose image [*formam*; French, *l'image*] we ought to express in our life" (III.6.3). Does Calvin then operate with two norms, the law and Christ, as Rothlisberger maintains? Hardly. Granted, in III.6.1 Calvin says that we have been adopted as sons so that his image may be restored in us through the *law*; and in III.6.3 he says that we have been adopted as sons (note the identical language) on the condition "that our life express [*repraesentet*] *Christ*, the bond of our adoption." But there is no contradiction here. Since Christ is the "very soul [*vere anima*],"[25] the life,[26] the goal and end (fulfillment) of the law,[27] "the law in all its parts has reference to him . . . indeed, every doctrine of the law, every command, every promise always points to Christ."[28] Christ is thus not only the best interpreter of the law; he is also its substance and fulfillment. Hence, for Calvin there is no inconsistency in referring sometimes to the law and other times to Christ as the norm or rule of godly living and as the expression of the will of God. Nevertheless, it is not without significance that in his discussion of the Christian life, he prefers to refer to Christ, rather than the law, as the model and image to which God would have us conform and whose life we are to emulate.

We find much the same approach in chapter 7 of book III: "The Sum of the Christian Life: The Denial of Ourselves." Again Calvin begins with a reference to the law (its third use), and again he quickly passes on to "an even more exact plan [*accuratiore etiamnum ratione*]." "Even though the law of the Lord provides the finest and best-disposed method of ordering a man's life [*constituendae vitae*], it seemed good to the Heavenly Teacher to shape his people by an even more exact plan (or precise principle) to that rule [*regulam*] which he had set forth in his law" (III.7.1). Note that just as in the beginning of chapter 6, here too the law is spoken of in the highest terms. Calvin has not forgotten the law; nor is he about to reject it in favor of some alleged antithetical New Testament insight or principle. He knows no either/or—either the Old Testament or the New Testament, either the law or Christ. At the same time, however, he tacitly acknowledges that in the law we have not exhausted the meaning and purpose of God's will for our lives. Hence, in both chapters the praise of the law is followed by a crucial qualification. In chapter 6 he spoke of a means by which God awakens us "more effectively" (III.6.1), and in chapter 7 he speaks of a "more exact plan" (III.7.1).

The "beginning of this plan" (*principium rationis*) in chapter 7 is found in Romans 12:1–2. For Calvin this is a programmatic text of special significance: "I appeal to you therefore brothers and sisters, by the mercies of God, to present your bodies as a living sacrifice, holy and acceptable unto God, which is your spiritual worship. Do not be conformed to this world but be transformed by the renewal of your minds, so that you may discern what is the will of God . . ." (NRSV; *Inst.* III.7.1). After citing this passage, Calvin proceeds to elaborate the nature of the Christian life in terms of a repeated contrast: "We are not our own. . . . We are the Lord's" (see Rom. 14:8; 1 Cor. 6:19). This is Calvin's "Christian philosophy" (*Christiana philosophia*) which "bids reason give way to, submit, and subject itself to, the Holy Spirit so that the man himself may no longer live but bear [*ferat*] Christ living and reigning within him" (Gal. 2:20; *Inst.* III.7.1).

In the above section Calvin also refers to Ephesians 4:23, another key text in his understanding of the Christian life. For in Ephesians 4:22–24 he finds the two basic principles of Christian living, namely, putting off the old nature and putting on the new nature. (These are also the two elements of repentance, i.e., mortification and vivification.)[29] In reference to this passage Calvin refers to two rules for a godly and holy life. The first is "the denial of ourselves and the regeneration of the Holy Spirit." The second—and here again we have an echo of III.7.1—is "to live, not by our own spirit, but by the Spirit of Christ."[30]

These are not the only texts which Calvin considers important for a "well-ordered life" (*vitae bene compositae*). In the *Institutes* he also points to Titus 2:11–14 (III.7.3) and "the rule of love" as found in 1 Cor. 13:4, 5 (III.7.5–7). But the important thing to keep in mind is that this is what Calvin means by the third use of the law![31]

6
EXCURSUS:
CHRISTIAN FREEDOM
(Section 31)

I. JUSTIFICATION, FREEDOM, AND PRAYER

It is often assumed that because Calvin stressed the third use of the law[1] whereby the law serves as a norm and guide in the Christian life, he relegated justification and Christian freedom to a secondary role. Calvin was indeed more concerned about growth and progress in the Christian life than Luther, but he was equally emphatic in affirming that justification by faith is "the main hinge on which religion turns" (*praecipuum esse sustinendae religionis cardinem*). This is the foundation both of our relationship to God and the life of godliness (*Inst.* III.11.1). The daily life of repentance and renewal, no less than our first turning to God in faith, is the work of God and the result of his grace.[2]

When it comes to the freedom of the Christian, Calvin again is as concerned as Luther.[3] He deals briefly with this subject in his Catechism, section 31, "On Human Traditions,"[4] and set apart a whole chapter for this subject in the *Institutes* (III.19). He begins by affirming that "He who proposes to summarize the gospel teaching ought by no means to omit an explanation of this topic . . . for unless this freedom is comprehended, neither Christ nor gospel truth, nor inner peace of soul can be rightly known" (III.19.1). Concerning this chapter, Paul Wernle comments: "This brief section concerning Christian freedom is a jewel in the *Institutes*. . . . How many words about Calvin's legalism [*Gesetzlichkeit*] would have remained unspoken if this chapter had been read more often."[5]

Before proceeding to the content of this crucial chapter, it is important to note its place in the structure of the *Institutes*. It follows the chapters on justification and precedes the one on prayer. The relation to justification is made clear by Calvin at the outset. "Freedom is especially an appendage [*appendix*] of justification and is of no little avail in understanding its power" (*Inst.* III.19.1). While Calvin emphasized the importance of Christian freedom from the first edition of the *Institutes* (1536) until the last, the sentence just quoted was not added until the 1559 edition. Benjamin Reist may be on target then in surmising, "The longer Calvin reflected on all this [the relation of justification and freedom], the more he came to understand that justification has its central significance in freeing the conscience from the paralysis of guilt."[6]

What is not as clear is the relation of justification to prayer. Calvin says nothing specific in this regard, but here, too, Reist may be correct in his conviction that "it is no accident that Calvin's great chapter on Christian freedom is followed by his equally memorable chapter on prayer." Reist reasons that Calvin's constant concern for true piety is an underlying motif in his understanding of Christian freedom and that this in turn is inseparable from prayer "which is the chief exercise of faith" (part of the title of chapter 20 on prayer).[7]

One more thing should be noted before moving on to specific aspects of Christian freedom. Our freedom is grounded in the freedom of God and is derivative of it.

> Christian freedom, as Calvin sees it, is rooted in the freedom of God. God's freedom is reflected in the freedom of the first human beings and expressed in God's will to recreate humanity through the work of Christ in the incarnation. Christ the liberator has freed fallen humanity from bondage to sin and from bondage to tyrannical human institutions that usurp God's sovereignty.[8]

II. FREEDOM FROM THE LAW

Over half of this chapter (III.19) in the *Institutes* deals with freedom from the law and freedom of the conscience. Moreover, in his discussion of the third use of the law in book II, chapter 7, Calvin devotes more space to a discussion of the abrogation of the law and the Christian's freedom than he does to the positive explication of the meaning of the law for the Christian! The apparent reason is that before advancing to the exposition of the Decalogue in chapter 8, he wants to make sure that one thing is clear: the Decalogue, which contains the rule of God's righteousness, is "useful" only for that person who is reconciled, justified, and *free*.

But we must understand in what sense the Christian is free from the law. "Paul teaches clearly enough," notes Calvin, "that the law has been abrogated" (*Inst*. II.7.14). But it would be a tragic mistake to conclude from this "that the righteousness which God approves in his law is abolished when the law is abrogated. This abrogation, however, does not at all apply to the precepts which teach us the way of living rightly, for Christ confirms and sanctions these and does not abrogate them. The proper solution to the objection is that the only part of the law which is removed is the curse, to which all men who are beyond the grace of Christ are subject."[9] Consequently, when Paul says that we are "dead to the law" (Rom. 7:4), this means, according to Calvin, that we are free from its power:

Paul is referring here only to that office of the law which is peculiar to the ministry of Moses. We must never imagine that the law is in any way abrogated in regard to the ten commandments, in which God has taught us what is right and has ordered our life, because the will of God must stand forever. The release here mentioned, we must carefully notice, is not from the righteousness which is taught in the law, but from the rigid demands of the law and from the curse which follows from its demands. What is abrogated, therefore, is not the rule of living well which the law prescribes, but that quality which is opposed to the liberty which we have obtained through Christ, namely, the demand for absolute perfection.[10]

III. FREEDOM OF CONSCIENCE

In short, the law is abolished, once and for all, insofar as it is able to threaten and bind the conscience with a curse. The believer has been freed from the burden of the "unending bondage" of a conscience agonizing with the fear of death (*Inst*. II.7.14, 15). This is one of the major differences between the old and the new dispensations. Under the old, "consciences were struck with fear and trembling," but the benefit of the new is that "they are released unto joy. The old [dispensation] held consciences bound by the yoke of bondage; the new by its spirit of liberality emancipates them unto freedom" (*Inst*. II.11.9).[11]

Freedom of conscience is one of the chief gifts of the gospel. This is possible only because Christ, the Son of God, who had the right to claim exemption from every kind of subjection, voluntarily became subject to the law. Why did he do this? "That in our name he might obtain freedom for us."[12] Thus "the bond which stood against us with its legal demands" was canceled (Col. 2:14). "This is full liberty, that Christ has by his blood blotted out not only our sins, but every handwriting which might declare us to be exposed to the judgment of God. . . . For he has fastened to the cross our curse, our sins, and also the punishment due to us, so also that bondage of the law and everything that tends to bind consciences."[13]

Therefore we turn to Christ because "there is found in him everything necessary for setting consciences at peace."[14] Just as we have nothing more to do with the law as far as justification is concerned, so too our consciences "embrace God's mercy alone, turn our attention from ourselves and look only to Christ. . . . The consciences of believers, in seeking assurance for their justification before God, should rise above and advance beyond the law, forgetting all law righteousness" (*Inst*. III.19.2).[15]

This is the first aspect of Christian freedom. We are freed *from* the legal requirements of the law. Our righteousness is found in Christ. He alone can give peace of conscience.

In his Catechism Calvin goes further and emphasizes that we are also freed from human traditions, whether in the form of civil observances or ecclesiastical regulations. Here it is clear that he has certain Roman Catholic rules and regulations in mind.

> We are stoutly to resist those regulations which under the title of "spiritual laws" are in force to bind consciences as if necessary for the worship of God. For they not only overturn the freedom which Christ won for us, but also obscure true religion and violate God's majesty, who alone wills to reign in our consciences through his Word (sec. 31).

However, Calvin was not satisfied with a mere formal, negative definition of freedom. He was also concerned to show what the Christian is freed *for*. In the *Institutes* he continues this discussion of freedom from the positive side also in terms of conscience. And this brings him again to the *usus tertius legis* (third use of the law).

IV. FREE TO OBEY GOD'S WILL

The second aspect of freedom, Calvin continues, "is that consciences observe the law, not as if constrained by the necessity of the law, but that freed from the law's yoke they willingly obey God's will. For since they dwell in perpetual dread as long as they remain under the sway of the law, they will never be disposed with eager readiness to obey God unless they have already been given this sort of freedom" (III.19.4). It is only the free person who is capable of the willing, spontaneous obedience desired by God.

Obedience to God's will is required under the gospel as well as under the law, but there is a difference. No longer is strict, rigorous obedience to the commands of the law required, but rather an obedient disposition. Christ, by his perfect obedience, has fulfilled the requirements of the law, so for the person in Christ the *will* to obedience suffices. Hence, if we are united to Christ by faith, it is enough "if we strive after the form of living [*vivendi formam*]" prescribed in the law. For "even though we be wide of the mark of perfection, the Lord gives us what is lacking" (*Geneva Catechism*, 1545, Q. 225). When our good works "proceed from the love of Christ," no matter how imperfect they may be, "God is pleased with the obedience of those who sincerely aspire to this goal," that is, keeping the commandments of Christ out of love for him.[16]

This is the glory of the freedom of the gospel! Our works are no longer measured by the strict requirements of the law but are judged leniently by the gracious Father. Without this comfort and assurance, no one would strive to serve God with much enthusiasm. But if believers "hear themselves called with fatherly gentleness by God from this severe requirement of the law, they will cheerfully and with great eagerness answer and follow his leading" (*Inst.* III.17.10). Wilhelm Niesel notes that this doctrine of the "justification of works"—which was developed in the Reformed Church—"is of the greatest consequence for ethics. It makes clear that the man who belongs to Christ need not be the prey of continual remorse. On the contrary, he can go about his daily work confidently and joyfully."[17]

It is in this spirit and on this basis that Calvin teaches the third use of the law. The only obedience and service that is acceptable to God is that which is spontaneous and free. Unless it springs from love and gratitude, it is not the obedience of faith. Christians obey God and seek to do his will not because they must, but because they want to. This joyous obedience is only possible because they are freed from the constraint and bondage of the law. Now, being truly free, they are free to love, free to obey, free to submit to the leading of the Spirit.

The difference, in short, between the unbeliever's and the believer's relation to the law is that between a slave and a son. The former are bound to their master by the yoke of the law; they are strictly required to perform their tasks. The relation of a son to a father is completely different. Even the incomplete and defective works of children are accepted by their fathers as long as they are done in a spirit of sincere effort. For a father compassionately overlooks the faults of those whom he loves (*Inst.* III.19.5). In relation to the law, therefore, everything depends on the transformation effected by our adoption as children into the family of God. "One must be personally related to the Law-Giver to obey the law rightly. Obedience must be within the family."[18]

Freedom is not autonomy or anarchy but finding one's true master. In the words of the hymn, "Make me a captive, Lord, and *then* I shall be free." Or, as Calvin puts it, echoing Luther, the freedom of a Christian is "a free servitude and a serving freedom (*libera servitus, et serva libertas*)."[19] True freedom is freedom in obedience. "Only those who serve God are free. . . . We obtain liberty in order that we may more promptly and more readily obey God."[20]

V. THE REALM OF "ADIAPHORA"

The third part of Christian freedom lies in the sphere of neutral or "indifferent things" (*adiaphora*), discussed by the apostle Paul in Romans 14 and 1 Corinthians 8 and 10:14f. Since these things are external and are in themselves neither good nor bad, "we are not bound, therefore, before God by any religious obligation preventing us from sometimes using them and other times not using them, indifferently" (*Inst.* III.19.7). Calvin attaches great importance to this matter, as is apparent from the lengthy discussion of this subject in the *Institutes* III.19.7–16. As Calvin himself observes elsewhere, "Wise and experienced persons know that this is one of the most important questions in the doctrine of salvation."[21]

Our freedom in this regard, however, has one limitation: it must never become an offense or cause of stumbling for the simple and weak fellow believer. (In this connection Calvin cites such passages as Rom. 14:1, 13; 15:1, 2; 1 Cor. 10:25, 29; Gal. 5:13 in the *Institutes*, III.19.11.) "Our freedom is not given against our feeble neighbors, for love makes us their servants in all things; rather it is given that, having peace with God in our hearts, we may also live at peace with men" (*Inst.* III.19.11). Freedom from human scruples, convention, and opinion must be preserved at all costs, but at the same time it must always be tempered by love of fellow Christians. "Nothing is plainer than this rule: that we should use our freedom as it results in the edification of our neighbor, but if it does not help our neighbor, then we should forego it. . . . It is the part of a godly man to realize that free power in outward matters has been given him in order that he may be the more ready for all the duties of love" (III.19.12). All of this is summarized succinctly by Hendrikus Berkhof: "Freedom exists for the sake of love, and love is made possible through freedom."[22]

However, there is an even higher rule which must guide us in the use of our freedom in the realm of *adiaphora*: "As our freedom must be subordinated to love, so in turn ought love itself to abide under purity of faith" (*Inst.* III.19.13). That is, under the pretext of love of neighbor, we must do nothing which will offend God. For his authority must not be compromised—nor that of our consciences. In our concern for the weaker brother or sister we must also beware of the claims and charges of the Pharisees (III.19.11, 12). Under no circumstances should we allow others to rule our consciences. For "if we let men bind our consciences, we shall be despoiled of an invaluable blessing and at the same time an insult will be offered to Christ, the author of freedom."[23]

This is obviously a complex and difficult matter. For if we are sensitive to the weaknesses and scruples of weak Christians in our midst, there is the danger that they, not the Word of God, will govern our decisions and behavior. Then we are susceptible to a new kind of bondage. Calvin resolves this difficulty by making a distinction between outward actions and a free conscience (*Inst.* III.19.16). In reference to Galatians 5:13—"For you were called to freedom . . ."—Calvin comments, "Liberty lies in the conscience and looks to God. Its use lies in externals and deals not only with God but also with men."[24] In Ronald Wallace's words, "Even when we are subjecting the outward expression of our liberty of conscience to the law of charity, our consciences can at the same time remain free before God and unbound by our outward behavior."[25]

Calvin is quite sensitive to the different accents in different passages of

Scripture. Thus, in reference to 1 Corinthians 10:29 he cautions, "We must observe that in this verse the word conscience is used in its strict sense, whereas in Romans 13:5 and 1 Timothy 1:5 it has a broader significance."[26] Calvin accordingly

> can speak of conscience in the broad sense as well as the narrow. In the narrow sense, the conscience before the judgment seat of God looks only to the freedom procured for it by Jesus Christ and is bound by no necessity or law with regard to other human beings. In the broad sense, however, our consciences are under obligation to others. This obligation is not based on external actions that are in and of themselves necessary, but on external actions that are required because of their consequences. A law is binding on the conscience in the narrow sense when it is commanded in and of itself, regardless of the consequences, and in this sense the consciences of believers are bound only by the law of God and by the Lordship of Jesus Christ. However, a law may be observed by the conscience in the broad sense when it is not held to be necessary in and of itself but is rather observed because of the good purposes or consequences that it entails.[27]

But we must also beware of ensnaring our own consciences with a slavishly literal and over-scrupulous interpretation of Scripture (Comm. Luke 3:10). "For when consciences once ensnare themselves, they enter a long and inextricable maze, not easy to get out of" (Inst. III.19.7). Moreover, if we do anything against our conscience, or even when our conscience is in doubt about it, this is a serious sin. Whenever we go our own way in opposition to our conscience, "we are rushing headlong to disaster."[28]

Freedom of conscience before God is the pearl of great price. Calvin recognizes the difficulty of preserving this liberty as we seek to avoid the snares of over-scrupulousness on the one hand and self-indulgence on the other. There is no simple, sure safeguard, but we shall not go far astray as long as throughout our lives we strive to follow the will of God. For "going against his will is the one thing which vitiates all our actions."[29] Consequently, in the last analysis, not only in regard to freedom of conscience, but also in regard to the whole Christian life, "his will ought to precede all our plans and actions" (Inst. III.19.7).

VI. THE ROLE OF
THE HOLY SPIRIT

Discerning God's will, however, is not always an easy matter, and doing God's will is even more difficult. As was noted earlier, the believer is not only freed from the legal demands of the law (and an enslaved will) but is freed for grateful obedience to God's will. However, sincere, spontaneous obedience only issues from a heart that is governed by the Holy

Spirit. And this is precisely the "peculiar office [*proprium munus*]" of the Holy Spirit, namely, to engrave the law on our hearts and inculcate in us a spirit of obedience. Our wills, being naturally depraved, incline to sin, but God through his Spirit changes them so that they seek after righteousness. "From this arises that true freedom which we obtain when God frames our hearts, which before were in thraldom to sin, unto obedience to himself."[30]

Therefore, when Paul says, "If you are led by the Spirit, you are not under the law" (Gal. 5:18), according to Calvin, the meaning is that the Spirit frees us from the *yoke* of the law. If you walk according to the Spirit, "you will then be free from the dominion of the law, which will only be a liberal teaching [*liberalis doctrina*] to advise you. It will no longer hold your consciences in bondage."[31] Governed now by the grace of the Holy Spirit, the commandment is no longer "above us" (Deut. 30:11). Freed from the yoke of the law, we "perceive how sweet the yoke of Christ is, and how light his burden is" (Matt. 11:30). Since the rigor of the law has been taken away, "the instruction of the law will not only be tolerable, but even joyful and pleasant; nor must we refuse the bridle which governs us mildly and does not urge us more severely than is expedient."[32]

The real test of Christian freedom is whether it turns believers back upon themselves or outward in the service of God and neighbor. "Christ does not reconcile believers to the Father that they may indulge themselves with impunity, but that by governing them with his Spirit, he may keep them under the hand and rule of his Father. From this it follows that Christ's love is rejected by those who do not prove by true obedience that they are his disciples."[33] Consequently, believers rejoice not only in the liberty which is granted to them, but also in the fact that God prescribes "a certain rule" for them. It would be no blessing to be left in uncertainty as to what the Lord's will is. Hence this subjection is not a burden but "a true and real happiness."[34]

In the above paragraphs almost all of the main elements in Calvin's doctrine of the didactic or third use of the law have emerged. Christians are free, not from the abiding meaning of the law, but from the rigid requirements, curse, and consequent burden of the law. By faith and union with Christ, who has borne that burden and suffered that curse in their place, believers have become children of God. Since they are children and not servants, they enjoy the freedom of the Spirit. The special office of the Spirit is to mold and remake them according to the image of God. The Spirit does this by means of the law, which is no longer an external accusing power but a helpful friend implanted in their being.

Thus through the Spirit believers seek more and more to do God's will, not their own. In joyful gratitude they seek to serve their rightful Lord in whom they find perfect freedom. They rejoice in their newfound power through the Spirit to obey the will of their heavenly Father.

7

ELECTION AND PREDESTINATION[1]

(Section 13)

The law, as we have seen, is a means by which we are humbled and brought to an awareness of our sinfulness. Thus it indirectly makes us ready to receive Christ and the gospel of the free forgiveness of sins. But the actual reception and enjoyment of Christ is only possible through faith (sec. 12). Before Calvin proceeds to describe the nature of faith in sections 14 and 15, however, he takes up a practical problem which was of great concern for him. That is, why is it that when some people hear the gospel proclaimed they respond with faith whereas others are unmoved and react negatively? Is it because some people are more intelligent or naturally pious than others?

I. THE PRACTICAL AND PASTORAL MOTIVES

No, says Calvin, the answer to this perplexing question is not to be found in the personalities of people but in the decree of God. This is how Calvin comes to discuss the doctrine of predestination within the context of his discussion of faith. This is very significant for understanding the Genevan Reformer's much maligned position here. For the doctrine of election—and even the frightening notion of double predestination—does not derive from a speculative, dogmatic interest of Calvin's but primarily from a practical, experiential concern. Had it been the former, he would have taken up the theme in his discussion of God or providence as was true of Augustine, Aquinas, and later Reformed theology. However, it must be conceded that Calvin's placement of this doctrine in his Catechism is not followed in the *Institutes* until the last edition.[2]

As François Wendel points out, Calvin's point of departure here,

> as in the *Institutes,* is the fact that the preaching of the Word does not equally move all those who hear it, but bears its fruits only in the elect, whereas to the reprobate it brings only death. The practical and ecclesiological point of view is evident and clear, as it is also in St. Augustine and Bucer. And this, in spite of the theoretical developments, is what dominates the exposition of predestination to the end.[3]

Accordingly, his first motive in taking up this doctrine, aside from the fact that it is scriptural,[4] is to explain the phenomenon that "the word of the gospel calls us all to share in Christ, but most men, blinded and hardened by unbelief [see Matt. 22:14] spurn such singular grace" (sec. 12).

Later in the *Institutes* a more pastoral motive comes to the fore. For Calvin, this doctrine not only answers the question of why some believe the gospel and others reject it; rightly understood, it should also give us assurance that our salvation is grounded in God's free mercy and grace. "We shall never be clearly persuaded, as we ought to be, that our salvation flows from the wellspring of God's free mercy until we come to know his eternal election, which illumines God's grace by this contrast . . ." (*Inst.* III.21.1).

In this context Calvin points to the apostle Paul's argument in Romans 11:5–6 that "a remnant has been saved according to the election of grace. But if it is by grace, it is no more of works; otherwise grace would no more be grace." This, Calvin maintains, should make us both humble and grateful. Hence the doctrine of election is "useful" and should yield "sweet fruit," for it makes "clear that our salvation comes about solely from God's mere generosity" (ibid.).

II. THE QUESTION OF REPROBATION

The reference above to those who are "blinded and hardened"[5] leads naturally to the first statements of section 13. "For the seed of God's word takes root and bears fruit only in those whom the Lord, by his eternal election, predestined as his children and heirs of the kingdom of heaven." Here we have only predestination to salvation. This much is generally accepted by many Protestant and Roman Catholic theologians, but few of them are willing to draw the conclusion which Calvin makes, namely, that it follows that those who do not believe are therefore rejected by God and are predestined to eternal damnation (reprobation). In Calvin's words, all those who do not respond to God's grace are "condemned by this same plan [*consilium*] of God before the foundation of the world." For such people "the utterly clear preaching of the truth can be nothing but the stench of death unto death" (sec. 13; cf. 2 Cor. 2:15–16). Or, to put the matter more boldly, as he does in his definition of predestination in the *Institutes:*

> We call predestination God's eternal decree, by which he compacted with himself what he willed to become of each man. For all are not created in equal condition; rather, eternal life is fore-ordained for some, eternal damnation for others. Therefore, as any man has been created to one or the other of these ends, we speak of him as predestined to life or to death (*Inst.* III.21.5).

This is the doctrine of double predestination, which is falsely attributed to Calvin as if he were its originator! Augustine, Gottschalk (a ninth-century theologian), Luther, Bucer (the Strasbourg reformer), and others had taught this doctrine before Calvin.[6]

It is also false to assert that the doctrine of predestination or that of the sovereignty of God is the central doctrine in Calvin's theology.[7] There are four confessions attributed to Calvin, and of these, three allude only incidentally to predestination. The same is true of his later Catechism of 1541, the Geneva Catechism (see Qs. 100 and 157), where again there is no mention of reprobation (i.e., election to damnation). It was unquestionably an important doctrine for Calvin, for he devotes four chapters to this subject in the *Institutes* (IV.21–24). But this was due largely to various attacks on the doctrine.[8] In the first edition of the *Institutes* (1536) it is mentioned briefly only in two places.

Not surprisingly, this doctrine is a stumbling block to human reason, particularly double predestination. It appears unjust and arbitrary and would seem to make people unresponsible for their decisions. Calvin recognizes these difficulties and himself raises the question, "Why should the Lord deem the former [the predestined] worthy of his mercy, but exercise his severe judgment on the latter?" He answers simply, "Let us leave the cause in his hand, for he has for the best of reasons willed to hide it from us" (sec. 13). He also warns his readers against trying to fathom the hidden decree of God. We should instead recognize the paucity of our wisdom and marvel at God's "unsearchable judgments" (Rom. 11:33). Calvin would remind us of the words of the apostle Paul: "Who are you, a human being, to argue with God? Will what is molded say to the one who molds it, 'Why have you made me like this?'" (Rom. 9:20; cf. *Inst.* III.23.1, 4, 5, where Calvin quotes this and similar texts). In any case, we should not accuse God of being unjust. Rather, "let us acknowledge among ourselves that this dispensation of the Lord, although hidden to us, is nonetheless just and holy" (sec. 13).

Despite Calvin's admonitions about not trying to probe into this great mystery—and his constant warnings about the danger of speculation in other contexts—the question can be raised as to whether he heeded his own advice. He is quite emphatic in asserting, "Let us leave the cause [of God's election] in his hand, for God has for the best of reasons willed to hide it from us." Not only that, Calvin urges us not to "seek to penetrate into heaven itself, and to fathom what God from eternity decreed for us" (sec. 13). To indulge in such "wanton curiosity . . . is both foolish and dangerous, nay, even deadly" (*Inst.* III.21.2).[9]

And yet, particularly in regard to his doctrine of reprobation, Calvin at times seems to go beyond the bounds of Scripture. Even though he described this doctrine of reprobation as "a dreadful decree" (*decretum horrible*) (*Inst.* III.23.7), he still felt he had to teach it because he was convinced it was scriptural. In particular, he found the doctrine taught by the apostle Paul in Romans 9:11–23, which can be interpreted as teaching double predestination. There is no consensus, however, on the interpretation of that key passage. It is noteworthy that even a conservative Calvinist such as G. C. Berkouwer believes that Calvin fails to understand part of Paul's argument in Romans 9:17f. For in the hardening of Pharaoh's heart Calvin sees a revelation of eternal damnation, whereas Berkouwer (and most exegetes) maintain that Paul here "is not concerned primarily to expound the 'ruin of the wicked' which is 'ordained by his counsel and will' [so Calvin], but rather to point to God's power and freedom in the history of salvation as he proceeds to manifest his mercy".[10] However, Calvin at least took this passage seriously, which is more than can be said of some recent biblical scholars.

The renowned English New Testament scholar of a past generation, C. H. Dodd, for example, in his commentary on Romans, accuses the apostle Paul of pushing "an unethical determinism to its logical extreme."[11] A. M. Hunter, the Scottish New Testament theologian, is just as bad in his commentary on Romans. He too charges the apostle Paul with teaching in Romans 9:18 that "we are simply puppets controlled by a cruelly capricious God. . . ."[12] The great German New Testament theologian Rudolf Bultmann simply avoids any discussion at all of Romans 9–11 in his two-volume *Theology of the New Testament*.[13]

It is to Karl Barth's credit that he has seriously wrestled with this problem, although his unique restatement of the doctrine of reprobation has an even more slender exegetical base than the traditional view. For Barth, Jesus Christ is at the same time the electing God, the elect man, and the rejected man. Since Christ has assumed the damnation that we deserved, rejection is no longer possible for humanity. This eliminates any possibility of a hidden decree of condemnation and thus makes the doctrine of election the most comforting doctrine of all. But it also leads to what I have called an "incipient universalism."[14]

III. ELECTION IN CHRIST

In any case, Calvin does not teach that there is a symmetry or parallel between election and reprobation as is the case with a few neo-Calvinists. Nor does he speculate concerning who is elect or non-elect. The assurance of our salvation comes from trusting in God's gracious promises and, above all, looking to Jesus Christ. Recall that Calvin's original purpose in discussing this doctrine was a pastoral one. Hence the accent in his discussion is on God's electing grace in Christ. He wants to stress above all that our salvation is grounded in the unfathomable grace of God and his gratuitous mercy. This doctrine should be a source of comfort, not uncertainty and confusion. Apparently in Calvin's time some people were troubling themselves with the question as to whether they were elect or not. (This problem became more acute in some Calvinistic groups in later centuries.) Calvin admonishes such people: "Let us not—in order to fix the assurance of our salvation—seek to penetrate into heaven itself, and to fathom what God from eternity decreed for us. Such thinking can only vex us with miserable anxiety and trouble" (sec. 13).[15]

Rather, urges Calvin, let us shun such fruitless speculation and look to Jesus Christ, the pledge of our election, in whom we were chosen before the foundation of the world (see Eph. 1:4).[16] We should simply look to Christ, who is "set before us as life, that all who believe in him may not die but have eternal life" (sec. 13). The simplest answer thus is found in the well-known verse, John 3:16.

Elsewhere Calvin suggests that rather than looking inward we should look to Scripture as a whole for guidance in this regard. For "the Word of the Lord is the sole way that can lead us in our search for all that is lawful to hold concerning him and the sole light to illumine our vision of all that we should see of him . . . " (*Inst.* III.21.2).

Calvin closes this section on election with a pastoral note of comfort: "If while possessing Christ in faith, we at the same time possess life in him, we have no business investigating anything beyond this concerning God's eternal plan. For Christ is not simply the mirror wherein God's will is shown to us, but the pledge (*pignus*) wherewith it is, so to speak, sealed" (sec. 13).

Wherever Calvin discusses this subject, he rings the changes on the theme of Christ as the mirror and pledge of our election. In the *Institutes*, his favorite metaphor is that of a mirror. This usage he picked up from Augustine, who, Calvin says, "wisely notes . . . that we have in the very Head of the church the clearest mirror of free election that we who are among the members may not be troubled about it" (*Inst.* III.22.1).

Later Calvin speaks for himself in what has become a classic statement. Again, appealing to Ephesians 1:4, he writes:

> If we have been chosen in him, we shall not find assurance of our election in ourselves; and not even in God the Father, if we conceive him as severed from his Son. Christ, then, is the mirror wherein we must, and without self-deception may, contemplate our own election. For since it is into his body the Father has destined those to be engrafted whom he has willed from eternity to be his own, that he may hold as sons all whom he acknowledges to be among his members, we have a sufficiently clear and firm testimony that we have been inscribed in the book of life [cf. Rev. 21:27] if we are in communion with Christ (III.24.5).[17]

In his separate treatise on predestination Calvin has a whole section on Christ's place in election in which Christ is not only the mirror and pledge of our election but also its earnest (*arrabon*). Here, too, Calvin takes up the question of the assurance of salvation and again urges us to turn to Christ alone. "Since the certainty of salvation is set forth in Christ, it is wrong and injurious to Christ to pass over this professed fountain of life from which supplies are available, and to toil to draw life out of the hidden recesses of God."[18]

Calvin supports this contention with a quotation of that key passage, Ephesians 1:4, and refers to John 1:12; Galatians 4:7; and Romans 8:17. He then concludes: "Christ, therefore, is for us the *bright mirror* of the eternal and hidden election of God, and also the *earnest and pledge*. We contemplate by faith the life which God represents to us in this *mirror;* and by faith we lay hold on this *pledge and earnest*" (emphasis added).[19]

This, as J.K.S. Reid comments, "is indeed eloquent testimony to the place that Christ has in the election of men."[20] For in Christ we have the revelation of God's purpose for humanity, the instrument by which God secures our election (salvation), and its assurance and guarantee. Predestination is in Christ, through Christ, and on account of Christ.[21] But for Reid this is not enough. He repeats Barth's complaint that Christ is not also the *fundamentum* (foundation) of our election. "He is not there as God frames his purpose to elect." According to Reid (and Barth), it "appears [N.B.] that into these deep counsels [of God], Christ has not been admitted."[22]

But how does Reid know whether Christ is the *fundamentum* of election and is or is not involved in the secret counsels of God? And if he is, does this necessarily justify Barth's and Reid's conclusion that therefore rejection of some people is impossible? Scripture is not clear on this matter. We are simply not privy to these mysteries. Here, as Calvin admonishes us again and again, it is best not to speculate.

IV. GOD'S CALL
AND OUR CALLING

Where both Calvin and Reid may err is in trying to surmise what God in all eternity has decreed and on what basis. But whereas Reid seems to know what role Christ plays in God's "secret counsels," Calvin makes an important distinction that Reid and other critics of Calvin have not noticed or sufficiently appreciated. This is the distinction between God's secret counsel (*consilium*) and God's call. The former is unknown to us and should not be investigated apart from the Word. The latter is both known through faith and confirmed through experience. Therefore, says Calvin, we are to "begin with God's call [*vocatione*] and to end with it . . . since God wills to confirm to us by this as by a token [*tessera*] as much as we may lawfully know of his plan" (*Inst.* III.24.4).

A key text in this connection for Calvin in his treatise on *Eternal Predestination* is Romans 8:28, particularly the latter part of the verse: "We know that all things work together for good for those who love God, *who are called according to his purpose*" (emphasis added).[23] Here we have an illustration of God's efficacious calling. This calling, as over against a general or external calling, is "a certain and specific calling which seals and ratifies the eternal election of God so as to make manifest what was before hidden in God."[24] Note well! What is hidden in God is revealed through our experience of his call.

This is made very clear in one of Calvin's commentaries: "The election of God is in itself hidden and secret; the Lord manifests [*patefacit*] it by calling, that is, when he bestows on us this blessing of calling us."[25] Moreover, "this inner call is a pledge of salvation that cannot deceive us" (*Inst.* III.24.2). Calvin then points to 1 John 3:24 as relevant in this connection: "We recognize that we are his children from the Spirit, which he has given us" (Calvin's tranlation).

There is thus an intimate connection between the Word, our awareness of God's special calling, the testimony of the Spirit in our lives, our adoption as God's children, and our assurance of salvation. Hence, in all our considerations of election, which is "the fountain from which our salvation flows," the proper approach is not to seek to plumb the secret counsel of God, but to turn to our calling, "which is his outward testimony to it [our election], and follows that gratuitous adoption which is hidden within himself."[26]

V. THE ISSUE AT STAKE

Whereas Luther opposed Pelagianism (the view that people take the initial and fundamental step toward their salvation apart from God's assistance) and the Roman Catholic errors of his day by stressing the doctrine of justification by faith, Calvin sought to anchor our salvation in God's election. Thus the doctrine of election is primarily an expression of the evangelical doctrine of grace.[27] Again and again in his discussion of predestination he returns to this theme of God's sovereign grace as the ground of our salvation. Our salvation is sure, ultimately, not because of our faith but because of God's sovereign goodness and mercy. This is why for Calvin this doctrine should be a source of confidence and comfort. Never for him is there any hint of fatalism. To the contrary, Calvin himself and generations of his spiritual heirs have combined strong convictions about God's providence and predestination with a very active evangelistic and social witness. As the Baptist historian Timothy George points out, "throughout the history of the church some of the most effective evangelists and missionaries have been staunch defenders of a high doctrine of predestination."[28] And as John T. McNeill, the former "dean" of American Calvin scholarship, has emphasized in all his writings, no reformer was—and few theologians since have been—more actively involved in social and political affairs than Calvin, despite his heavy pastoral and teaching responsiblities. One can criticize Calvin for a variety of things, McNeill acknowledges, but "at least one of the charges leveled against him, that of a de-energizing fatalism, is without foundation." For

> In his writings we are not in the atmosphere of fate, but in the company of the living God. Life consists of *negotium cum deo*, a series of transactions with God; and the life of faith is not a resigned aquiescence, but is distinguished by an energizing gratitude that bears fruit in vigorous action.[29]

George concludes his discussion of Calvin on predestination in a way that can well conclude this chapter:

> Predestination as Calvin understood it, is neither a church steeple from which to view the human landscape, nor a pillow to sleep on. It is rather a stronghold in times of temptation and trials and a confession of praise to God's grace and to his glory.[30]

Nothing can "separate us from the love of God in Christ Jesus our Lord" (Rom. 8:39) because God "chose us in him before the foundation of the world" (Eph. 1:4). "O the depth of the riches and wisdom and knowledge of God!" (Rom. 11:33).[31]

8

FAITH

(Sections 12, 14–21)

I. A KNOWLEDGE OF THE HEAD AND HEART

After this brief interlude on election, Calvin returns to the main subject of faith in section 14, where he defines true faith. "Now we are to conceive the Christian faith as no bare knowledge of God or understanding of Scripture which rattles around in the brain and affects the heart not at all. . . .[1] But it is a firm and staunch confidence of the heart by which we securely repose in God's mercy promised us through the Gospel." Thus, according to Calvin, faith is not merely knowledge of various historical facts and fundamental doctrines; it is above all a certain confidence of heart in God's gracious promises. This presupposes, of course, a knowledge of these promises. Faith, after all, "rests not on ignorance, but on knowledge" (*Inst.* III.2.2).

But this is a special kind of knowledge, as we shall see. For the knowledge of faith "is more a matter of the heart than the brain, and more of the disposition (*affectus*) than of the understanding (*intelligentiae*)" (III.2.8). Calvin cannot emphasize this too much. He devotes three sections to this theme in the *Institutes* (III.2.14, 34, 36).[2] In one passage he explains what is distinctive about this kind of knowledge, the goal of which is not so much intellectual comprehension as heartfelt persuasion.

> When we call faith "knowledge" we do not mean comprehension of the sort that is commonly concerned with those things which fall under human sense perception. For faith is so far above sense that man's mind has to go beyond and rise above itself in order to attain it. Even where the mind has attained, it does not comprehend what it feels. But while it is persuaded of what it does not grasp, by the very certainty of its persuasion it understands more than if it perceived anything human by its own capacity (III.2.14).[3]

The text that best illustrates this kind of knowledge for Calvin is Ephesians 3:18–19. Here, says Calvin, Paul "beautifully describes" this knowledge as "the power 'to comprehend what is the breadth and length and depth and height, and to know the love of Christ which surpasses knowledge.'" Calvin then comments: "He means that what our mind embraces

101

by faith is in every way infinite, and that this kind of knowledge is far more lofty than all understanding" (*Inst.* III.2.14).

In one of Calvin's commentaries he simply describes the knowledge of faith in this way: "Let us note that the seal of faith is not in the head but in the heart." He quickly adds that he is not trying to make any sharp psychological distinction between the heart and the head. "I am not going to argue about the part of the body in which faith is located, but since the word *heart* generally means a serious and sincere affection, I maintain that faith is a firm and effectual confidence and not just a bare idea."[4]

II. CHRIST THE
OBJECT OF FAITH

Since these promises in which the gospel consists culminate in Jesus Christ, he is "the perpetual object of faith" (sec. 16). "Since all God's promises are confirmed in Christ, and so to speak are presented and fulfilled, it is beyond a shadow of a doubt that Christ himself is the everlasting object of faith in whom we are to contemplate all the riches of divine mercy" (sec. 14). This thesis is developed in the *Institutes*, where Calvin begins by noting that in a more general sense, faith rests upon God's Word, for "there is a permanent relationship between faith and the Word." God "could not separate one from the other any more than we could separate rays from the sun from which they come" (*Inst.* III.2.6). But this does not mean that the Bible itself is the object of faith, as we have seen. Here Calvin proceeds to explain that the Word is indispensable because "it is like a mirror in which faith may contemplate God" (ibid.).

What is especially necessary to know about God, however, is his will toward us.[5] Since some passages in the Bible speak of sin and judgment, this does not offer us much comfort or hope. Therefore, a general knowledge of God's will is not faith as such. Accordingly, what is required for a genuine faith is more specifically the knowledge that God is mercifully inclined toward me, that he loves me, and that he will forgive my sins through his Son, Jesus Christ. We need, in other words, "the promise of grace," for "upon grace alone the heart of man can rest" (*Inst.* III.2.7). Since the "sole pledge" of God's love and mercy is Christ, Calvin concludes that the object of faith, properly speaking, is the "freely given promise" which is based on the redeeming work of Jesus Christ. Calvin concludes this section with his most formal and complete definition of faith: It is "a firm and certain knowledge of God's benevolence toward us, founded upon the truth of the freely given promise in Christ, both revealed to our minds and sealed upon our hearts through the Holy Spirit" (ibid.).[6]

III. THE HOLY SPIRIT,
DOUBT, AND ASSURANCE

The closing reference to the Holy Spirit is similar to a passage in the Catechism where faith is described as "the enlightenment of the Holy Spirit by which our minds are illumined and our hearts confirmed in a sure persuasion . . ." (sec. 15). Faith, in fact, is the "principal work" of the Holy Spirit (*Inst.* III.1.4; III.2.4) who "is the bond by which Christ effectually unites us to himself" (III.1.1).

Since faith would be impossible apart from the aid of the Spirit, faith is ultimately "an excellent and singular gift of God" (Catechism, sec. 15). In this section Calvin alludes to passages like 2 Corinthians 1:22, Ephesians 1:13, and Romans 8:16 to stress that our faith would soon falter and fail if it were not for divine assistance. "The Spirit accordingly serves as a seal, to seal up in our hearts those very promises the certainty of which it had previously impressed upon our minds; and takes the place of a guarantee to confirm and establish them" (*Inst.* III.2.36.) Here, too, Calvin appeals to Ephesians 1:13–14 and 2 Corinthians 1:21–22.[7]

Yet Calvin is enough of a realist to recognize that even the most zealous Christian is plagued at times by moments of doubt. Although he insists that faith is "distinguished from . . . doubtful and uncertain opinions, . . . it would be inconsistent that faith should waver."[8] Faith is contrary to doubtfulness,[9] for God's truth is sure and God's promises will not fail. Existentially, however, Calvin concedes that "while we teach that faith ought to be certain and assured, we cannot imagine any certainty that is not tinged with doubt, or any assurance that is not assailed by some anxiety." To the contrary, "believers are in perpetual conflict with their own unbelief" (*Inst.* III.2.17; a prime illustration here for Calvin is King David's experience as recorded in Psalms 42:5, 11; 43:5; 77:9, etc.). But as long as we are aware of these temptations and doubts and struggle to overcome them we are "already in large part victorious" (III.2.17). The life of faith is inevitably one of struggle and conflict because we can never escape the "imperfection of faith" (III.2.18). But even weak faith is real faith (III.2.19).[10]

In any case, our confidence is not based on our faith but on God's grace. The indestructible certainty of faith rests ultimately upon Christ's oneness with us. For we must not think of Christ as dwelling in the heavens remote from us and our existence. Rather, through faith (and baptism) Christ "makes us, ingrafted into his body, participants not only in all his benefits but also in himself" (III.2.24). We are "deprived" of all these benefits, Calvin says later in another context, "until Christ is made ours." Then follows an oft-quoted passage where Calvin speaks of this union with Christ as a "mystical union."[11]

That joining together of Head and members, that indwelling of Christ in our hearts—in short, that mystical union—are accorded by us the highest degree of importance, so that Christ, having been made ours, makes us sharers with him in the gifts with which he has been endowed. We do not, therefore, contemplate him outside ourselves from afar in order that his righteousness may be imputed to us but because we put on Christ and are engrafted into his body—in short, because he deigns to make us one with him. For this reason, we glory that we have fellowship of righteousness with him. (Inst. III.11.10)

This is the real basis of our confidence and the guarantee of the victory of faith. For "with a wonderful communion, day by day, Christ grows more and more into one body with us, until he becomes completely one with us" (III.2.24). Faith, in short, is a uniquely intimate fellowship with the living Christ. "All its stability rests in him" (III.2.1; cf. III.17.1).

IV. JUSTIFICATION BY FAITH

This is but another way of expressing what is considered a key Protestant doctrine, namely, justification by faith. (However, Hans Küng and other Roman Catholic theologians insist that this doctrine is also maintained in Catholicism.)[12] Luther stressed this particular doctrine more than Calvin, but this does not mean that Calvin considered it secondary. Rather, he insists that this doctrine is "the main hinge on which religion turns" (*Inst.* III.11.1). Yet in several ways Calvin's treatment of this doctrine varies somewhat from that of Luther. For example, in the *Institutes* he takes up this doctrine *after* he has discussed regeneration and sanctification. In his 1538 Catechism he follows the more Lutheran order: justification is treated in sec. 16, sanctification in sec. 17.[13] But even here Calvin characteristically finds the basis for this doctrine in our faith-union with Christ. Christ "makes us sharers [*participes*] in himself," he explains, "that although we in ourselves are sinners, we may be adjudged righteous before God's throne. Thus stripped of our own righteousness, we are clad with Christ's righteousness; unrighteous in our own works, we are justified by faith in Christ" (sec. 16). In the *Institutes* Calvin briefly defines justification as "the acceptance with which God receives us into his favor as righteous men" (III.11.2). Later, in his discussion of good works he gives a more complete definition: "We define justification as follows: the sinner, received into communion with Christ, is reconciled to God by his grace, while cleansed by Christ's blood, he obtains forgiveness of sins, and clothed with Christ's righteousness as if it were his own, he stands confident before the heavenly judgment seat" (III.17.8).[14]

It is important to see that for Calvin justification is not simply a forensic matter. That is, that we are only *declared* righteous and regarded by God *as if* we were not sinners on the basis of our faith in Christ. This is certainly an important truth and is clearly scriptural. This is the gist of the apostle Paul's argument in Romans 4: "Abraham believed God and it was *reckoned* to him as righteousness" (v. 3; emphasis added).[15]

However, the justification of the ungodly (Romans 4:5b) is not a legal fiction as is occasionally alleged. The believer is not simply "declared" or "reckoned" righteous, but is "clad with Christ's righteousness" and is "cleansed in him" (Catechism, sec. 16), phrases which are virtually repeated in the full definition cited above from the *Institutes* (III.17.8). Another benefit of justification is the forgiveness of sins, also noted in the above definition. Hence, after listing all the characteristics or benefits of justification in his Catechism, Calvin concludes: "in a word one may call this righteousness [Christ's righteousness, the righteousness of faith] truly 'forgiveness of sins'" (sec. 16). Similarly in the *Institutes:* "Therefore, we explain justification simply as the acceptance with which God receives us into his favor as righteous men. And we say that it consists in the remission of sins and the imputation of Christ's righteousness" (III.11.2).[16]

Thus to be justified is to be accepted, to be forgiven, to be clothed with the righteousness of Christ. Not only that, one of the wonderful benefits of being justified by faith is a "peace and quiet joy" of conscience (*Inst.* III.13.5). Moreover, on the last day, when we are called before God's judgment seat, we can do so with consciences that have "peaceful rest and serene tranquillity" (*Inst.* III.13.1). Either/or! At the last judgment a conscience which rests in its own righteousness will be "besieged by the terrors of hell"; or a conscience which "looks to God" and his righteousness will have "sure peace with his judgment" (*Inst.* III.13.3). The latter will "have in heaven instead of a Judge a gracious Father" (*Inst.* III.11.1).

It is clear that for Calvin justification is no mere forensic legal transaction or a formal technicality. It is an experiential reality, one of the greatest gifts of the gospel.[17]

V. SANCTIFICATION AND GOOD WORKS

For Calvin, however, *sanctification* is just as important as justification; and both are derived from our union with Christ. "Just as Christ by his righteousness intercedes on our behalf with the Father in order that with him as our sponsor we may be reckoned as righteous, so by participation in his Spirit he sanctifies to all purity and innocence" (sec. 17). By partaking of Christ we "receive a double grace," that is, justification and sanctification. The key text here is 1 Corinthians 1:30, especially the phrase, Christ "became for us . . . righteousness and sanctification and redemption."[18] On the basis of this passage Calvin concludes: "Therefore Christ justifies no one whom he does not at that same time sanctify. . . . He bestows both of these benefits at the same time, the one never without the other" (*Inst.* III.16.1).

In this way Calvin also answers the Roman Catholic charge that Protestants have so emphasized justification by faith that the importance of good works and holiness of life fades into the background.[19] With Luther and some of his disciples there may be some basis for this criticism, although one of Luther's later battles was with the antinomian flank on his left. Moreover, Luther would have agreed with Calvin's statement that "we dream neither of a faith devoid of good works nor of a justification that stands without them" (ibid.). And both reformers were agreed that good works are never the cause of our justification but only its fruit. In section 19 Calvin makes this crystal clear. But in this life we never measure up to the standards of God's righteousness, even when we are at our best. Hence "we always have need of Christ, by whose perfection our imperfection is covered, by whose purity our uncleanness is cleaned, by whose obedience our iniquity is wiped out, and finally on account of whose righteousness, righteousness is freely imputed to us, without any reckoning of our works, which are in no way great enough for us to stand up in God's judgment" (sec. 19).

The best of our good works are never perfect. "For even though this fact could seem incredible, it is nonetheless very true. No work at all leaves our hand accomplished with complete perfection, and unmarked by some defect" (Catechism, sec. 19). Hence even our best works must also be justified if they are to be acceptable to God. This leads Calvin to "formulate a doctrine of double justification":[20] the first is the justification of the sinner and then the justification of the justified person's works.

> As we ourselves, when we have been engrafted in Christ, are righteous in God's sight because our iniquities are covered by Christ's sinlessness, so our works are righteous and are thus regarded because whatever fault is otherwise in them is buried in Christ's purity, and is not charged to our account. Accordingly, we can deservedly say that by faith alone not only we ourselves but our works as well are justified (*Inst*. III.17.10).[21]

It is not that our good works are unimportant. They are a sign of our gratitude and bring honor to God. Keep in mind that "through faith we are sanctified unto obedience to the law" (title of sec. 17). Accordingly, "we must ever strive in the direction of our call" as we "are directed to the good by the Spirit of the Lord" (*Inst*. III.17.6).

VI. REPENTANCE AND REGENERATION

The observant reader of the Catechism may well think we are going backward! For the normal way of treating the various loci (topics) of theology when dealing with the doctrine of salvation would be to begin with regeneration, then take up repentance, faith, and justification, and conclude with sanctification (or glorification). Here in section 18 Calvin seems to reverse that order. He begins with faith (secs. 14 and 15), then discusses

justification (sec. 16) and sanctification (sec. 17), which is the usual procedure; but how can we explain the placement of section 18 with the simple
title: "Repentance and Regeneration"?

At least two answers can be given. First, there is Calvin's fluid use of
terminology, or to put it more negatively, his lack of precision in his use
of key theological words. It was left to the seventeenth-century orthodox
theologians to "clean up" this lack of tidiness and develop a more orderly,
logical system. That, however, is not all gain, for there is a dynamism in
the sixteenth-century reformers which sometimes gets domesticated by
their successors.

As a result of this fluidity or lack of precision, it is sometimes difficult
to distinguish between Calvin's use of key concepts such as regeneration
and sanctification, on the one hand, and repentance and conversion on the
other. However, if we accept Calvin on his own terms, many of the difficulties can be resolved. Generally he defines his terms quite carefully, although occasionally there is some overlapping. Thus repentance and
conversion are often virtually identical. The same can be said of regeneration and sanctification,[22] although for Calvin regeneration is generally a
more comprehensive term.[23]

In the Catechism, Calvin begins with repentance and quickly identifies
it with rebirth and conversion. Then, almost in passing, he alludes to regeneration.[24] In order to understand Calvin's progression here, it is necessary to quote most of this highly condensed section and then unpack its
various components.

> We are now ready to understand why *repentance* is always joined with
> *faith* in Christ, why also the Lord affirms that no one can enter into the
> kingdom of heaven, unless he is *reborn*. For *repentance* signifies *conver-
> sion*, by which, having said farewell to the perversity of this world, we
> betake ourselves into the Lord's way. Moreover, Christ is not the minis-
> ter of sin, and for that reason he does not *clothe with participation in his
> righteousness* those cleansed of the corruptions of sins, in order that we
> may profane with new filth repeatedly his great grace, but that we,
> *adopted* as God's children, may *consecrate our lives* forever to our Father's
> glory. But this effect of *repentance* depends upon our *regeneration,* which
> *consists of two parts:* the *mortification* of our flesh, that is, the mortification
> of the corruption inborn in us, *and spiritual rightness.* We must press our
> whole life toward this meditation, that dead to sin and to ourselves, we
> may live to Christ and his righteousness (sec. 18; emphasis added).

What Calvin does here in one paragraph is developed at length in a
long chapter in the *Institutes* (III.3). Here he clarifies and amplifies the
points made in the closely packed paragraph in the Catechism.

Note first that repentance is linked to faith. "Repentance is always
joined with faith in Christ" (sec. 18). In the *Institutes* Calvin is more specific: repentance *follows* faith. In fact, he says that "it ought to be a fact

beyond controversy that repentance not only constantly follows faith but is born of faith" (III.3.1). Not that there is a temporal sequence. Rather, one will not repent apart from a knowledge of God; and not just a general knowledge, for "no one is truly persuaded that he belongs to God unless he has first recognized God's grace" (III.3.2).

Moreover, repentance is not a one-time act but a life-long process. "There must be an unflagging pursuit of repentance even unto death" (sec. 18). Luther had already stated this in the first of his 95 theses.[25] Calvin also equates repentance with conversion and defines it as having two parts: "mortification of our flesh" and "spiritual rightness" or "vivification through which man's nature is restored to integrity" (sec. 18).[26] In short, repentance or conversion consists of mortification and vivification.[27] The former consists of being "dead to sin and ourselves"; the latter consists in living "to Christ and his righteousness" (ibid.). That is, mortification involves denying our old nature. But this can only happen when we are "violently slain by the Spirit and brought to nought" (*Inst.* III.3.8).

Vivification, our renewal in Christ, consists in "the desire to live in a holy and devoted manner, a desire arising from rebirth; as if it were said that a man dies to himself that he may begin to live to God" (*Inst.* III.3.3). Note that the presupposition here is that one has experienced a "rebirth" or is "reborn" (sec. 18). On the basis of Romans 6:6 Calvin concludes that "both things [mortification and vivification] happen to us by participation in Christ" (*Inst.* III.3.9). Calvin accordingly interprets repentance as equivalent to regeneration[28] "whose sole end is to restore in us the image of God" (*Inst.* III.3.9). After citing several passages that speak of this renewal—2 Corinthians 3:18; Ephesians 4:23; and Colossians 3:10—Calvin concludes:

> Indeed, this restoration does not take place in one moment or one day or one year; but through continual and sometimes even slow advances God wipes out in his elect the corruptions of the flesh, cleanses them of guilt, consecrates them to himself as temples renewing all their minds to true purity that they may practice repentance throughout their lives and know that this warfare will end only at death (ibid.).[29]

V. CHRISTIAN HOPE

After discussing these various aspects of faith, Calvin gives a brief analysis of the Apostles' Creed, which he calls the "symbol of the faith" (sec. 20). His introductory statement is important, for it indicates that though faith may be more a matter of the heart than of the head, it nevertheless has a specific content. Hence he begins, "Now we must hear what our faith ought to look to in Christ and to ponder how it is to be strengthened" (sec. 20). Following his discussion of the Creed, he describes the relation of faith and hope (sec. 21). Here he does not discuss love, the other member of St. Paul's famous triad (see 1 Cor. 13:13), but this was taken up earlier in his treatment of the law (secs. 8 and 9). Calvin's discussion here is based on the famous definition of faith in Hebrews 11:1, where faith and hope are conjoined. Calvin sees in this passage the following contrasts:

> Thus faith believes God to be truthful; hope waits for him to show his truth at the right occasion. Faith believes God to be our Father; hope waits for him ever to act as such toward us. Faith believes eternal life has been given us; hope waits for it sometimes to be revealed. Faith is the foundation on which hope leans. Hope nourishes faith and sustains it (sec. 21).

Calvin concludes his chapter on faith in the *Institutes* with two sections on faith and hope. The one is largely polemical; Calvin counters Lombard's contention that hope has two foundations: God's grace and the merit of works. Calvin vehemently protests that hope, like faith, has only one foundation, that is, God's mercy (III.2.43).

The previous section, however, contains a paragraph which Karl Barth calls "one of the most striking passages in the *Institutes*."[30] It begins with the sentence, "Wherever this faith is alive, it must have along with it the hope of eternal salvation as its inseparable companion." Calvin then notes that both faith and hope are grounded in "a sure persuasion" of God's truth and particularly God's gracious promises. Then he adds this eloquent paragraph, which is an amplification of the lines from the Catechism quoted above:

> Accordingly, in brief, hope is nothing else than the expectation of those things which faith has believed to have been truly promised by God. Thus, faith believes God to be true, hope awaits the time when his truth shall be manifested; faith believes that he is our Father, hope anticipates that he will ever show himself to be a Father toward us; faith believes that eternal life has been given to us, hope anticipates that it will some time be revealed; faith is the foundation upon which hope rests, hope nourishes and sustains faith. For as no one except him who already believes his promises can look for anything from God, so again the weakness of our faith must be sustained and nourished by patient hope and expectation, lest it fail and grow faint. For this reason, Paul rightly sets our salvation in hope [Rom. 8:24]. For hope, while it awaits the Lord in silence, restrains faith that it may not fall headlong from too much haste. Hope strengthens faith, that it may not waver in God's promises, or begin to doubt concerning their truth. Hope refreshes faith, that it may not become weary. It sustains faith to the final goal, that it may not fail in mid-course, or even at the starting gate. In short, by unremitting renewing and restoring, it invigorates faith again and again with perseverance (III.2.42).[31]

9

THE APOSTLES' CREED

(Section 20)

Part I: "I Believe in God"

I. THE PLACE OF THE CREED IN CALVIN'S THEOLOGY

Ironically, early in his career Calvin's orthodoxy was slightly suspect for a while because of his refusal to subscribe to the three catholic creeds (Apostles', Nicene, and Athanasian). His lifelong nemesis, Pierre Caroli, an unreliable rogue, at a disputation in Bern in 1537 accused Farel and Calvin of Arianism, that is, of a faulty doctrine of the Trinity.

Calvin's response was (1) he had already affirmed his belief in one God; (2) he insisted that Caroli had no right to demand such a subscription; and (3) he pointed out that the authenticity of the Athanasian Creed was questionable and that it had never been adopted by a church council. In the Catechism he also acknowledges that he is not sure about the author(s) of the Apostles' Creed either: "Who the author was or rather who wrote down this epitome of the faith is not of great concern to us, for it contains nothing merely human but has been assembled from very sure testimonies of Scripture" (sec. 20, Introduction).[1]

It was not that Calvin did not have a high regard for the creeds, especially the Apostles' Creed; it was rather that he felt that the new Genevan Confession was adequate and faithfully reflected the teachings of the Bible. Moreover, all those present at the disputation would have needed to do was to check Calvin's newly published Catechism (available only in French at this juncture) to see with what respect he treats the Apostles' Creed.

He refers to it as "The Symbol of the Faith" (for some reason not so translated by Battles even though the Latin title is *Symbolum Fidei*). The word "symbol" in this context reflects an early Christian usage to denote that which stood for the faith, in particular the Apostles' Creed. Hence the study of Christian creeds is often called "Symbolics."[2]

The significance of the Apostles' Creed for Calvin's thinking is reflected in the later editions of the *Institutes*. Prior to 1543, whether in his first Catechism or the first two editions of the *Institutes*, the Creed was discussed in one lengthy chapter. In the third edition of the *Institutes* (Latin, 1543; French, 1545) he divides the discussion of the Creed into four chapters, which in the final 1559 edition became the framework for the structure of the whole *Institutes*, in other words, the four books of the *Institutes* which correspond more or less with the four parts of the Creed: Father, Son, Holy Spirit, Church.

It should be noted, however, that Calvin does not follow this order consistently; hence Edward Dowey, I believe, is correct in stressing that it is not so much the framework of the Creed as the notion of the twofold knowledge of God—God the Creator and God the Redeemer—which really determines the structure and distinctive character of the *Institutes*.[3] A staunch defender of the other view, that the Creed is the clue to the structure of the *Institutes,* is the English Calvin scholar T.H.L. Parker, who defends his thesis in *The Doctrine of the Knowledge of God*.[4] The strength of Parker's contention is that only one book is devoted to the knowledge of God the Creator, whereas three books are given over to the knowledge of God the Redeemer, an admittedly lopsided arrangement.

II. THE GOD OF CALVIN

This heading may sound strange, for normally one would speak of "Calvin's concept of God" or something similar. However, this phrase is a deliberate takeoff on the extremely negative and scornful references to "the God of Calvin" by certain popular writers and historians of an earlier era who, relying on old caricatures and secondary sources, often depicted Calvin's understanding of God as being cold, cruel, and capricious. Their conclusion was usually based on a superficial understanding of the discipline exercised in Geneva, the execution of Servetus, and a distaste for the doctrine of predestination.

An example of this kind of judgment comes from the popular historian Will Durant, in his volume *The Reformation,* volume 6 in the series The Story of Civilization. He concludes his fascinating but very uneven treatment of Calvin and the Genevan Reformation with the incredible sentence: "We shall always find it hard to love the man who darkened the human soul with the most absurd and blasphemous conception of God in all the long and honored history of nonsense."[5]

It is hard to take seriously such an intemperate blast, but one is nonplussed to find even a Reformation scholar of the stature of Harold J. Grimm, professor emeritus of history at Ohio State University, stating that whereas Luther "placed the loving and forgiving God of the New Testament in the foreground . . . Calvin followed Bucer in stressing the autocratic God of the Old Testament."[6]

That these caricatures have no basis in fact will be demonstrated later, but first we should take a look at Calvin's views of the Trinity and the providence of God.

A. The Trinity

In the Catechism Calvin makes only a passing reference to the Trinity. "When we name Father, Son, and Holy Spirit, we are not fashioning three Gods, but in the simplest unity (Lat.; cf. Fr. *essence*) of God, Scripture and the very experience of godliness [*pietatis*] disclose to us God the Father, his Son, and the Spirit" (sec. 20, introductory paragraph, my translation). He proceeds to point out that we cannot think of the one "person" of the Trinity without thinking of the others and hence our attention should be focused on the one God even when we experience him in three different forms.

There is nothing unusual about this description of the Trinity. The same is true of the later and fuller treatment in the 1559 *Institutes*, book I, chapter 13. Crucial here is Calvin's understanding of the difficult notion of the "persons" of the Trinity. He is obviously aware of the subtle distinctions made by various church fathers, in particular Hilary of Poitiers, Jerome, and Augustine. However, says Calvin, "I am not, indeed such a stickler as to battle doggedly over words" (I.13.5). He then tries to give as simple a definition as possible:

> "Person," therefore, I call a "subsistence" in God's essence, which, while related to the others, is distinguished by an incommunicable quality. By the term "subsistence" we would understand something different from "essence." For if the Word were simply God, and yet possessed no other characteristic mark, John would wrongly have said that the Word was always with God [John 1:1]. When immediately after he adds that the Word was also God himself, he recalls us to the essence as a unity. But because he could not be with God without residing in the Father, hence emerges the idea of a subsistence, which, even though it has been joined with the essence by a common bond and cannot be separated from it, yet has a special mark whereby it is distinguished from it. Now, of the three subsistences I say that each one, while related to the others, is distinguished by a special quality. This "relation" is here distinctly expressed; because where simple and indefinite mention is made of God, this name pertains no less to the Son and the Spirit than to the Father. But as soon as the Father is compared with the Son, the character of each distinguishes the one from the other. Thirdly, whatever is proper to each individually, I maintain to be incommunicable because whatever is attributed to the Father as a distinguishing mark cannot agree with, or be transferred to, the Son (*Inst.* I.13.6).

This is a fairly traditional definition and relatively nontechnical as far as discussions of the Trinity go. What is characteristically Calvinian, however, is his appeal not only to Scripture but also to "the very experience of godliness" (Catechism, sec. 20) as a source of our knowledge of the Trinity. He takes a similar tack later in his discussion of the divinity of the

Spirit. "For what Scripture attributes to him [the Holy Spirit] we ourselves learn by the sure experience of godliness" (*Inst.* I.13, 14).

These observations are significant for two reasons. One is that Calvin does not hesitate to appeal to the experience of believers, more particularly their godliness or piety, as that which can and should confirm the witness of Scripture. This is not atypical, for Calvin frequently appeals to experience with expressions like "Experience teaches . . ." or "with experience as our teacher we find God just as he declares himself in his Word" (*Inst.* I.11.2). Experience for Calvin is far preferable and more valuable than "high-flown speculation" (ibid.).

The second point is that for Calvin the doctrine of the Trinity was not an abtruse doctrine only of interest to theologians, but a vital belief for faith and life. He can deal with this question on a scholarly level when he discusses the shades of meaning in the Greek word *hypostasis* and the Latin *persona* (person), which he would translate as either "substance" or "subsistence" (*Inst.* I.13.2), the point being that each "person" or "hypostasis" in the Trinity is shared by the other and is conjoined in one essence or hypostatic union.[7] Here contemporary scholars frequently applaud Calvin not only for his awareness of the nuances in these technical words but also for his balanced presentation.[8]

All this notwithstanding, Calvin's primary concern is of a practical and religious nature, rather than theoretical and philosophical. Recall how in the beginning of his discussion in the Catechism and the *Institutes* he appeals to "the very experience of godliness." Similarly, in the *Institutes* he warns against "evanescent speculation" (I.13.19), and affirms that "this practical knowledge [of the Trinity] is doubtless more certain and firmer than any idle speculation" (I.13.13). B. B. Warfield is quite correct, therefore, in asserting that for Calvin "the doctrine of the Trinity did not for him stand out of relation to his religious consciousness but was a postulate of his profoundest religious emotions; was given, indeed, in his experience of salvation itself."[9]

B. The Providence of God

It is significant—and again typical—that in Calvin's very brief discussion of the first article of the Creed, "I believe in one God, Father Almighty . . . ," he does so first in terms of God's covenant with his people and then God's providence. Note the language: The point of this confession, he observes, is not simply to believe in God (Fr.,"to believe that God exists") but to "recognize him to be our God, and to trust that we are among the number of those to whom he promises he will be God and whom he receives as his people" (sec. 20). Calvin is clearly thinking of the one covenant promise that runs throughout Scripture: "I will be your God and you shall be my people." Thus, for Calvin, to believe in God the Creator is to believe in the God of the covenant.

Next, to believe in God the Almighty means to believe in God's providential care and concern for his creation. For God's omnipotence signifies that "he administers all things by his providence, governs by his will, and directs by his hand" (ibid.). Calvin's interpretation of God the Creator runs along similar lines, that is, that we are to understand by this "that all he once created he everlastingly nourishes, sustains and quickens" (ibid.). It is interesting to see that later when Calvin discusses the phrase, "I believe in the Holy Spirit," he explains, "Through that power [the Spirit of Christ] he empowers and sustains all things, causes them to grow and quickens them . . ." (sec. 20, vi). This only bears out the point made earlier that despite the distinctions between the "persons" of the Trinity, for Calvin what is true of one is true of all.

In the *Institutes* three chapters (I.16–18) are devoted to the theme of God's providence. Calvin begins by observing: "Moreover, to make God a momentary Creator, who once for all finished his work, would be cold and barren, and we must differ from profane men especially in that we see the presence of divine power shining as much in the continuing state of the universe as in its inception" (I.16.1). This is reminiscent of Calvin's positive view of the revelatory character of this creation as a "theater of God's glory" (see *Institutes* I.14.20; cf. I.5.1, 2, 8, 11; I.6.2).

God as the "everlasting Creator and Preserver" (I.16.1) governs not only the created order of nature by "his fatherly favor" but also directs the lives of individuals. God's gracious providence is evident above all in his special concern for the church (I.17.1, 6). Calvin's concern is that we allow nothing to fate, fortune, or chance. At the same time, he is concerned to establish our responsibility (I.17.3, 4) and the significance of intermediate or secondary causes (I.16.9; cf. I.17.1). This does not mean that there are no riddles or enigmas in human existence. Yet God's "wonderful method of governing the universe is rightly called an abyss, because while it is hidden from us, we ought reverently to adore it" (I.17.2). Our response should be that of humble submission "under the Spirit's guidance"[10] as we seek to learn God's revealed will in the Scriptures (I.17.4, 5; cf. I.17.2).

Whereas later Calvinists have sometimes misread, distorted, or ignored the reformer's position, in stressing the providence of God they have been true to their ecclesiastical mentor. For as Calvin says, "nothing is more profitable than the knowledge of this doctrine" (I.17.3). "The ignorance of providence is the ultimate of all miseries, the highest blessedness lies in the knowledge of it" (I.17.11). In the midst of adversity, nothing is more comforting than the conviction that God is in control (I.17.8).

Yet, when that light of divine providence has once shone upon a godly man, he is then relieved and set free not only from the extreme anxiety and fear that were pressing him before, but from every care. For as he justly dreads fortune, so he fearlessly dares commit himself to God. His solace, I say, is to know that his Heavenly Father so holds all things in his power, so rules by his authority and will, so governs by his wisdom, that nothing can befall except he determine it. Moreover, it comforts him to know that he has been received into God's safekeeping and entrusted to the care of his angels, and that neither water, nor fire, nor iron can harm him, except in so far as it pleases God as governor to give them occasion.

(Inst. I. 17.11)

III. KEY MOTIFS IN
CALVIN'S CONCEPT OF GOD

Finally, we must come back again to Calvin's much maligned doctrine of God. It must be conceded at the outset that it is not only second-rate historians and older foes of all that Calvin stood for but also some serious, responsible, and basically appreciative theologians who find Calvin's concept of God problematic. The leading example of this type is Karl Barth, who admires much in Calvin's understanding of God but feels that ultimately Calvin's portrayal is vitiated by his doctrine of reprobation (predestination to damnation). This results in an abstract God who can and does seemingly operate at times—at least in reprobation—apart from Jesus Christ. This, Barth is convinced, casts a shadow over Calvin's whole concept of God.[11] Barth's many references to Calvin are generally positive, but in his treatment of the doctrine of election Barth's discontent with Calvin—and all traditional views of predestination—becomes apparent.[12]

However, it should be pointed out that Barth's solution to the problem results in what I would call an incipient universalism. That is, the eternal will of God and his election of grace are so identified with Jesus Christ that it is almost impossible to escape from God's determination to save all people in Jesus Christ, the elect man who has already, once and for all, taken our condemnation and rejection on himself.[13]

From this it is clear that there is no simple solution to this problem, while at the same time acknowledging that one's view of God and one's doctrine of election are bound to interpenetrate and color each other. Still, we must move beyond that problem to see how Calvin sought to describe the nature and ways of God.

This should also be our procedure in responding to another criticism of Calvin's doctrine of God: that he was influenced by a philosophical school known as nominalism or terminism. This asserts that we cannot really know the real; by an act of faith we must believe that what things are called corresponds in some way to the reality behind the object. William of Ockham and Duns Scotus are the two names usually associated with this movement, which developed in the fourteenth century. Scotus's influence was mediated through one of his leading disciples, John Major, a Scottish theologian who taught in Paris during Calvin's student days.

Since Scotus emphasized the will rather than the being of God, and since Calvin frequently appeals to God's will as "the sole rule of righteousness, and the truly just cause of all things" (*Inst.* I.17.2; cf. III.23.2), Calvin is often identified with Scotus and the nominalists, some of whom ascribed to God an absolute power divorced from his justice. The result is an arbitrary God of lawless caprice. Twice Calvin explicitly denies that he believes anything like that (*Inst.* I.17.2 and III.23.2), but until recently he has been accused of echoing Scotus in some of his statements.[14]

This is a very complex matter that again admits of no simple solution, but it should be noted first that most Calvin scholars today are convinced that Calvin is free from the idea that behind the God we know is some capricious God who is different from the God revealed in Jesus Christ. Second, recent research reveals that Calvin's alleged mentor, Scotus (through Major), did not teach some of the things attributed to him.[15] T. F. Torrance, in fact, staunchly maintains that Scotus has been frightfully misrepresented in this regard and was not a nominalist at all, but a realist![16]

How, then, does Calvin depict God in his writings, particularly in his catechisms and the *Institutes*? Here the average Calvinist is in for some surprises, for it is generally thought that the sovereignty of God is Calvin's central doctrine. However, that is not the case. The idea is certainly there, for Calvin frequently refers to God's omnipotence, majesty, glory, and power.[17] (The key word in the first three chapters of the Catechism is "majesty.") But the word "sovereignty" in reference to God does not appear in the *Institutes*.[18]

No, the key concepts in Calvin's portrayal of God, especially God the Redeemer, are "gratuitous [free] mercy" (*gratuita misericordia*) and variations such as "gratuitous goodness" and "gratuitous love" (*Inst.* III.21.7; Comm. Gen. 12:1 and Rom. 8:3; *Inst.* II.7.14; Comm. Gen. 17:15 and Ex. 34:5; *Inst.* III.21.5; Comm. 1 John 4:9. These precise expressions are not found in the Catechism, but on the mercy of God see sec. 8.2 and sec. 13, and on God's goodness see sec. 23), as well as "fatherly goodness," "fatherly love," and similar expressions denoting the fatherly character of God (*Inst.* I.10.1; I.14.2, 22; III.2.12, 16; III.14.17; cf. I.2.1 and 2, and the Catechism, secs. 12 and 15). Edward Dowey, after an extensive investigation of this subject in his book *The Knowledge of God in Calvin's Theology*, concludes that the two most prominent attributes Calvin employs for describing God the Redeemer are really one, that is, gratuitous mercy. "These two words represent the two poles of saving knowledge 'of God' as Redeemer and 'of ourselves' as redeemed. Both poles are on one axis: Christ."[19]

In a later study of the doctrine of God, Garret Wilterdink, former professor at Western Theological Seminary, confirms the findings of Warfield and Dowey in regard to Calvin's conception of God. He finds a key expression in God's "fatherly goodness." Contrary to many caricatures of Calvin's view of God, Wilterdink demonstrates that for the Genevan reformer the understanding of God as Father "is constitutive to his very outlook on Christian faith and life."[20] Although Wilterdink sees a tension in Calvin's views of divine fatherhood and the irresistibility of grace, he concludes that the "use of mystery allows Calvin to emphasize the personal, paternal care of the Father alongside an equally strong emphasis on the immutability and autonomy of grace, and leave them juxtaposed without systematic resolution."[21]

An English scholar, R. A. Finlayson, comes to a similar conclusion: "The sense of divine Fatherhood is as fundamental to Calvin's conception of God as that of divine sovereignty. Indeed, his doctrine is outstanding among Reformed statements in the commanding place it gives to the divine Fatherhood."[22]

Calvin, of course, lists other attributes of God: life, wisdom, might, power, justice, clemency, and truth, as well as mercy and goodness. (All of these are found in two lists in the Catechism, one in sec. 3, the other in sec. 24 under the first petition of the Lord's Prayer.)

Such lists, however, are not as meaningful as particular places where Calvin is appealing to the character of God. One is in his comments on the preface to the Decalogue ("who brought you out of the land of Egypt . . ."). Here in the context of the *law* Calvin stresses God's kindness, power, and mercy.

> There is no one, I say, who ought not to be captivated to embrace the Lawgiver, in the observance of whose commandments he is taught to take especial delight; from whose kindness he expects both an abundance of all good things and the glory of immortal life; by whose marvelous power and mercy he knows himself freed from the jaws of death (*Inst.* II.8.1).

Another passage, rich with meaning, is found in Calvin's discussion of the Lord's Prayer, the first petition ("Our Father"). First, he observes that whenever we call God "Father" we ought to think of Christ through whom we have become God's children. Then he adds:

> By the great sweetness of this name he frees us from all distrust, since no greater feeling of love can be found elsewhere than in the Father. Therefore he could not attest his own boundless love toward us with any surer proof than the fact that we are called "children of God" (1 John 3:1). But just as he surpasses all men in goodness and mercy, so is his love greater and more excellent than all our parents' love (*Inst.* III.20.36).

So much for the so-called "God of Calvin"!

10

THE APOSTLES' CREED
(Section 20)

Part II: "And in Jesus Christ"

I. INTRODUCTION

One of the distinctive contributions of Wilhelm Niesel's modern classic in Calvin studies, *The Theology of Calvin*,[1] was to point out the Christocentric character of Calvin's theology. Prior to the first edition of this work in 1938, the traditional approach had been to focus on the theocentric character of Calvin's theology. However, B. B. Warfield and others have with considerable justice also dubbed Calvin "the theologian of the Holy Spirit."[2]

All three positions are true. It is fruitless to pit one against the other. Yet Niesel performed an important service by highlighting a neglected aspect in older Calvin studies, namely, the evangelical thrust of Calvin's theology. The reformer may not be thoroughly Christocentric in the Barthian sense, but there is no denying the force of the quotations Niesel cites in his second chapter, which show that for Calvin Jesus Christ is the center, purpose, and goal (*scopus*) of the Scriptures.[3] In Calvin's words, "We must read Scripture with the intention of finding Christ therein. If we turn aside from this end, however much trouble we take, however much time we devote to our study, we shall never attain the knowledge of truth."[4]

However, Calvin's Christology has not attracted the same attention as several other aspects of his theology, partially because it is assumed that his treatment of the person and work of Christ is rather traditional. Moreover, the space devoted to this subject in his 1538 Catechism and the *Institutes* is relatively slight.[5] Nevertheless, Calvin does make several distinctive contributions to theology in his treatment of the two natures of Christ: the work of Christ as prophet, priest, and king; the death of Christ not only as sacrificial and substitutionary but also as a victory over death and the devil; his stress on the significance of the resurrection of Christ; and finally, the special place he assigns to the ascension of Christ and his heavenly priesthood.

These themes will be taken up in order in this chapter, albeit with the brevity befitting a study of this sort—and mindful of Calvin's own love of brevity!

II. THE THREEFOLD
OFFICE OF CHRIST

For all of his theological prowess, there are few doctrines that can be said to be uniquely Calvinian. One of those is Calvin's development of the threefold office of Christ (*munus triplex Christi*) to describe the work of Christ the Mediator.

The early church taught a twofold office of Christ (as priest and king), although Eusebius also referred to a prophetic office, as did Thomas Aquinas and Bucer centuries later. Calvin originally taught only a twofold office, as we see in the Catechism (sec. 20, iii), but the following year, in the second edition of the *Institutes* (1539), he added the prophetic office, as well as in his Geneva Catechism (1541).[6]

Although the idea was not original with Calvin, his formulation of it was unique and was taken over by both Reformed and Lutheran Orthodox theologians in the next century. Even the nineteenth-century liberal theologians Ritschl and Schleiermacher employ this schema, though in quite a different manner. Many modern works on dogmatics continue to use this formula for describing the person and work of Christ.[7]

Calvin begins his discussion of the phrase in the Creed, "And in Jesus Christ our Lord," with the observation: "Earlier we taught that Christ is the proper object of faith. From this it readily appears that in him are represented all parts of our salvation" (sec. 20, ii).

Then he comments briefly on the two Christological titles "Jesus" and "Christ" and points out that in his anointing as the Christ (Messiah) Jesus "was first appointed King by the Father, to subject to himself all power in heaven and on earth . . ." (ibid.). There is nothing unusual in this description of the kingship of Christ. What is noteworthy, however, is what Calvin adds to his description: "*that in him we might be kings,* having sway over the devil, sin, death, and hell." The privileges and powers of Christ's offices are shared by his people!

The same is true of his priestly office. For Christ "was also consecrated priest to placate by his self-sacrifice and reconcile the Father to us, *that in himself we might be priests,* with him as our Intercessor and Mediator, offering our prayers, our thanks, ourselves, and our all to the Father" (ibid., emphasis added).

In the Geneva Catechism (1541) where Calvin adds the third office, that of prophet, there is a similar emphasis. First he explains in Question 39 that Christ is a prophet "because on coming down into the world [Isa. 7:14] he was the sovereign messenger and ambassador of God his Father, to give a full exposition of God's will toward the world and so put an end to all prophecies and revelations [Heb. 1:2]." Then Calvin asks in typical fashion (Q. 40), "But do you derive any benefit from this?" The answer applies to all three offices: "All this is for our good. For Jesus Christ has received all these gifts in order that he may communicate them to us, and that all of us may receive out of his fullness." Later he speaks more specifically concerning the personal benefit to be derived from Christ's prophetic office. "Since this office was given to the Lord Jesus to be the Master and Teacher of his own, its end is to bring us the true knowledge of the Father and of his truth, so *that we may be scholars in the household of God*" (Q. 44, emphasis added).[8]

In the *Institutes* a whole chapter is devoted to this theme. The title is revealing: "To Know the Purpose for Which Christ Was Sent by the Father, and What He Conferred Upon Us, We Must Look Above All at Three Things in Him: The Prophetic Office, Kingship, and Priesthood" (II.15).[9] Here too Calvin emphasizes that Christ was anointed by the Spirit with these three offices "not only for himself . . . but for his whole body . . ." (*Inst.* II.15.1). "The emphasis on 'for us' is the central theme of all that Calvin has to say about the 'office' of Christ. Nothing happens here 'for itself' but everything is 'for us.' Soteriology is nothing other than Christology properly understood."[10]

This is beautifully and succinctly expressed in a passage in the Catechism where Calvin is commenting on the phrase, "He was conceived of the Holy Ghost, born of the Virgin Mary": "Here we see how he became for us the Son of God, and Jesus, that is, Savior. . . . He put on our flesh in order that having submitted to our weakness, he might strengthen us by his power; having accepted our mortality, he might give us immortality; having descended to earth, he might raise us to heaven" (sec. 20, iii).[11]

Christ's birth, life, ministry, and reconciling deeds are thus all "for us and for our salvation." Over against scholastic theologians such as Lombard and Aquinas, who taught that Christ acquired merit for himself through his obedience and death, Calvin cites Romans 8:32, John 17:19, and similar passages and comments: "He who gave away the fruit of his holiness to others testifies that he acquired nothing for himself. . . . To devote himself completely to saving us, Christ in a way forgot himself" (*Inst.* II.17.6).

It is impossible, therefore, to sharply separate the person and work of Christ, as is often done in systematic theologies. What Christ did is inseparably related to who he is.[12]

Moreover, Calvin would also have us not separate the doctrine of Christ (Christology) from the doctrine of salvation (soteriology). Although the formal discussion of the appropriation of Christ's benefits by the believer takes place in book 3, Calvin cannot refrain from pointing out even here in the context of the kingship of Christ that our participation in Christ's benefits is thanks to the work of the Holy Spirit.

Especially with regard to heavenly life, there is not a drop of vigor in us save what the Holy Spirit instills. For the Spirit has chosen Christ as his seat, that from him might abundantly flow the heavenly riches of which we are in such need. The believers stand unconquered through the strength of their king, and his spiritual riches abound in them. Hence they are justly called Christians (*Inst.* II.15.5).

III. CHRIST'S RECONCILING DEATH

Although the redemptive significance of Christ's death was touched on in the brief discussion of Christ's priestly work, this subject calls for more attention. It is often assumed in discussions of the atonement that Calvin's view is only a refinement of the Anselmic approach, which is usually described as the "satisfaction" or "penal" theory.

There are, admittedly, many similarities. Calvin does not hesitate to use the word "satisfaction," and he gives the impression at times that Christ appeased the wrath of God the Father by taking our sins upon himself. Note, for example, the key words in the following passage from the Catechism (sec. 20, iv):

For because God was provoked to wrath by man's disobedience, by Christ's own obedience he wiped out ours, showing himself obedient to his Father, even unto death. And by his death he offered himself as a *sacrifice* to his Father, in order that his justice might once for all be *appeased* for all time, in order that believers might be eternally sanctified, in order that the eternal *satisfaction* might be fulfilled. He poured out his sacred blood in *payment* for our redemption, in order that God's anger, kindled against us, might be extinguished, and our iniquity might be cleansed [emphasis mine].

Calvin continued to use such language in the final edition of the *Institutes.* "The priestly office belongs to Christ alone because by the sacrifice of his death he blotted out our guilt and made satisfaction for our sins [Heb. 9:22]" (*Inst.* II.15.6). Calvin finds support for such a view not only in the passage cited above, but also in texts such as 1 John 2:2 and 4:10; 2 Corinthians 5:19, 21; Colossians 1:19–20; Ephesians 1:6 and 2:15–16; all of which are cited in II.17.2. Then he comments, " . . . if Christ made satisfaction for our sins, if he paid the penalty owed by us, if he appeased God by his obedience—in short, if as a righteous man he suffered for unrighteous men—then he acquired salvation for us by his righteousness . . ." (II.17.3). After citing Romans 5:10–11 and 5:19 he concludes: "The meaning, therefore, is: God, by whom we were hateful because of sin, was appeased by the death of his Son to become favorable toward us" (ibid.).

Taken out of context, these quotations give the impression that there is a tension within the Godhead concerning the mode of redemption. It might be concluded that God the holy Father is only inclined to judge and punish a rebellious humanity, whereas Christ, the loving and compassionate Son, by virtue of his substitutionary sacrifice for sin, persuades the Father, almost against his will, to save a fallen race.

Calvin clearly does not hold such a crude view of the atonement. In all of his writings he emphasizes that the origin of our salvation is in the love and mercy of God. "The ground of our redemption is that immense love of God toward us by which it happened that he did not even spare his own Son" (Comm. Heb. 2:9). As he puts it tersely in the *Institutes:* "God is one; Christ is God and the Son of God; our salvation rests in God's mercy" (IV.1.12).

How then should we interpret those passages cited above where Calvin speaks of Christ's appeasing the wrath of God and satisfying his justice? Calvin concedes that there is "some sort of contradiction" (*aliqua repugnantae species*) here, i.e., the tension between God's wrath and love. He cites Romans 5:9–10, Galatians 3:10, 13, and Colossians 1:21–22, which speak of God's wrath and our being enemies of God and under a curse, and observes that "Expressions of this sort have been accommodated to our capacity that we may better understand how miserable and ruinous our condition is apart from Christ." Then follows a typically Calvinian explanation: "For if it had not been clearly stated that the wrath and vengeance of God and eternal death rested upon us, we would scarcely have recognized how miserable we would have been without God's mercy, and we would have underestimated the benefit of liberation" (*Inst.* II.16.2).

Two things are to be noted here: (1) God's wrath is a response to sin, but God initiates our liberation from sin by his mercy. (2) This mercy cannot be experienced apart from Christ. "For apart from Christ, God is, so to speak, hostile to us . . ." (ibid.).

Though we are by nature deserving of wrath, God "is moved by pure and freely given love of us to receive us into grace" (*Inst.* II.16.3)—and such grace is to be found in Christ. "Therefore, by his love God the Father goes before and anticipates our reconciliation in Christ. Indeed, 'because he first loved us' [1 John 4:19], he afterward reconciles us to himself" (ibid.).

Nowhere is this stress on the love of God as being the ground of our salvation expressed more strikingly than in a paraphrase of Augustine:

"God's love," says he, "is incomprehensible and unchangeable. For it was not after we were reconciled to him through the blood of his Son that he began to love us. Rather, he has loved us before the world was created, that we also might be his sons along with his only-begotten Son—before we became anything at all. The fact that we were reconciled through Christ's death must not be understood as if his Son reconciled us to him that he might now begin to love those whom he had hated. Rather, we have already been reconciled to him who loves us, with whom we were enemies on account of sin. The apostle will testify whether I am speaking the truth: 'God shows his love for us in that while we were yet sinners Christ died for us' [Rom. 5:8]. Therefore, he loved us even when we practiced enmity toward him and committed wickedness. Thus in a marvelous and divine way he loved us even when he hated us. For he hated us for what we were that he had not made; yet because our wickedness had not entirely consumed his handiwork, he knew how, at the same time, to hate in each one of us what we had made, and to love what he had made" (*Inst.* II.16.4).

This should suffice to show that there is no tension in the Godhead, that Christ the Son, does not have to "twist the Father's arm," so to speak, in order to win our salvation. The initiative is with God the Father, the implementation by God the Son and Holy Spirit. Such distinctions can lead to misunderstanding, however, for Christ is not merely the instrument or means of our redemption. Our reconciliation from beginning to end is the work of the one God: Father, Son, and Holy Spirit. "One must go all the way back to the eternal counsels of the triune God to reach the primary source of Calvin's doctrine of the atonement."[13]

One more question must still be clarified. In Gustaf Aulén's famous little book *Christus Victor: An Historical Study of the Three Main Types of the Idea of the Atonement*,[14] he submits that there are three main approaches to the doctrine of the atonement: (1) The "classic," or dramatic, view which, he maintains, "dominates the whole of Greek patristic theology from Irenaeus to John of Damascus";[15] (2) The so-called "Latin" view of the atonement, which found classic form in Anselm's *Cur Deus Homo?* (Why Did God Become Man?); (3) The moral influence theory, whose chief representative is Abelard.

Aulén favors the dramatic view, whereby the atonement is understood primarily in terms of Christ's victory over sin, death, and the devil. This is also basically Luther's view, he affirms. He ignores Calvin, but in books on the history of the atonement it is usually assumed that Calvin fits best in the second category, that is, the Latin type, where the idea of penal substitution is predominant.[16] Since "satisfaction" is a key word in the Anselmic theory and since Calvin also uses that word, as we have seen, it might be concluded that Calvin's approach is basically the same as Anselm's. However, the differences are significant. First, Anselm argues philosophically, not biblically as Calvin does. For Anselm, that in God which must be satisfied is his honor; for Calvin it is God's justice. More important, Anselm, like the later scholastics, sees Christ as obtaining excess merit by virtue of his perfect obedience. His reward is the salvation of those who believe in him. There is nothing like this in Calvin. Moreover,

Calvin, unlike Anselm, views the atonement as grounded in the love of God and flowing from it. For Calvin, Christ's life of obedience and resurrection also play a significant role in our redemption, whereas this is not the case with Anselm.[17]

Aulén's typology is too simplistic, for he ignores other key biblical motifs in regard to the death of Christ, such as obedience and sacrifice. He also underestimates the idea in Luther of Christ as our penal substitute.[18] Not only that, he fails to recognize that the *Christus Victor* motif—the so-called "classic" view of the atonement—is also found frequently in Calvin.[19]

One quotation will have to suffice, but note that here sacrificial and forensic motifs are combined with that of *Christus Victor:*

> Our common nature with Christ is the pledge of our fellowship with the Son of God; and clothed with our flesh he vanquished sin and death together that the victory and triumph might be ours. He offered as a sacrifice the flesh he received from us, that he might wipe out our guilt by his act of expiation and appease the Father's righteous wrath (*Inst.* II.12.3; cf. II.12.2; II.16.7).[20]

Space limitations do not allow a discussion of two major themes in Calvin's doctrine of reconciliation, that is, the redemptive significance of Christ's obedience and the sacrificial nature of his death. Two brief quotations must suffice. In his Catechism, Calvin begins his discussion of the phrase in the Creed—"Suffered under Pontius Pilate"—with the explanation that our redemption was accomplished "because God was provoked to wrath by man's disobedience, by Christ's own obedience he wiped out ours, showing himself obedient to his Father, even unto death. And by his death he offered himself as a sacrifice to the Father . . ." (sec. 20, iv). In the *Institutes,* after pointing out that Christ's sacrificial death would have been meaningless unless it had resulted from his willing obedience, Calvin concludes: "We must hold fast to this: that no proper sacrifice to God could have been offered unless Christ, disregarding his own feelings, subjected and yielded himself wholly to his Father's will" (II.16.3; Calvin's key text here is Heb. 10:7).

It should be clear that Calvin's understanding of the atonement is very complex. Unlike Anselm, he has no *theory* of the atonement. In his study of Calvin's sermons, T.H.L. Parker also finds a variety of images and motifs in Calvin's presentation of Christ's reconciling work, five to be exact: (1) sacrifice; (2) satisfaction; (3) obedience; (4) cleansing (expiation of sin); (5) victory.[21]

We have already encountered all five of these themes in passages cited from the Catechism, the *Institutes,* and commentaries. It is significant, however, that Calvin nowhere tries to blend them into a systematic unity.

If there is any one overarching theme, it is that of Christ as our substitute.[22] In this regard, Calvin might well echo Luther's description of Christ's death in our place as a "wonderful exchange."[23]

There are still, however, many "rough edges," as Robert Peterson puts it, in Calvin's formulation of the doctrine of the atonement. He refused to "oversystematize doctrine, for he was too much of a biblical scholar to impose an artificial unity on his materials. The result was that sometimes he left rough edges in his doctrinal formulations. So it was with his doctrine of the atonement."[24]

This does not mean that Calvin leaves us with an incoherent presentation of our reconciliation in Christ. Rather, there is a breadth and sophistication in his treatment of this theme beyond that of Aquinas or Luther.[25] Consequently Robert Culpepper, who is not altogether sympathetic to Calvin's view, still concludes that "Calvin's doctrine of the atonement is truly a milestone in Christian theology"[26]

IV. THE SIGNIFICANCE OF CHRIST'S RESURRECTION AND ASCENSION

When we take up this topic we are not moving to a completely separate aspect of Christ's work,[27] for the resurrection, ascension, and exaltation of Christ are an integral part of our redemption. Although "the whole of redemption is contained in the cross," the "resurrection of Christ does not lead us away from the cross,"[28] but rather represents its consummation. It is true that "we have in Christ's death the complete fulfillment of salvation, for through it we are reconciled to God. . . . Nevertheless, we are said to 'have been born anew to a living hope' not through his death but 'through his resurrection' [1 Peter 1:3]" (Inst. II.16.13).

Though the death and resurrection of Christ are inseparable, and both are indispensable to our salvation, there is an order and distinctive benefit in each. As the apostle Paul notes in Romans 4:25: Christ "was put to death for our sins, and raised for our justification." Therefore, says Calvin, "we divide the substance between Christ's death and resurrection as follows: through his death sin was wiped out and death extinguished; through his resurrection, righteousness was restored and life raised up, so that—thanks to his resurrection—his death manifested its power and efficacy in us" (Inst. II.16.13).

Calvin does not discuss at great length the significance of Christ's resurrection, for it was not for him a problematic area.[29] However, in the French edition of the Institutes J. Pannier "calls attention . . . to the victorious note in Calvinist piety [deriving] from its view of the resurrection,"[30] on the basis of passages like this: "From his resurrection one may infer a sure confidence we will obtain victory over the power of death" (Catechism, sec. 20, v). For as Christ "in rising again came forth the victor over death, so the victory of our faith over death lies in his resurrection alone" (*Inst*. II.16.13).

Accordingly, there are two special benefits we derive from the resurrection of Christ: (1) His resurrection is "the surest truth and substance [*hypostasis*] of our resurrection"; and (2) it is also the assurance of "the present quickening by which we are aroused into newness of life" (Catechism, sec. 20, v). It is this latter motif that is prominent in Calvin's discussion of the Christian life. The resurrection is not simply something that was experienced by Christ and eventually by all his followers. It is also something which has significance for our daily lives here and now. For we only "know Christ in the right way when we experience the meaning of his death and resurrection *within us* and as they become effective *in us*"(emphasis added).[31]

The same can be said of the ascension of Christ. Here a peculiarly Calvinian accent and interest comes to the fore. According to Joseph Haroutunian, "No one after Paul in the history of the church, so far as we know, made so much of the ascension of Christ and his sitting at the right hand of the Father, as did Calvin."[32]

Why is this so? It follows from Calvin's constant emphasis on the unity of Christ, the Head, and believers, the body. What he experiences, we experience. In faith-union with Christ we too have ascended and begin to enjoy the heavenly life and inheritance. Thus the first of many benefits we enjoy is that "the Lord by his ascent into heaven opened for us the entry into the kingdom of heaven . . ." (Catechism, sec. 20, v, repeated almost verbatim in *Inst*. II.16.16). For Christ "entered heaven *in our flesh*"—see Ephesians 2:6—"so that we do not await heaven with a bare hope, but in our Head already possess it" (*Inst*. II.16.16). It is by virtue of this "holy brotherhood" with Christ whereby he has adopted us as his brethren (see Rom. 8:17) that we are "assured of the inheritance of the heavenly kingdom" (*Inst*. II.12.2). Today we call this realized—or better, inaugurated— eschatology.[33]

The second benefit of Christ's ascension is that we recognize that "Christ resides with the Father." This may seem unimportant, but for Calvin it is crucial because our Lord "appears before the Father's face as our constant advocate and intercessor [Heb. 7:25; 9:11–12; Rom. 8:34]" (ibid.). Here we have another key motif in Calvin's theology: the royal priesthood of Christ, a theme largely ignored in Calvin research until recent studies by the Torrance clan.[34] One must read Calvin's great Commentary on the Hebrews to appreciate how much this doctrine means to him. However, in the *Institutes* he goes on to explain briefly that Christ, having reconciled us to the Father and provided access to his throne, "fills with grace and kindness the throne that for miserable sinners would otherwise have been filled with dread" (*Inst.* II.16.6).

The third benefit[35] is the power and might symbolized by Christ's victory over the powers of hell. "When he ascended into heaven, he led captivity captive" (Eph. 4:8). Having despoiled his enemies, Calvin adds, "he enriched his own people and daily lavishes spiritual riches upon them."

> He therefore sits on high, transfusing us with his power, that he may quicken us to spiritual life, sanctify us by his Spirit, adorn his church with divers gifts of his grace, keep it safe from all harm by his protection, restrain the raging enemies of his cross and of our salvation by the strength of his hand, and finally hold all power in heaven and on earth (ibid.).

With this explanation Calvin has already passed over to the meaning of the next phrase in the Creed, "He sits at the right hand of the Father." In fact, the passage just quoted from the *Institutes* is a paraphrase of a similar sentence in the Catechism that is used to explain the meaning of the above phrase from the Creed. Calvin continues, "Therefore, although lifted up into heaven, he has removed his bodily presence from our sight, yet he does not refuse to be present with his believers in help and might, and to show the manifest power of his presence" (Catechism, sec. 20, v). Thus, for Calvin, Christ's sitting at the right hand of God is "the source of all the benefits Christians receive from God the Father. It is not too much to say that if one takes away Christ at God's right hand, the whole gospel as addressed to the suffering church falls to pieces, because Christians are left without their Christ, and therefore without their God."[36]

Even Christ's exaltation at the right hand of God, however, does not complete our redemption. For our salvation is not complete until Christ *"shall come to judge the living and the dead."* This could strike fear in the hearts of believers, but characteristically Calvin points to the comfort of this doctrine. "From this a remarkable comfort comes to us, because we hear that judgment has been transferred to him whose coming could be only for our salvation" (Catechism, sec. 20, v). "Far indeed is he from mounting his judgment seat to condemn us! . . . How could the Head scatter his own members? How could our Advocate condemn his clients?" (*Inst.* II.16.18).

How, indeed, since the Judge is also the Redeemer. This is why the thought of the return of Christ should not be a cause for consternation but a "wonderful consolation"[37] and source of assurance. "No mean assurance, this—that we shall be brought before no other judgment seat than that of our Redeemer, to whom we must look for our salvation" (ibid.).

Calvin may have been intimidated by the book of Revelation, the one book in the New Testament on which he wrote no commentary, but of one thing he was sure: Our Lord is coming in glory, and this conviction should be a source of anticipation and hope, a major motif in the proclamation of the gospel. For "teachers of the church are commanded to lift up the minds of the faithful with the confidence of the Lord's coming, even though God seems to be far from his people."[38] As the years pass by and his coming seems interminably delayed, we should not become doubtful and discouraged. Rather, "we must gather strength, and be firm, and from what better source, than from the hope, the virtual sight, of the coming of the Lord!"[39]

V. CONCLUSION:
SALVATION IN CHRIST ALONE

Calvin concludes his discussion of the article in the Creed—"and in Jesus Christ"—with a section that confirms the opening affirmation in this chapter, that is, that he is thoroughly Christocentric. He begins by saying, "We see that our whole salvation and all its parts are comprehended in Christ [Acts 4:12]. We should therefore take care not to devise the least portion of it from anywhere else." Then follows a packed, eloquent paragraph which is a paean of praise to the all-sufficiency of Christ:

> If we seek salvation, we are taught by the very name of Jesus that it is "of him" [1 Cor. 1:30]. If we seek any other gifts of the Spirit, they will be found in his anointing. If we seek strength, it lies in his dominion; if purity, in his conception; if gentleness, it appears in his birth. For by his birth he was made like us in all respects [Heb. 2:17] that he might learn to feel our pain [cf. Heb. 5:2]. If we seek redemption, it lies in his passion; if acquittal, in his condemnation; if remission of the curse, in his cross [Gal. 3:13]; if satisfaction, in his sacrifice; if purification, in his blood; if reconciliation, in his descent into hell; if mortification of the flesh, in his tomb; if newness of life, in his resurrection; if immortality, in the same; if inheritance of the Heavenly Kingdom, in his entrance into heaven; if protection, if security, if abundant supply of all blessings, in his Kingdom; if untroubled expectation of judgment, in the power given to him to judge. In short, since rich store of every kind of good abounds in him, let us drink our fill from this fountain, and from no other (*Inst.* II.16.19).

11

PRAYER

(Sections 22–25)

I. INTRODUCTION

One of the most important aspects of the life of faith is prayer. Calvin accordingly devotes considerable space to this subject: four chapters in his Catechism, one being a fairly long exposition of the Lord's Prayer. In the *Institutes* only one chapter is devoted to prayer (III.20), largely because this was not a contested subject that required additional polemical chapters (as was the case with the doctrine of justification). But, as the editors of the McNeill-Battles edition of the *Institutes* comment: "This thoughtful and ample chapter, with its tone of devout warmth, takes its place in the forefront of historically celebrated discussions of prayer"[1]

II. PRAYER AND FAITH

Prayer is integrally related to faith because a "man duly versed in true faith" recognizes his spiritual poverty and his need of God's continued help. He realizes that by himself he will surely fail. He accordingly will "seek resources to succor himself in his need" and "must go outside himself and get them elsewhere." This he finds in his Creator and Lord "who willingly and freely reveals himself in his Christ, and in him opens all heavenly treasures that his whole faith may contemplate his beloved Son, his whole expectation depend upon him, and his whole hope cleave to and rest in him . . ." (sec. 22).[2]

Faith is thus the foundation and necessary condition of genuine prayer. "Faith grounded upon the Word is the mother of proper [*rectae*] prayer. . . . Prayer rightly springs from faith, and faith from hearing God's Word [Rom. 10:14, 17]" (*Inst.* III.20, 27). In his commentaries Calvin frequently mentions the special relationship between prayer, faith, and the Word. In one place he likens Scripture, particularly its promises, to the fuel that stirs up the desire to pray. "The faithful feel that their hearts soon languish in prayer unless they are constantly stirring themselves up to it by new incitements. . . . Just as one must lay on fuel in order to preserve a fire, so the exercise of prayer requires such help," that is, recalling God's goodness as revealed in the Word.[3] For genuine and earnest prayer "proceeds from faith in the promises of God."[4] Prayer, moreover, is "the chief exercise [*praecipuum exercitium*] of faith" (*Inst.* III.20).[5] Both focus on and find their proper object in Jesus Christ. Consequently, prayer, like faith, is primarily a response to God's goodness and grace manifest in Christ.

To fail to take advantage of these rich resources available to us is like neglecting a great treasure buried and hidden in the earth even after we are aware of its existence (sec. 22; *Inst.* III.20.1, 2). In prayer, however, we can "dig up the treasures that were pointed out by the Lord's gospel, and which our faith gazed upon" (*Inst.* III.20.2).

The merciful Father wishes to supply all our needs—both felt needs and needs of which we ourselves are not aware (sec. 24). But we must claim God's promises for ourselves. Otherwise they are of no use to us. Hence failure to pray is a costly error, for we thus deprive ourselves of countless blessings. So many of our frustrations and failures in the Christian life could be avoided if only we were faithful in prayer. For among the many blessings that result from prayer, one of the greatest is "an extraordinary peace and repose to our consciences" (*Inst.* III.20.2).

III. WHY PRAY?

It might be objected that since God is so kind and generous, it should not be necessary to ask him for what we need. After all, God is omniscient and knows our needs even better than we do. Then why does he command us to pray? Calvin replies that God "ordained prayer not so much for his own sake as ours" (*Inst.* III.20.3). For our faith must be exercised lest it become lazy and weak. In the *Institutes* Calvin proceeds to suggest six ways in which prayer contributes toward strengthening our faith: (1) it inflames our hearts with the desire to seek, love, and serve God; (2) it trains us to expose the secrets and desires of our hearts to God; (3) it promotes gratitude; (4) it leads to meditation on God's kindness as a result of his having answered our prayers; (5) it produces even greater joy in those things which we have obtained through prayer; and (6) finally, it serves as a personal confirmation of God's providence (III.20.3).

Before examining the rules of praying properly, we should note how Calvin defines prayer in the Catechism. He describes it as "a sort of agreement [*arbitrii*] between God and us whereby we pour out before him all the desires, joys, sighs, and finally, thoughts of our hearts . . ." (sec. 23). In the *Institutes* Calvin calls prayer an "intimate conversation (*familiare colloquium*) with God" (III.20.5, 6). It is "a pure affection of our heart" whereby we approach God (sec. 23).

It is not an optional activity which we can indulge in when we feel like it. For God commands us to pray; but with the command comes also the promise "assuring us we will receive whatever we ask" (ibid.). God's command and promise are both a motive for prayer and the ground of our confidence. For it would be rash to approach the Almighty Creator with our requests if we were not assured that we were welcome (*Inst.* III.20.13). On the other hand, when we do not pray, we in effect rebelliously reject God's command and show a lack of faith in God's promises (ibid.). Consequently, Calvin might well concur with P. T. Forsyth's judgment that "the worst sin is prayerlessness."[6]

IV. RULES FOR
PRAYING PROPERLY

In the *Institutes* (III.20.4–12) Calvin lists and discusses four laws or rules for "framing our prayer duly and properly":

1. The first is "that we be disposed in mind and heart as is suitable for those who enter into conversation with God" (III.20.4). Here Calvin is warning against undisciplined and irreverent prayer. However, he also reminds those who might therefore be timid or afraid that they can rely on the help of the Holy Spirit as promised in Romans 8:26 (III.20.5).
2. "That in our petitions we always have a sense of our own insufficiency, and earnestly pondering how we need all that we seek, join with this prayer an earnest—nay, burning—desire to attain it" (III.20.6). Prayers that are not offered sincerely and seriously are a mockery to God (ibid.). The presupposition for lawful prayer is a spirit of repentance and a zeal for the Kingdom of God (III.20.7).
3. "That anyone who stands before God to pray, in his humility giving glory completely to God, abandon all thought of his own glory, cast off all notion of his own worth, in short, put away all self-assurance . . ." (III.20.8). We are to offer our prayers "not in our own righteousness but in his great mercies, that he may answer us for his own sake . . ." (Catechism, sec. 23). Thus we can and should be confident as we approach God in prayer, but this confidence derives solely from God's mercy. Every prayer must be accompanied by a confession of guilt and a plea for pardon (III.20.9).
4. "The fourth rule is that, thus cast down and overcome by

true humility, we should nevertheless be encouraged to pray by a sure hope that our prayer will be answered." Confident faith and reverent fear go together (III.20.11; cf. III.20.14). "Only that prayer is acceptable to God which is born . . . out of such presumption of faith and is grounded in unshaken hope" (III.20.12). But this is possible only for those who know the good news that God in Jesus Christ is "gentle and kind" to all who call upon him in repentance and faith (III.20.14; cf. III.20.12).

It is noteworthy, as Wilhelm Niesel has pointed out, that in this long chapter on prayer in the *Institutes* Calvin does not give a doctrine of prayer as such, but rather practical instructions about how to pray.[7] This is a further illustration of the point made at the beginning of this commentary, namely, that Calvin's theology—even when he writes a systematic treatise—is not an abstract, speculative system. It is eminently practical and suffused with the warmth of his own faith and piety.

V. THE LORD'S PRAYER[8]

In both the Catechism (sec. 24) and the *Institutes* (III.20.34–42) Calvin then gives an exposition of the Lord's Prayer.[9] God in his mercy gives us this model prayer as a guide. In this prayer, which our Lord taught us, we are requesting "nothing unacceptable to him—since we are asking almost in his own words" (sec. 24). Consequently, it is a tremendous honor and responsibility whenever we pray the Lord's Prayer. In its six brief petitions is "comprehended everything that is legitimate and expedient for us to pray for" (*Geneva Catechism*, Q. 255). The first three petitions are concerned with the glory of God alone; the latter three are concerned with our welfare and what is useful for us. However, even that which glorifies God works to our benefit, and in the latter three petitions we in turn must keep in view the glory of God (sec. 24, p. 71; cf. the *Geneva Catechism*, Qs. 258, 9).[10]

A. Significance of the mediatorial work
of Christ and the Spirit

Rather than give an exposition of each of the petitions of the Lord's Prayer, which are quite clear, I will focus on four special motifs. First, everything that Calvin says about prayer revolves about the reconciling work of Jesus Christ. The christocentric nature of prayer was apparent already in the first statements of section 22 of the Catechism. This is brought out even more clearly in Calvin's comments on the opening words of the Lord's Prayer: "Our Father . . ." For, according to Calvin, these words signify that "all prayer ought to be offered to God by us in Christ's name as no prayer can be commended to him in another name. . . . And as a rule for calling upon God has been established, and a promise given that those who call upon him shall be heard, so too we are particularly bidden to call upon him in Christ's name; and we have his promise that we shall obtain what we have asked in his name" (sec. 24, i; cf. John 14:13; 16:23–26).

We pray in or through the name of Jesus because he is the only mediator between God and humankind (see 1 Tim. 2:5, 6). He is also our intercessor, continually interceding with the Father for us (sec. 24; cf. *Inst.* III.20.17–20). Thus, every time we pray, we can do so with the assurance that we have a friend in the presence of the heavenly Father, "by whose intercession the Father is for us rendered gracious and easily entreated" (*Inst.* 20.19).[11] This does not mean, however, that the risen Christ, "kneeling before God, pleads as a suppliant for us; rather, . . . he so appears before God's presence that the power of his death avails as an everlasting intercession in our behalf [see Rom. 8:34], yet in such a way that, having entered the heavenly sanctuary, even to the consummation of the ages [see Heb. 9:24f.], he alone bears to God the petition of his people, who stay afar off in the outer court" (*Inst.* III.20.20). Referring to the imagery of the Old Testament cultus where the priests offered the prayers for the people who stood afar off in the court (see Ex. 28:9–21), Calvin adds that this "foreshadowing ceremony of the law" teaches us that "we are all barred from God's presence and consequently need a mediator who should appear in our name and bear us upon his shoulders and hold us bound upon his breast so that we are heard in his person" (*Inst.* III.20.18).[12]

Calvin makes two more points of great importance in his explication of the meaning of the words "Our Father" in the *Institutes*. One is that although we should be freed from all fear and distrust by the privilege of calling God our Father (III.20.36), it is difficult to believe this without reservation. God, therefore, adds a further guarantee, so to speak, to the gift of his son as our savior. Closely related to the gift of the savior is the gift of the guidance of the Holy Spirit. "Because the narrowness of our hearts cannot comprehend God's boundless favor, not only is Christ the guarantee and pledge of our adoption, but he gives the Spirit as witness to us of the same adoption, through whom with free and full voice we may cry, 'Abba, Father' [Gal. 4:6; Rom. 8:15]. Therefore, whenever any hesitation shall hinder us, let us remember to ask him to correct our fearfulness and to set before us that Spirit that he may guide us to pray boldly" (III.20.37).[13]

B. The corporate nature
of the Lord's Prayer

Calvin also emphasizes that the Lord's Prayer is a corporate prayer. We do not pray "My Father" but rather "*Our* Father." This distinction has great social implications. "For as one father is common to us all [Matt. 23:9], and every good thing that can fall to our lot comes from him, there ought not to be anything separate among us that we are not prepared gladly and wholeheartedly to share with one another, as far as the occasion requires" (III.20.38). Every time we pray the Lord's Prayer, therefore, we would be reminded of our common bond of faith and fellowship with Christians all over the world, as well as our responsibility for them. This also applies to all people, whether they are Christians or not, but we are to have a special concern for those who are "of the household of faith" (Gal. 6:10).[14] We cannot love God without loving our neighbor—a point Calvin also stresses in his discussion of the two tables of the law. "To sum up, all prayers ought to be such as to look to that community which our Lord has established in his kingdom and his household" (ibid.).

C. The nature of the kingdom

In his exposition of the second petition, "Thy kingdom come," Calvin tends to stress God's reign within the lives of believers and the church. For example, in the Catechism he defines the kingdom of God in this way: "By his Holy Spirit, to act and rule over his own people, in order to make the riches of his goodness and mercy conspicuous in all their works" (sec. 24, iii). However, note that the works of believers are to testify to God's rule. Moreover, Calvin immediately points to the negative side of God's reign, that is, to "confound" and "lay low" the arrogance of the wicked "in order to make it clear that there is no power which can withstand his power" (ibid.).

Nevertheless, in a fuller definition which follows, the personal aspect dominates. For when we pray "Thy kingdom come," we also are asking

> that the Lord may day by day add new believers to his people so that they may celebrate his glory in every way; also, that he may pour out ever more widely upon them his rich graces, through which he may live and reign day by day more and more in them, until he completely fulfills their perfect union with himself (ibid.).

At the same time, however, Calvin sees in this petition what might be called cosmic and eschatological dimensions. For the coming of the kingdom also includes the spread of God's light and truth in the world so as to "dispel, snuff out, and destroy the darkness and falsehoods of Satan and his kingdom." In addition, in praying this petition we also desire that God's kingdom "at last may be perfected and fulfilled" and Satan's kingdom "utterly disrupted and laid low" (ibid.).

In the *Institutes* Calvin defines the kingdom of God a little differently, to wit: "God reigns where men, both by denial of themselves and by contempt of the world and of earthly life, pledge themselves to his righteousness in order to aspire to a heavenly life" (IV.20.42). Again, the focus is on personal godliness, and a little later, on "the zeal for daily progress" in the faith. God "spreads his kingdom" as believers pray that God will enable them to mortify the flesh and bear the cross—two key aspects of the Christian life.

However, Calvin also mentions the church specifically here for the first time. He does not distinguish between the church and the kingdom, but suggests that the latter is realized by the increase of the former. God, says Calvin, "sets up his kingdom by humbling the whole world, but in different ways." One of those ways is through the growth of the church. Hence

We must daily desire that God gather churches unto himself from all parts of the earth; that he spread and increase them in number; that he adorn them with gifts; that he establish a lawful order among them; on the other hand, that he cast down all enemies of pure teaching and religion; that he scatter their counsels and crush their efforts (IV.20.42).

This is not too different in substance from one of the passages quoted earlier from the Catechism, except that there the goal was that the Lord might "day by day add new believers to his people."

What is mentioned only in passing in the Catechism, however, is developed more fully in the *Institutes* and particularly in Calvin's commentary on the synoptic gospels, namely, the role of the Word and the Spirit, particularly the latter. For "God by the power of his Spirit" enables believers to mortify the flesh. And it is to the "royal scepter" of God's Word that we must bring our "minds and hearts into voluntary obedience." This happens when God "manifests the working of his Word through the secret inspiration of the Spirit" (*Inst.* IV.20.42). Meanwhile, as we wait for the full coming of the kingdom, the Lord "protects his own, guides them by the help of his Spirit into uprightness, and strengthens them to perseverance" (ibid.).

It is in his harmony of the gospels, however, that Calvin spells out the role of the Word and the Spirit in the realization of the kingdom. In this prayer, says Calvin, God realizes his reign "partly [as] the effect of the word of preaching, partly of the hidden power of the Spirit."

He would govern men by His Word, but as the voice alone, without the inward influence of the Spirit, does not reach down into the heart, the two must be brought together for the establishment of God's Kingdom.

So we pray that God will show His power both in Word and in Spirit, that the whole world may willingly come over to Him. . . . So the sum of this supplication is that God will illuminate the heart by the light of His Word, bring our hearts to obey His righteousness by the breathing of His Spirit, and restore to order at His will, all that is lying waste upon the face of the earth (Comm. Matt. 6:10).[15]

In his commentary, Calvin also makes clear what was only implied before, namely, that God reigns in two ways: in the renewal of the lives of believers and in the overcoming of Satan and all God's enemies. The goal in both cases is to restore order in a confused and disordered world, for disorder and confusion are "the opposite of the kingdom of God" (ibid.). For ultimately the goal is that "God will be all in all" (1 Cor. 15:28).[16]

D. The necessity of
perseverance in prayer

Calvin closes his exposition of prayer in the Catechism with a discussion of the necessity of perseverance in prayer (sec. 25). He recognizes that many times it seems as if God does not answer our prayers. We are then prone to impatience and skepticism. The way to avoid this, submits Calvin, is to seek first of all that God's will be done. If we learn to submit our wills to his will, we will not become frustrated but will wait patiently until God's will becomes clear. Yet Calvin acknowledges that there will be times when "finally, even after long waiting, our senses cannot learn the benefit received from prayer or perceive any fruit from it . . ." (ibid.). In such cases, we must simply rely in faith upon God, with the confidence that he will ultimately do what is good for us. "For though all things fail us, yet God will never forsake us, who cannot disappoint the expectation and patience of his people" (ibid.).

Calvin amplifies this theme in the *Institutes*. Here he discusses briefly the importance of set times for prayer, suggesting when we awake, before leaving for work, before and after meals, and before we retire in the evening. But he also warns about an undue rigidity in this regard (III.20.50). The important thing, in any case, is to be faithful and to persevere in prayer so that we will not become discouraged or give up. However, "if with minds composed to this obedience [a disciplined prayer life], we allow ourselves to be ruled by divine providence, we shall easily learn to persevere in prayer and, with desires suspended, patiently to wait for the Lord" (III.20.51).

It is important to keep in mind, therefore, that in prayer, as in the whole of the Christian life, it is faith, not our feelings, that counts. As Ronald Wallace points out in his chapter on "Prayer as the Principal Exercise of Faith" in *Calvin's Doctrine of the Christian Life:*

We will not pray unless we make ourselves pray, in spite of our feelings. If we were left to our own inclination in this matter our prayer life would die out [see Calvin's Commentary on Ps. 55:18]. Even affliction, which should drive us to our knees and stimulate us in prayer, can have the contrary effect and can stupefy us and render us prayerless unless we "stir up our minds to pray" [Comm. Ps. 103:1, 2 and Ps. 106:58].[17]

In the words of the apostle Paul, which Calvin cites twice: "Rejoice always, pray constantly, give thanks in all circumstances, for this is the will of God in Christ Jesus for you" (1 Thess. 5:18; cf. Eph. 6:18).

APPENDIX

In addition to discussing Calvin's understanding of prayer and its importance in the Christian life, it may be instructive to examine some of Calvin's prayers. Unfortunately, there is no complete collection of the reformer's prayers, but we do have access to some of his set prayers for special occasions, such as a morning and evening prayer, a prayer before one goes to work, a grace before meals, and the prayers he ordinarily used before and after his sermons.[18]

I. THE FORMAL, SET PRAYERS

These prayers are longer than the very brief extemporaneous prayers Calvin offered after each of his lectures on the prophets, and differ somewhat in their nature. In the former the following characteristics stand out:

1. *The form of address to God.* It is not so much the sovereignty or majesty of God but rather the fatherhood of God that is prominent. For example, "My God, my Father and preserver"; "O Lord God, most merciful Father and Savior"; or "Let us call upon our good God and Father".[19]
2. *Confession of sin.* Invariably Calvin acknowledges specific sins, even in these generic prayers: indolence, torpor, the cravings of the flesh, greedy affection or desire of gain, distrust (of God), and lack of patience.
3. *An appeal to God's mercy and grace in Jesus Christ.* May it please God "to look upon us in the face of his well-beloved Son our Lord Jesus." "May I look for all happiness only to thy grace and kindness." "Increase the gifts of thy grace to

me from day to day, while so much the more I cleave to thy Son Jesus Christ, whom we justly call the true Sun, perpetually shining in our hearts."

4. *A request for God's guidance, particularly that of the Holy Spirit.*[20] "As thou dost illumine this world by the sun . . . , so enlighten my mind by the illumination of thy Spirit and guide me through him in the way of righteousness." "So govern my heart that I may willingly and eagerly set myself to profit. . . . " "May it please God to guide with his Holy Spirit all kings, princes, and magistrates. . . . "

5. *Exhortation to glorify God in all of life.* "May all my actions conduce to the glory of thy name (and the welfare of my brethren)." May we "serve and honor God by glorifying his holy name in all our life. . . . " May God give his faithful ones who are persecuted "such a true steadfastness that his holy name may be glorified by them both in life and death." And in his evening prayer Calvin prays that while sleeping God will keep him "chaste and pure" and "safe from all perils, so that even my sleep may yield glory to thy name."

II. THE EXTEMPORANEOUS PRAYERS[21]

The brief prayers that follow Calvin's lectures on the prophets were apparently given extemporaneously. Most of the above themes are found also in these prayers, but they usually reflect the subject of the preceding biblical exposition. More important and especially noteworthy is the way Calvin concludes the vast majority of these prayers, that is, with an eschatological motif—with a view to the consummation of all things and the full coming of the reign of God. For example, these prayers typically end with phrases like "until at length . . . we be gathered into the celestial kingdom," or "that having finished our warfare we may at last enjoy that blessed rest which thou hast promised to us and which is laid up for us in heaven. . . . "[22]

The following four prayers illustrate this point and show how these eschatological endings are integrated into the prayer as a whole.[23]

Almighty God, since you so kindly invite us to yourself and do not cease, even if we are deaf, to extend your grace toward us, grant that we obey you willingly and allow ourselves to be ruled by your Word. And grant that we might obey you steadfastly, not only for a day or a short time, but *until we have completed the course of our journey and are gathered together in your heavenly rest,* through Christ our Lord. Amen.[24]

Almighty God, since you have today made yourself known to us so intimately in the gospel of Christ our Lord, grant that we might learn to lift our eyes to the light set before us, and keep them there fixed, so that we may be directed ever to hold to the path and struggle to reach the goal to which you call us; *until at last, having completed the course of our calling, we attain to you and enjoy with you that glory which your only-begotten Son has won for us by his blood.* Amen.[25]

Almighty God, since you have condescended to approach us so intimately, grant that we in turn may eagerly approach you and abide in firm and holy communion. While we continue in the legitimate worship that you prescribe for us in your Word, may your benefits to us also increase, *until you lead us to their fullness when you gather us together into your heavenly kingdom,* through Jesus Christ, our Lord. Amen.[26]

Almighty God, since we are the work and creation of your hands, grant us to realize that we do not live and move except in you alone. And grant, we pray, that we would be so subject to you that we are not only ruled by your hidden providence but also give such evidence of our willing obedience and submission to you, as children should, that we zealously glorify your name on earth, *until we attain to the enjoyment of that blessed inheritance which is laid up for us in heaven,* through Christ our Lord. Amen.[27] [emphasis added]

There could hardly be a better illustration of Calvin's conviction that a key component of the Christian life is a "meditation on the future life."[28] In these expositions Calvin is very concerned with the issues of daily life, but as these prayers indicate, the affairs of this world must always be seen in the light of eternity (*sub specie aeternitatis*).

12

THE SACRAMENTS

(Sections 26–29)

Baptism and the Lord's Supper

I. SACRAMENTS AS A MARK OF THE CHURCH

Calvin now turns to the doctrine of the church. In the Catechism, however, the church as such is not discussed, but rather only a few aspects of the church, namely, the two evangelical sacraments (secs. 26–29), "The Pastors of the Church and Their Power" (sec. 30), and "Excommunication" (sec. 32). In the *Institutes* the church is discussed at length in book IV, which takes up almost one-third of the reformer's classic. Much of this is a polemic against the Roman Catholic Church, but this is at the same time the most important treatise on the church to appear during the Reformation. The British scholar J. S. Whale even maintains that, "Along with doctrine, churchmanship is the second constitutive principle of Calvin's system."[1]

The title of book IV is both interesting and significant: "The External Means or Aids by Which God Invites Us into the Society of Christ and Holds Us Therein." At least one theologian (Emil Brunner) has been put off by this title and concludes that this suggests a low view of the church, one where the church is simply "an external support of faith," something "accidental and subsidiary to faith rather than something that belongs to its nature."[2] However, just the opposite is the case, as is indicated by the title of chapter 1 of book IV: "The True Church with Which as Mother of All the Godly We Must Keep Unity."

The church is a visible society with visible marks by which it can be distinguished. Calvin accordingly says that we have a church wherever the Word of God is purely preached and heard and where the sacraments are properly administered. Wherever these two marks are present, a true church exists (*Inst.* IV.1.9; cf. secs. 10–12). This definition of the church is almost the same as that found in the Lutheran Augsburg Confession, Article 7.[3] In short, the Word and the sacraments are the two marks of the church. And these two are in the last analysis one, for the sacraments are—in the words of Augustine—"the visible word of God" (*Inst.* IV.14.6).[4]

II. WHY SACRAMENTS?

It may be asked, if we have the written Word of God, the Bible, why do we need anything else (besides the help of the Holy Spirit) to communicate God's will and grace to us? The answer is that because of our small and weak faith, we need some special concrete and visible aids to help us appropriate God's grace and to confirm our faith. They are also "an exercise of our faith both before God and among men" (sec. 26).[5] Our understanding of God's revelation is so limited that we require a visible sign (*signum,* token or proof; Calvin also uses *marque* [mark], *sceau* [seal], and *enseigne* [badge]) to confirm and seal God's promises. A sacrament, therefore, is defined as "an outward sign by which the Lord represents and attests to his good will toward us in order to sustain the weakness of our faith." Or, to put it more briefly and simply, a sacrament is "a testimony of God's grace, declared to us by an outward sign" (sec. 27).[6]

The reformers recognized only two sacraments, baptism and the Lord's Supper. Roman Catholics—at least since 1439—observe seven sacraments: baptism, confirmation, the Eucharist, penance, extreme unction, orders (i.e., the ordination of priests), and matrimony. The principal reason the reformers rejected the other five is that they are not clearly taught in Scripture. Some Protestants, such as the Quakers and the Non-church Movement in Japan (*Mukyōkai*), maintain no sacraments at all, and Karl Barth, among others, maintains that the idea of sacraments is not to be found in the Bible. But he does recognize the significance of the rites of both baptism and the Lord's Supper.[7]

Calvin, in any case, had a high view of the sacraments, as high in most respects as Luther. (The same cannot be said of many modern Reformed/ Presbyterian Christians, in contrast to their Lutheran counterparts.) He regards the sacraments as "lofty and heavenly mysteries" (sec. 26) and "pillars of our faith" (*Inst.* IV.14.6), which are testimonies of God's goodness and grace toward us in Jesus Christ. They do not offer us anything different from what is given us in the written Word, which is the foundation of our faith, but they strengthen and confirm our weak faith. Because the eye of faith is so dim, we need these visual aids that speak to our other senses as well as to our faculty of hearing.

Calvin uses very graphic language to describe the weakness of our faith. This, in addition to our "dull capacity," is why we require additional helps beyond the Word. "So scanty and weak is our faith that, unless it is propped up on all sides and sustained by every means, it trembles, wavers, and totters" (sec. 26).[8] Therefore, "our Lord, according to his infinite kindness, so tempers himself to our capacity that, since we are creatures who always creep on the ground, cleave to the flesh, and do not think about or even conceive of anything spiritual, he condescends to lead us to himself even by these earthly elements, and to set before us in the flesh a mirror of spiritual blessings" (*Inst.* IV.14.3).

Three more things need to be pointed out before turning to the specific sacraments, that is, the role of the Holy Spirit, the importance of faith, and the place of Christ in making the sacraments powerful and efficacious. In the Catechism there is no reference to the Spirit in the brief treatment of the nature of sacraments (secs. 26 and 27), but in the lengthy chapter on the sacraments in the *Institutes* this motif becomes prominent. Here Calvin repeats that the sacraments were given by God to establish and increase our faith, but, he adds, they only

> properly fulfill their office when the Spirit, that inward teacher, comes to them, by whose power alone hearts are penetrated and affections moved and our souls opened for the sacraments to enter in. If the Spirit is lacking, the sacraments can accomplish nothing more in our minds than the splendor of the sun shining on blind eyes, or a voice sounding in deaf ears (*Inst.* IV.14.9).

In short, "the sacraments profit not a whit without the power of the Holy Spirit" (ibid.). Or, as Calvin puts it in his Geneva Catechism, "The power and efficacy of a sacrament does not lie in the external elements, but wholly emanates from the Spirit of God" (Q. 313).[9]

On the human side, however, faith is also indispensable. For it is "certain that the Lord offers us mercy and the pledge of his grace both in his sacred Word and in his sacraments. But it is understood only by those who take Word and sacraments with sure faith. . . ." Then Calvin cites Augustine to the same effect, that "the efficacy of the Word is brought to light in the sacrament, not because it is spoken, but because it is believed" (*Inst.* IV.14.7). The reformer expresses himself even more forcibly in a polemical treatise: "He who separates faith from the sacraments does just as if he were to take the soul away from the body."[10]

Sacraments are thus not magical means by which recipients are automatically blessed. On God's side the Word and the Spirit are crucial, and on our side faith is essential if the promises of God in Jesus Christ are to be realized. Yet even the faith by which we believe is a gift of the Holy Spirit, for "faith is the proper and entire work of the Holy Spirit, illumined by whom we recognize God and the treasures of his kindness and without whose light our mind is so blinded that it can see nothing, so dull that it can sense nothing of spiritual things" (*Inst.* IV.14.8).[11]

The third idea that is fundamental to Calvin's understanding of the sacraments is that they find their meaning in Christ. For "Christ is the matter [*materiam*] or (if you prefer) the substance [*substantiam*] of all the sacraments; for in him they have all their firmness [*soliditatem*], and they do not promise anything apart from him" (*Inst.* IV.14.16). For the benefits of the sacraments "are conferred through the Holy Spirit, who makes us partakers in Christ; confined, indeed, with the help of outward signs, if they allure us to Christ; but when they are twisted in another direction, their whole worth is shamefully destroyed" (ibid.). In other words, if we focus on the elements and not on the Christ to whom they point, we misunderstand and misconstrue the sacraments.

More particularly, baptism for the believer is a "kind of entry into the Church," whereas the Lord's Supper is a means by which the heavenly Father continually "feeds and refreshes the members of his household" (Geneva Catechism, Q. 323). In both cases we are thereby united more closely to Jesus Christ. For sacraments "are aids and means to our incorporation in Jesus Christ, or, if we are already [members] of his body, to confirm us therein more and more until he unites us wholly with himself in the life of heaven."[12]

III. BAPTISM

"Baptism has been given to us by God: first, to serve our faith before him; secondly, to serve our confession before men" (sec. 28). The first purpose concerns the religious content of the sacrament, the second is more of a public testimonial of our faith. Concerning the religious content, Calvin mentions three benefits (only two are specified in the Catechism) we receive through baptism: First, it is a sign of the remission of sins which we receive through the blood (i.e., sacrificial death) of Christ (see Matt. 28:19; Acts 2:38; 1 Peter 3:21). Baptism is thus "like a sealed document to confirm to us that all our sins are so abolished, remitted, and effaced that they can never come to his sight, be recalled, or charged against us" (*Inst.* IV.15.1). Believers, therefore, when troubled and in doubt about their salvation, should remind themselves of their baptism. This should be a constant source of comfort and assurance.

Second, baptism is a sign of the mortification of our flesh through our identification with Christ. This is expressed by the apostle Paul in Romans 6:3–11 where he says that we have been baptized into the death of Christ so that we might be raised with him and walk in the newness of life (cf. Col. 2:11, 12). Third, through baptism we are "not only engrafted into the death and life of Christ, but so united that we become sharers in all his blessings" (*Inst.* IV.15.6). As noted above, this is not listed in the Catechism as a third benefit, but almost the same expression is found in the beginning of the discussion of baptism: "Faith looks at the promise by which our merciful Father offers the communication of his Christ, that clothed with him we may share in all his goods" (sec. 28).

The second general purpose of baptism is to acknowledge our faith before others and thus "openly profess that we wish to be numbered among God's people, in order to worship one God in the same religion along with all godly men" (sec. 28; cf. *Inst.* IV.15.13). God is not glorified nor is the church strengthened by hidden, isolated Christians. To become a Christian means to join a fellowship, and baptism is the visible mark or sign of belonging to that fellowship which is the spiritual body of Christ (see Rom. 12:4–8; 1 Cor. 12:12–27).

IV. INFANT BAPTISM

Calvin makes only a brief reference in the Catechism to the baptism of children. "Since the covenant of the Lord with us is principally ratified by baptism, we rightly baptize our infants as sharers in the eternal covenant by which the Lord promises us he will be the God not only of us but also of our descendants" (cf. Gen. 17:7) (sec. 18). In the *Institutes*, however, he devotes a special chapter to this subject, for this practice was rejected by the Anabaptists of that time (and by Baptists today) on the ground that in the New Testament there is no specific command to baptize children. They conclude, therefore, that only those who are capable of making a personal confession of faith should be baptized. Calvin, along with other reformers, points to such texts as Matthew 19:13–15 and Acts 16:15, 32; but his basic appeal is not to isolated texts but to the eternal covenant of grace (Gen. 17:1–14; cf. *Inst.* IV.16.3–6).[13] In particular, he draws a parallel between circumcision and baptism and stresses the "anagogic relationship" between the two (*Inst.* IV.16.3). Calvin then reasons that "if the covenant still remains firm and steadfast, it applies no less today to the children of Christians than under the Old Testament it pertained to the infants of the Jews" (*Inst.* IV.16.5).

The question inevitably arises concerning the fact that in the New Testament baptism is linked with faith and infants are incapable of faith. Whereas Luther answered this objection by either pointing to the objective value of the sacrament or, more often, to the latent faith of the infant,[14] Calvin's response is that God's regenerative work can and does begin at times even prior to birth, in one's mother's womb. Here he points to John the Baptist (see Luke 1:15) and Jesus (*Inst.* IV.16.17–18), and might well have pointed to Jeremiah (see Jer. 1:5) and the apostle Paul (see Gal. 1:15). Thus "infants are baptized into future repentance and faith, and even though these have not yet been formed in them, the seed of both lies hidden within them by the secret working of the Spirit" (*Inst.* IV.16.20).[15] "Infants are renewed by the Spirit of God according to the capacity of their age, until the power [*virtus*] which was concealed in them grows by degrees and becomes fully manifest at the proper time."[16]

This line of reasoning is admittedly rather speculative, but it does not lead to cheap grace in Calvin's view, for he also insists that there must eventually be evidence of faith at an appropriate level. When children "come of age they are to acknowledge the truth of their baptism" (Geneva Catechism, Q. 139).[17] In the last analysis, however, Calvin's case for infant baptism rests on his doctrine of election. He does not make a specific appeal to this doctrine in his chapter on infant baptism but here and there he suggests that it is God's sovereign grace which is the ultimate basis for believing that the regenerative work of the Holy Spirit is at work in the lives of those infants who are chosen for eternal life. What Calvin says of God's calling of Abraham could well apply to all those who come after Christ: "God's election alone rules as of free right" (*Inst.* IV.16.15).[18]

Although we cannot fully comprehend the gracious work of God in the life of an infant, there is no doubt about the joys and benefits of this sacrament. For God's gracious promises and "boundless generosity" to godly parents and their children in this sign should move them to proclaim God's glory and flood their hearts "with uncommon happiness" and move them "to a deeper love of their kind Father, as they see his concern on their behalf for their posterity" (*Inst.* IV.16.9).

Other benefits of infant baptism are that parents are thereby "aroused to a surer confidence because they see with their very eyes the covenant of the Lord engraved on the bodies of their children."[19] The children themselves also receive the benefit that "they are somewhat more commended to the other members" of the congregation. As they grow up they should be "greatly spurred to an earnest zeal for worshiping God." And finally, the threat of God's punishment should be a sobering reminder to those who refuse God's "proffered grace" (Gen. 17:14) (ibid.).

Although Calvin feels strongly about this doctrine and attributes to Satan the attempt "to take from us the singular fruit of assurance and spiritual joy which is to be gathered from" it (*Inst.* IV.16.32), he concedes that God's work in the life of an infant is "beyond our understanding" (*Inst.* IV.16, 17). However, such humility is appropriate not only in regard to baptism; Calvin also acknowledges, as we shall see, that what takes place in the Lord's Supper is also a mystery beyond our comprehension.

V. THE LORD'S SUPPER

The second evangelical sacrament is the Lord's Supper, which has an important place not only in Calvin's theology but also in his churchmanship. Here, as in many other areas, Calvin's heirs have often failed to understand and appreciate the depth and sophistication of Calvin's understanding of this sacrament. Everything hinges on the interpretation of

Jesus' words at his last supper with the disciples. For what does Jesus mean when he breaks the bread, gives it to his disciples, and says, "This is my body"; and later shares the cup of wine and says, "This is my blood" (Mark 14:22–25; cf. 1 Cor. 11:23–26)? Contrary to much popular opinion, even in Reformed and Presbyterian churches, Calvin does *not* teach that the bread and wine are mere symbols of Christ's body and blood. This was the view of Zwingli, the Zurich reformer. Calvin was actually closer to Luther in this regard, although there are differences between the positions of the two.[20] In any case, both believed that Christ is really present in some sense in the elements of the bread and wine when they are received by faith. Calvin emphasized more than Luther the role of the Holy Spirit, but at the same time he warned against conceiving of the sacraments as no more than a purely spiritual communion with the spirit of Christ.

Note how he expresses the matter in the Catechism: In the symbols of the bread and the wine "the Lord exhibits the true communication of his body and his blood—but a spiritual one . . ." (sec. 29).[21] These words might be interpreted in a "spiritual," that is, non-objective way, but he later says, "Accordingly, body and blood are represented under bread and wine, so that we may learn not only that they are ours, but that they are life and food for us" (ibid.). The same truth is expressed more clearly later in the *Institutes:* "If it is true that a visible sign is given to us to seal the gift of a thing invisible, when we have received the symbol of the body, let us no less surely trust that the body itself is also given to us" (IV.17.10).

At times Calvin seems to be engaging in a direct polemic against Zwingli's more symbolic view, where the recipient's faith is the key factor. Calvin also emphasizes the necessity of faith for the sacrament to be efficacious, but his emphasis is on God's grace and the inherent power in the sacrament. He sharply criticizes the Roman view and that of his high Lutheran critic Joachim Westphal,[22] but he does not hesitate to use concrete, graphic language and metaphors to show how seriously he believes that when we partake of the elements in the Lord's Supper we truly feed on the Lord Jesus himself.

A. Calvin's realism

Here are a few examples: In the Supper "it should be established beyond doubt that Christ with all his riches is shown to us, just as if he were set before our gaze and were touched by our hands" (sec. 29). Just as bread nourishes our bodies, so the body of Christ nourishes and quickens our souls. Similarly as wine "strengthens, refreshes, and rejoices a man physically, so his [Christ's] blood is our joy, our refreshing and our spiritual strength" (Geneva Catechism, Q. 341). When the sacrament reminds us that Christ "was made the bread of life which we continually eat, and which gives us a relish and savor of that bread, it causes us to feel the power of that bread." By "true partaking of him, his life passes into us and is made ours—just as bread when taken as food imparts vigor to the body" (*Inst.* IV.17.5).

Calvin can even say that "Christ's flesh enters into us to be our food" (IV.17.24). Taking his cue from Cyril of Alexandria and using the analogy of a spring, Calvin concludes: "In like manner the flesh of Christ is like a rich and inexhaustible fountain that pours into us the life springing forth from the Godhead into itself. Now who does not see that the communion of Christ's flesh and blood is necessary for all who aspire to heavenly life?" (IV.17.9).[23]

This kind of realistic language about "eating Christ's flesh" through faith (IV.17.5) and having Christ's blood offered "for us to taste" has been offensive to later Reformed theologians and may shock some contemporary Reformed/Presbyterian faithful.[24] Calvin himself concedes that "it seems unbelievable that Christ's flesh, separated from us by such great distance, penetrates to us so that it becomes our food . . ." (*Inst.* IV.17.10).

One would think that the passages cited above would dispose of criticisms from Calvin's Lutheran critics in particular who maintain that Calvin does not believe in a "real presence" of Christ in the Supper.[25] The real presence and partaking of Christ's flesh and blood in the Supper, however, should not be interpreted materialistically but spiritually; and "spiritual" in this sense does not mean unreal or that Christ is present only in spirit. At the same time, Calvin resists the notion that the body and blood of Christ are contained in the elements. Rather, the elements "are as instruments by which our Lord Jesus Christ distributes them to us."[26] Nevertheless, Christ is present to us in the Supper even though physically distant from us. The clue to Calvin's theology of the sacrament here, as with so many doctrines, is the Holy Spirit.

B. The role of the Holy Spirit

A fundamental presupposition of Calvin's in regard to the Lord's Supper is that the ascended body of Christ is localized, so to speak, in heaven. Hence the body of Christ cannot be ubiquitous, as it is for Luther.[27] What Calvin affirms briefly in the Catechism is repeated again and again in various later works, to wit: "For although Christ, having ascended into heaven, ceases to reside on earth . . . , still no distance can prevent his power from feeding his believers on himself and bringing it about that they still enjoy ever-present communication with him, though he is absent from that place" (sec. 29).

What is missing here, however, is how the distant, ascended Christ becomes one with us in the Supper. The answer is the Holy Spirit. In his *Short*

Treatise on the Lord's Supper, written only two years later, the role of the
Holy Spirit in this connection is still largely absent. Calvin only alludes to
the fact that it is the Holy Spirit who "gives efficacy to his ordinance" and
that the virtue [or power] of the Holy Spirit is joined to the sacraments
when they are duly received" (p. 149). In his Geneva Catechism, however,
written the following year (French ed., 1541) Calvin is much more explicit
as to how we are made "partakers of Christ's substance," even though
"Christ's body is in heaven and we are still pilgrims on earth." This gap is
bridged "by the miraculous and secret virtue of his [Christ's] Spirit, for
whom it is not difficult to associate things that are otherwise separated by
an interval of space" (Q. 353.5).[28]

In his commentary on Paul's account of the Lord's Supper in 1 Corinthians 11, written in 1546, Calvin is more precise about the way the Holy
Spirit unites things separated in the celebration of the sacrament. Here he
succinctly and clearly explains how the flesh of the ascended Lord spiritually nourishes us. In the following passage note particularly how he first
rejects Roman Catholic and Lutheran views of the real presence and then
states his own view:

> The sharing in the Lord's body, which, I maintain, is offered to us in the
> Supper, demands neither a local presence, nor the descent of Christ, nor
> an infinite extension of His body, nor anything of that sort; for, in view
> of the fact that the Supper is a heavenly act, there is nothing absurd
> about saying that Christ remains in heaven and is yet received by us. For
> the way in which He imparts Himself to us is by the secret power of the
> Holy Spirit, a power which is able not only to bring together, but also to
> join together, things which are separated by distance, and by a great dis-
> tance at that.[29]

Elsewhere in this commentary, he is even more explicit in distancing
himself from Zwinglians and those who see in the Supper "only a memo-
rial of something that is absent." His conclusion is that

> the body of Christ is really [*realiter*], to use the usual word, i.e., truly
> [*vere*] given to us in the Supper, so that it may be health-giving food for
> our souls. I am adopting the usual terms, but I mean that our souls are
> fed by the substance of his body, so that we are truly [*vere*] made one
> with him; or, what amounts to the same thing, that a life-giving power
> from the flesh of Christ [*vim ex Christi carne vivificam*] is poured into us
> through the medium of the Spirit, even although it is at a great distance
> from us, and is not mixed with us [*nec misceatur nobiscum*].[30]

The final edition of the *Institutes* is only an amplification of this thesis.
Here he refers to the Holy Spirit as "the bond of connection" which is "like
a channel through which all that Christ himself is and has is conveyed to
us." Calvin's key text here is Romans 8:9, which "teaches that the Spirit

alone causes us to possess Christ completely and have him dwelling in us" (IV.17.12). More specifically, in reference to the Supper, Calvin reiterates that this spiritual eating is no less real even though Christ remains in heaven and is not "enclosed" in the elements in a carnal fashion. The solution again is the secret and "incomprehensible power" of the Spirit (IV.17.33).

Here a slight complication arises. Do we then only lift up our hearts (*sursum corda!*) to the ascended Christ and somehow feed on him there? Or, is there a sense in which the risen Christ by his Spirit descends to us and nourishes us spiritually through the partaking of the elements? Both are true, but the accent is on the former. That is, for the most part, Calvin teaches that "in order to enjoy the reality of the signs our minds must be raised to heaven where Christ is" (*Geneva Catechism*, Q. 355). Calvin is so averse to any notion that Christ is physically contained or enclosed in the elements that he ridicules those who would "drag" Christ down from heaven (IV.17.31). "But if we are lifted up to heaven with our eyes and minds, to seek Christ there in the glory of his kingdom, as the symbols invite us to him in his wholeness, so under the symbol of bread we shall be fed by his body, under the symbol of wine we shall separately drink his blood, to enjoy him at last in his wholeness" (IV.17.18).

Yet Calvin can also speak figuratively of Christ's coming down to us in order to nourish us in the Supper.[31] For "in order to be present with us, he does not change his place, but from heaven *he sends down* the efficacy of his flesh to be present in us" (Comm. 1 Cor. 11:24, emphasis added). "We say Christ descends to us both by the outward symbol and by his Spirit, that he may truly quicken our souls by the substance of his flesh and blood" (IV.17.24). But this "descent" must not be misunderstood in such a way that Christ is literally brought down and enclosed within the elements. Those who so believe "do not understand the manner of descent by which he lifts us up to himself" (IV.17.16).

C. The mystery of it all

This may leave some readers confused—and understandably so—for this is a very complex matter. It may be of some comfort then to see that Calvin himself did not pretend to understand all of this. One cannot "reduce to words so great a mystery," he concedes, and then humbly adds, "which I see I do not even sufficiently comprehend with my mind. I therefore freely admit that no man should measure its sublimity by the little measure of my childishness."

> Rather, I urge my readers not to confine their mental interest within these too narrow limits, but to strive to rise much higher than I can lead them. For, whenever this matter is discussed, when I have tried to say

all, I feel that I have as yet said little in proportion to its worth. And although my mind can think beyond what my tongue can utter, yet even my mind is conquered and overwhelmed by the greatness of the thing. Therefore, nothing remains but to break forth in wonder at this mystery, which plainly neither the mind is able to conceive nor the tongue to express (IV.17.7).[32]

Since this heavenly mystery is beyond comprehension but is at the same time such a precious gift of God's generosity and kindness (sec. 29), our proper response should not be frustration because of our inability to understand the mysteries of the sacrament, but rather a reverent openness to what God would give us through it. We should emulate the spirit of Calvin, who was "not ashamed to confess" that the nature of Christ's presence in the Supper is "a secret too lofty for either my mind to comprehend or my words to declare." In short, he concludes, "I rather experience than understand it" (IV.17.32).[33]

D. What about the participation of unbelievers?

A highly controverted point between Calvin and some of his Lutheran and Catholic critics was whether unbelievers who participate in the Lord's Supper actually partake of Christ. This is the question of the *manducatio impiorum* or *indignorum*—the "partaking by the wicked or the unworthy."[34] Luther's emphasis on the objectivity of the sacrament and his view of the ubiquity of Christ's body leads to the conclusion that when the Supper is eaten by the wicked they receive Christ. Granted, they are not blessed thereby. The result is "poison and death."[35]

Calvin will also go so far as to say that "the flesh and blood are no less truly given to the unworthy than to God's believers." However, Calvin quickly adds—and this is a fundamental qualification—"just as rain falling upon a hard rock flows off because no entrance opens into the stone, the wicked by their hardness so repel God's grace that it does not reach them" (*Inst.* IV.17.33). Further, "From this we infer that all those who are devoid of Christ's Spirit can no more eat Christ's flesh than drink wine that has no taste. Surely, Christ is too unworthily torn apart if his body, lifeless and powerless, is prostituted to unbelievers" (ibid).[36] By an unworthy eating of the sacrament the wicked only "bring condemnation on themselves" (IV.17.40; See 1 Cor. 11:27).

The reason Calvin cannot tolerate such a view is that he places a greater emphasis on faith in regard to the effective participation in the Supper. "There is no other eating than that of faith. . . . I say that we eat Christ's flesh in believing, because it is made ours by faith, and that this eating is the result and effect of faith" (IV.17.5). The efficacy of the Supper, however, does not depend on our faith, but at the same time it cannot be separated from faith. As Kilian McDonnell points out,

> The presence of Christ in the Eucharist is an objective reality and as such is bound to faith, but it is not subjectively dependent on faith. Rather it leads to faith. Faith is not a condition of sacramental objectivity but another gift which precedes and accompanies the eucharistic gift.[37]

E. The horizontal dimension

Whereas the principal goal and benefit of the Supper is to strengthen our faith, and more particularly our union with Christ,[38] Calvin also made much of the horizontal dimensions of this sacrament. That is, it also implies mutual love and oneness among the faithful and evokes a spirit of gratitude. Note how he concludes his discussion of the Lord's Supper in the 1538 Catechism:

> Now this mystery, as it is a proof of God's very great bounty toward us, so at the same time it ought to admonish us not to be ungrateful for such lavish kindness, but rather to proclaim it with fitting praises and to celebrate it with thanksgiving. Then we should embrace one another in that unity, with which the members of this same body bound among themselves are connected. For there could be no sharper goad to arouse mutual love among us than when Christ, giving himself to us, not only invites us by his example to pledge and give ourselves to one another, but as he makes himself common to all, so also makes all one in himself (sec. 29).

In the *Institutes* Calvin approvingly cites Augustine's designation of the Supper as "the bond of love" (IV.17.38). As such, it also has ethical dimensions. Here Calvin becomes especially eloquent and must be quoted at length:

> The Lord also intended the Supper to be a kind of exhortation for us, which can more forcefully than any other means quicken and inspire us both to purity and holiness of life, and to love, peace, and concord. For the Lord so communicates his body to us there that he is made completely one with us and we with him. Now, since he has only one body, of which he makes us all partakers, it is necessary that all of us also be made one body by such participation. The bread shown in the Sacrament represents this unity. As it is made of many grains so mixed together that one cannot be distinguished from another, so it is fitting that in the same way we should be joined and bound together by such great agreement of minds that no sort of disagreement or division may intrude (ibid.).

Calvin here is obviously thinking of the apostle Paul's words in 1 Corinthians 10:16–17, which he quotes. Then follows another beautiful example of rhetoric in the service of pastoral care:

We shall benefit very much from the Sacrament if this thought is impressed and engraved upon our minds: that none of the brethren can be injured, despised, rejected, abused, or in any way offended by us, without at the same time, injuring, despising, and abusing Christ by the wrongs we do; that we cannot disagree with our brethren without at the same time disagreeing with Christ; that we cannot love Christ without loving him in the brethren; that we ought to take the same care of our brethren's bodies as we take of our own; for they are members of our body; and that, as no part of our body is touched by any feeling of pain which is not spread among all the rest, so we ought not to allow a brother to be affected by any evil, without being touched with compassion for him (ibid.).

F. Regarding frequency, benefits, and worthiness

Calvin had such a high view of this sacrament and all its benefits that he thought it should be celebrated at every Sunday service. This was intolerable for the Genevan leaders who, under Catholic rule, had celebrated the sacrament only once a year![39] The result was a compromise resulting in a quarterly celebration. (This compromise unfortunately later became the norm for most Presbyterian and Reformed churches, a practice now being gradually rectified.)

The reason for Calvin's zeal in this regard is related to the rich benefits he felt one derived from this spiritual banquet to which "all, like hungry men, should flock . . . " (IV.17.46). He alludes to two benefits in the Catechism: Celebration of the sacrament "not only brings us undoubted assurance of eternal life to our minds but also assures of the immortality of our flesh" (sec. 29).[40]

In his *Short Treatise,* Calvin lists three benefits. The first is closely related to the doctrine of justification. For the Supper

directs and conducts us to the cross of Jesus Christ and to his resurrection, in order to assure us that, whatever iniquity there may be in us, the Lord does not cease to regard and accept us as righteous; whatever material of death may be in us, he does not cease to vivify us; whatever the wretchedness we may have, yet he does not cease to fill us with all felicity.[41]

The second benefit which we receive from the Supper "is that it urges and incites us the better to recognize the blessings which we have received, and daily receive, from the Lord Jesus Christ, so that we may render him such an offering of praise as is his due."[42] The third benefit relates to sanctification, for here we have "a vehement incitement to holy living, and above all to observe charity and brotherly love among us." Thus, as we are drawn closer to Christ, with whom we are already united by faith, we are also drawn closer to each other in the bond of love." Therefore, "seeing that the virtue of the Holy Spirit is joined to the sacraments when they are duly received, we have reason to hope they will afford a good means and assistance for our growth and advance in sanctity of life and especially in charity."[43]

No wonder that Calvin urges frequent celebration of the Lord's Supper! Clearly, for Calvin, its benefits extend far beyond the actual time of celebration. Almost every dimension of the Christian life is enriched through the sacrament: confirmation of the Word, justification, forgiveness of sins, the strengthening of faith, assurance of salvation, mutual love, the bond of unity, the gratitude of praise, and closer conformity to our Head.[44]

Finally, there is the matter of who is worthy to partake of the Supper. Given the strict discipline carried out by Calvin and the consistory in regard to the Lord's Supper, his pastoral concern in this regard is remarkable. He takes very seriously the apostle's admonition about unworthily drinking judgment upon oneself (1 Cor. 11:27, 29) and decries those who "without any spark of faith, without any zeal for love, rush like swine to take the Lord's Supper" and "do not discern the Lord's body" (*Inst.* IV.17.40).

However, to those of a tender conscience who are all too aware of their sins and unworthiness Calvin speaks in quite a different way. First he complains about the "immoderate harshness" of the papacy which "deprives and despoils sinners, miserable and afflicted with trembling and grief, of the consolation of this sacrament" (IV.17.42). Unfortunately, a later generation of Calvinists, both Dutch and Scots, would deprive themselves of this heavenly feast because of a false pietism that would discourage all but a few elderly "saints" from partaking of the sacrament. To all such, Calvin writes with deep feeling,

> let us remember that this sacred feast is medicine for the sick, solace for sinners, alms to the poor; but would bring no benefit to the healthy, righteous, and rich—if such could be found. For since in it Christ is given to us as food, we understand that without him we would pine away, starve, and faint—as famine destroys the vigor of the body. Then, since he is given us unto life, we understand that without him in us we would plainly be dead. Therefore, this is the worthiness—the best and only kind we can bring to God—to offer our vileness and (so to speak) our unworthiness to him so that his mercy may make us worthy of him; to despair in ourselves so that we may be comforted in him; to abase ourselves so that we may be lifted up by him; to accuse ourselves so that we may be justified by him; moreover, to aspire to that unity which he commends to us in his Supper; and, as he makes all of us one in himself, to desire one soul, one heart, one tongue for us all. If we have weighed and

considered these things well, these thoughts, though they may stagger us, will never lay us low. How could we, needy and bare of all good, befouled with sins, half-dead, eat the Lord's body worthily? Rather, we shall think that we, as being poor, come to a kindly giver; as sick, to a physician; as sinners, to the Author of righteousness; finally, as dead, to him who gives us life. We shall think that the worthiness, which is commanded by God, consists chiefly in faith, which reposes all things in Christ, but nothing in ourselves; secondly, in love—and that very love which, though imperfect, is enough to offer to God, that he may increase it to something better, inasmuch as it cannot be offered in completeness. . . . For it is a sacrament ordained not for the perfect, but for the weak and feeble, to awaken, arouse, stimulate, and exercise the feeling of faith and love, indeed, to correct the defect of both (IV.17.42).[45]

What more consolation and what finer incentive could one want to desire earnestly this heavenly feast!

13

THE NATURE AND MARKS
OF THE CHURCH
(Sections 30, 32)

I. INTRODUCTION

As noted in the previous chapter, in the final edition of the *Institutes* the longest of the four books is devoted to the subject of the church, whereas in the Catechism of 1538 there is no discussion of the church as such except for chapters devoted to "Pastors of the Church and Their Power" (sec. 30) and "Excommunication" (sec. 32). Section 31, "Human Traditions," relates only indirectly to the matter of the church, for it is primarily concerned with the freedom of the Christian over against human traditions and should be read in conjunction with the great chapter on Christian freedom in the *Institutes* (chapter 19 of book III). In the Genevan Confession, however, there is also an article (sec. 18) that deals briefly with the nature and marks of the church.

II. CALVIN'S HIGH DOCTRINE OF THE CHURCH

Before taking up the matter of the marks of the church, it is important to note Calvin's high doctrine of the church. That is, Calvin laid great stress on the authority and indispensability of the visible, earthly church. For everything he has to say about the marks of the church presupposes this high evaluation of the church.

Some people (e.g., Emil Brunner) have concluded that Calvin regarded the church as something secondary because he describes it as "the external means or aid by which God invites us into the society of Christ and holds us therein" (title of book IV). But the title of chapter 1 of book IV immediately indicates that this is not the case at all. Here Calvin sounds more like a Roman Catholic than a Protestant! For (following Cyprian), he speaks of "the true church" as "the mother of all the godly with which we must keep unity."[1] He elaborates on this affirmation later: "Let us learn even from this simple title 'mother' how useful [N.B.!] indeed how necessary, it is that we should know her. For there is no other way to enter into life unless this mother conceive us in her womb, give us birth, nourish us at her breast, and lastly, unless she keep us under her care and guidance until, putting off mortal flesh, we become like the angels. Our weakness does not allow us to be dismissed from her school until we have been pupils all our lives" (*Inst.* IV.1.4; cf. IV.1.1 and Geneva Catechism, Qs. 104–5). In short, the church is our mother and apart from her there is no salvation. One can hardly speak of the church more highly than this!

One might conclude that this only applies to the invisible church, that is, the ideal church, to which our particular congregations bear only a faint resemblance. But Calvin specifies (at the beginning of IV.1.4) that he is speaking of the visible church, the empirical institutional church, with all its faults and weaknesses. He backs up this affirmation with numerous Scripture passages. Today we might question the validity of some of these passages, but on the whole Calvin's position is defensible.

There is, to be sure, an unbiblical concept of an invisible church as a sort of Platonic ideal.[2] In effect, this is what Emil Brunner and the *Mukyōkai* (a non-church Christian fellowship in Japan) do when they imagine that there can be an *ecclesia*, a fellowship of Jesus Christ which is "a pure communion of persons which has nothing of the character of an institution about it."[3] There is much about the visible church that causes us shame and embarrassment, but that does not justify our taking refuge in some ideal, invisible church. The Reformers, in any case, did not do this when they confessed in the Apostles' Creed, *credo ecclesiam.* They were admittedly thinking primarily of that fellowship which is hidden or invisible except to the eye of faith.[4] For in their conflict with Rome, they could not concede the title "church" to everything Rome represented. Nevertheless, when they confessed, "I believe [in] the church," they clearly had in mind the visible as well as the invisible church.[5] Calvin is explicit about this in the beginning of the discussion of this phrase of the Creed (*Inst.* IV.1.2).[6] As Jan Weerda points out, he distinguishes between the two but does not separate them as if the church as a historical reality had no relation to the church as the company of the elect. "The church of the elect lives in the visibility of historical existence and is known here as the church of God by definite marks."[7]

Granted, this distinction has sometimes been used in an unbiblical way, but some sort of distinction like this must be used to describe the various aspects or levels of the one reality known as the church.[8] There may be better ways of depicting this paradox or tension between the internal and the external, the hidden and the manifest, the historical and the eternal aspects of the church; but the visible-invisible contrast may still be useful. Roger Hazelton has expressed very well the function this distinction serves. "The Church of Christ," he notes, "is neither a simple nor a single thing." This is why the ancient distinction between the visible and the invisible church was necessary, for it serves "the purpose of marking a fundamental unity as well as an obvious diversity within the church." Moreover, this distinction "has its value for theology in safeguarding the essentially mysterious character of the church of Christ in speech and thought."[9]

With Calvin, in any case, the accent falls on the visible church. J. S. Whale discerns a development in Calvin's theology in regard to this question, but even in the first edition of the *Institutes* (1536) the church is seen as both visible and invisible. Here however, the accent is on the invisible church of the elect.[10] But in the important second edition of 1539 "the invisible church of the elect recedes into the background and gives place to the visible, ecclesiastical society. . . . Calvin now concerns himself more and more with the church in its empirical actuality, where holiness is potential rather than achieved, and is only in the process of becoming."[11] In the final edition of the *Institutes* (1559) the church is still defined in terms of election ("We must leave to God alone the knowledge of his church, whose foundation is his secret election"; IV.1.2.; cf. IV.1.7); but Calvin's main concern is with the visible church: its marks, authority, ministry, and organization. "He has indeed become the Cyprian of the Reformation."[12] A. Dakin, in fact, after summarizing Calvin's exposition of the church, concludes that "while Calvin certainly takes note of the invisible church, his interest is in the church visible."[13]

This is confirmed by even a cursory examination of book IV of the *Institutes,* one of the most notable discussions of the church in the history of theology. Apart from the two incidental references cited earlier (IV.1.2, 3), there is no discussion of the invisible church as such, except for one brief section (IV.1.7). The remainder of this lengthy discussion concerns the visible church, as Calvin indicates clearly at the beginning of section 4: "But because it is now our intention to discuss the visible church . . . ." It is this visible, empirical church which is necessary to our salvation (IV.1.4, 8), which is a mother to those for whom God is Father (IV.1.1), and a separation from which is "the denial of God and Christ" (IV.1.10).

Again we see Calvin's "high" view of the church. It was not that he was inexperienced or unrealistic! He recognizes that in the visible, historical church "there are many hypocrites who have nothing of Christ but the name and outward appearance." And there are "also many ambitious, greedy, envious persons, evil speakers, and some of quite unclean life" (IV.1.7). Nevertheless, Calvin insists that "we are commanded to revere and keep communion" with the visible church, despite all its flaws and weaknesses (ibid.).

This is strong medicine that will be hard for many church members to swallow. The problem is not only a low view of the church, its authority, and relevance, but also of its ministers and the worship services which are often regarded as dull and irrelevant. However, in Calvin's day also there were apparently many people who complained about the ministers and dull worship services. Note how contemporary the following sounds: "Many are led either by pride, dislike, or rivalry to the conviction that they can profit enough by private reading and meditation; hence they despise public assemblies [i.e., worship services] and deem preaching superfluous. But such people who think the authority of doctrine is dragged down by the baseness of the men called to teach it [i.e., the ministers] disclose their own ungratefulness" (IV.1.5).

To despise God's servants and their preaching is not only an act of ingratitude, but is also a sign of stubbornness and pride. In the last analysis, it means the rejection of God himself. For God's willingness to communicate his "heavenly doctrine" to us through ordinary ministers is another indication of God's grace and condescension. "For among the many excellent gifts with which God has adorned the human race, it is a singular privilege that he deigns to consecrate to himself the mouths and tongues of men in order that his voice may resound in them." Those who refuse to "submit to the yoke of being taught by human word and ministry" are guilty of "blotting out the face of God which shines in his teaching" (ibid.). To reject the ministry of the church is thus tantamount to rejecting God himself. For he "would have men recognize him as present in this institution" (ibid.; cf. IV.3.1).

It is easy to see how scholars can claim that "no ecclesiology has ever more exalted the ministry, under Christ, than Calvin."[14] "For," says Calvin, "neither the light and heat of the sun, nor food and drink, are so necessary to nourish and sustain the present life as the apostolic and pastoral office is necessary to preserve the church on earth" (IV.3.2).

But it must be kept in mind that this authority and power is not inherent in the church or the ministry itself. Rather, it is derived from and is always dependent on the head of the church, Jesus Christ. "He [God] alone should rule and reign in the church as well as have preeminence and authority in it, and this authority should be exercised by his Word alone" (IV.3.1).[15] Nevertheless, God condescends to use the mouths of humans in order to make his will known, and chooses some to be his ambassadors to represent himself (ibid.). Thus "there is nothing more notable or glorious in the church than the ministry of the gospel . . . " (IV.3.3).

Hence, just as the church is necessary for our salvation, so the ministry is indispensable for the welfare and unity of the church (ibid.).

III. THE MARKS OF THE TRUE CHURCH

But how can we determine where the true church exists? For the Reformers this was an existential question of paramount importance. For if

Rome could justify her claims to be *the* church, the body of Christ on earth, the Reformers would have been guilty of heresy and schism. Calvin himself would never have left the Roman church if he had not been convinced that it was hopelessly corrupt (see *Inst.* IV.2.7–11). But note well that Calvin did not acknowledge that he was guilty of schism when he departed from Rome. To the contrary, he insists that Rome was guilty of heresy and schism by its rejection of God's Word and above all by its rejection of Christ (IV.2.3, 4, 6). The papists, he maintains, have "so divided and mangled Christ that they have no Christ at all and are therefore removed from Christ."[16] Rome was guilty of many abuses, but this was not Calvin's main reason for leaving the Roman Catholic Church. The issue was ultimately the glory of Christ. Calvin felt that finally he had to make a choice between Christ and Rome. He concluded that it was necessary to withdraw from Rome that he "might come to Christ" (*Inst.* IV.2.6).

Thus there are times when it is necessary to withdraw from the visible church, or at least from a certain manifestation of it, although such occasions are rare. But we are still left with the important practical question of how we can distinguish between a true church and a false church. Calvin discusses this at some length in chapter 2 (of book IV), which has already been cited a few times above. His main point is that a true church exists wherever Christ is honored as the head of the church (IV.2.6). But how can we judge whether Christ is really acknowledged as the Head and Lord of the church? In other words, how, concretely, can we recognize where there is a real church? Calvin offers a definition of the church in the *Institutes*, IV.1.9: "The church universal is a multitude gathered from all nations; it is divided and dispersed in separate places, but agrees on the one truth of divine doctrine and is found by the bond of the same religion." This is helpful, but it still does not really answer the practical question of how to decide where we find "the one truth of divine doctrine." Calvin himself raises this question and concludes that there are fundamentally two marks or criteria by which the visible church can be recognized: the Word and the sacraments. More explicitly, "Wherever we see the Word of God purely preached and heard, and the sacraments administered according to Christ's institution, there it is not to be doubted, a church of God exists" (IV.1.9).[17] "Every congregation that claims the name 'church' must be tested by this standard as by a (Lydian) touchstone" (IV.1.11). A church may be defective in many ways, but as long as "the preaching of the gospel is reverently heard" and "the sacraments are not neglected" (IV.1.10), it can still be called a church.[18]

There may be hypocrisy, moral lapses, and scandals within the church, but as long as these two objective criteria are "sufficiently delineated" (*sufficienter descriptam*) we are not justified in separating from that church

(IV.1.11). A good example is the Corinthian church, which was tainted with all kinds of errors, both ethical and doctrinal, and yet the apostle Paul addresses these Christians as saints. Calvin regards this as highly significant. In his Commentary on 1 Corinthians 1:2 he admonishes his readers:

> We should give close attention to this verse lest we should expect in this world a church without spot or wrinkle, or immediately withhold this title from any group in which everything does not satisfy our standards. For it is a dangerous temptation to think that there is no church where purity is lacking. The point is that anyone who is obsessed by that idea, must cut himself off from everybody else, and appear to himself to be the only saint in the world, or he must set up a sect of his own along with other hypocrites (cf. *Inst.* IV.1.12–16).

In short, the idea of a pure church is a dangerous myth. Those who are too critical will eventually end up alone. Moreover, separation from any church where the means of grace are still found is "a denial of God and Christ" since the church is the body of Christ (IV.1.10).

It is rather surprising to see how broad and irenic Calvin is in this regard, even concerning doctrinal questions. He concedes that there are many doctrines where churches can differ from each other and still maintain "the unity of faith" (see IV.1.12). For Calvin, this even included the important doctrine of predestination, for he never forsook his friend Philipp Melanchthon, even though the latter was very weak on this point. Different interpretations of the meaning of baptism and the Lord's Supper would be another illustration. "A difference over these nonessentials [*de rebus istis non necessariis*] should in no wise be the basis of schism among Christians" (IV.1.12).[19] But it would be a serious error to conclude that Calvin did not therefore take this doctrine seriously. After all, Servetus was put to death for denying the doctrine of the Trinity! Other basic doctrines which "should be certain and unquestioned by all men" are: "God is one; Christ is God and the Son of God; our salvation rests in God's mercy, etc." (IV.1.12).

In his *Second Defence of the Faith Concerning the Sacraments in Answer to Joachim Westphal*, Calvin gives a more complete list of what he regarded as "leading articles" of the Christian faith.[20] Calvin was extremely concerned about the unity of the church, but never at the expense of truth (see *Inst.* IV.2.4–5; 8.8–9). For the Kingdom of Christ cannot exist apart from the scepter of his most Holy Word (IV.2.4). Indeed, "there is no church unless it is obedient to the Word of God and is guided by it."[21]

In the last analysis, then, there is really only one mark of the church, the Word; but it comes to us in two forms in the context of the church, namely, as proclamation and as sacrament. The Word, in turn, always refers us back to and mediates to us the Lord of the church, the living Word. "It is through these two means, preaching and the administration of the sacraments, that the church experiences Christ because in them the lordship of Christ is announced and realized. And where the lordship of Christ is actualized, there is the church."[22] But the lordship of Christ is only experienced and actualized where his voice is truly heard and where he is obeyed. Consequently, merely preaching sound doctrine and perfunctorily administering the sacraments in a proper way will not suffice. The Lord through his Word must be "reverently heard" (IV.1.10); Christ must be truly worshiped.[23] In sum, "This is the mark of the true church, by which it is to be distinguished from all other gatherings which falsely claim to speak in the name of God and presume to pass themselves off as churches: where the lordship and priesthood of Christ is earnestly recognized; but where Christ is not recognized as king and priest, there is nothing else but chaos."[24]

IV. CHURCH DISCIPLINE

In Calvin's very brief treatment of the church in his Catechism (the chapter on the Apostles' Creed, subsection vii) there is no mention of church discipline, which came to be a focal point of Calvin's whole ministry. Later, in section 32 he deals with excommunication, which is the most extreme form of church discipline. Even here, however, it is important to note that Calvin is concerned not only with the condemnation of the perverse but also with receiving those who repent "into grace" (sec. 32).

Unfortunately, the very word "discipline" evokes a negative reaction among many people, even pastors. For when "discipline" is mentioned, many people immediately think of punishment. And when we speak of *church* discipline most people think of excommunication. However, despite the strict and sometimes harsh way discipline was exercised in Calvin's Geneva,[25] discipline for him was essentially a positive thing, an aspect of pastoral care. It was an integral part of the proclamation of the Word of God. Its goal ultimately was nothing other than promoting the honor of Christ and the holiness of the church.

The establishment of a true church discipline not only was central to Calvin's doctrine of the church but also was one of the key issues in his long struggle in Geneva. From the outset he was concerned about a well-ordered church. Soon after his arrival in Geneva (January 1537), Calvin, together with Farel, submitted to the Genevan people three things he considered essential for a church: a series of articles for the organization of the church, a confession of faith, and a catechism. Originally the "Articles" and the "Confession" were accepted by the Magistracy (the Catechism apparently never became a problem), but eventually the Confession and certain Articles were rejected by the Councils. This whole matter is rather complicated, but the basic point of disagreement was Calvin's plan for discipline. For Calvin was something of a radical in his time in wanting to make the church independent of the civil authorities, that is, the state. Luther, Zwingli, and the other Swiss reformers—with the exception of Oecolampadius—all conceded to the civil authorities the right of the supervision of morals and excommunication.[26] The civil authorities in Geneva jealously wanted to maintain their supremacy in this realm, but at this point Calvin (and Farel) would not compromise. Thus the real reason he was expelled from Geneva in 1538 was his insistence upon an autonomous church. And central to the idea of an autonomous (but not independent!) church was the right to discipline its own members and, if necessary, excommunicate them.

In Strasbourg Calvin was largely able to realize his ideals in this regard. Although he happily took over the liturgies and adopted most of the practices of the Strasbourg churches, he was especially noted for the zeal with which he carried out church discipline in his congregation of refugees.[27] This was manifest particularly in the way he sought to give solemnity to the celebration of the Lord's Supper. However, it is noteworthy that there is no evidence to indicate that anyone was ever excommunicated in his congregation in Strasbourg. This shows that although Calvin always fought vigorously to reserve this right to the church, under normal circumstances he rarely resorted to it.

Upon his return to Geneva in 1541 he immediately presented the Magistracy with a new church constitution, the famous Ecclesiastical Ordinances of 1541. Again the key issue was church discipline, of which the cornerstone was the right to excommunicate. He finally got the Magistracy to compromise on this, but only at the price of adding an article which would allay their apprehensions.[28] This article was rather ambiguous and thus made possible a number of interpretations. In fact, this one article, according to Wendel, "was at the bottom of all the conflicts and arguments that went on for nearly fifteen years after."[29] And even after 1555, when Calvin finally became the unchallenged leader in the city, he never succeeded in totally withdrawing the Genevan Church from the control of the Magistracy. Hence we should keep in mind that even the Ecclesiastical Ordinances of 1541 represent a compromise, not only in regard to this question but also concerning such matters as the frequency of the celebration of the Lord's Supper.

This brief historical sketch reveals how seriously Calvin considered this matter. He literally risked his life for the sake of a proper church discipline. This was crucial to his whole life and ministry, for he felt that nothing less than the Lordship of Christ was at stake.

V. CALVIN'S VIEW
OF CHURCH DISCIPLINE

Calvin's practice is quite consistent with his theory, for in the *Institutes* and other writings he lays great stress on the importance of discipline in the church. As noted earlier, Calvin, like the Lutheran reformers, formally recognized only two marks (*notae*) of the church: the preaching of the Word and the administration of the sacraments. More specifically, "whenever we see the Word of God purely preached and heard, and the sacraments administered according to Christ's institution, there, it is not to be doubted, a church exists" (*Inst.* IV.1.9).[30] Very closely related to these two marks, however, is church discipline. In fact, he describes the necessity of church discipline in such strong terms that several distinguished Calvin scholars have concluded that for Calvin—as for Bucer and Knox—it was virtually a third mark.[31] (And it later becomes a third mark of the church in several Reformed confessions such as the Belgic Confession, Article 29; the Scots Confession, Article 18; and the Emden Catechism of 1554, Q. 51.) Calvin could hardly express himself more emphatically than this: "As the saving doctrine of Christ is the soul of the church, so does discipline serve as its own sinews, through which the members of the body hold together, each in its own place" (*Inst.* IV.12.1).[32] Moreover, Calvin felt so strongly about this that he maintained that those who do not practice discipline or who oppose it "are surely contributing to the ultimate dissolution of the church" (ibid.).

How prophetic these words have proved to be! Even in most Presbyterian and Reformed churches in the United States and Great Britain the practice of church discipline is almost extinct.[33] The basic reasons for neglecting church discipline are unbelief, a spirit of relativism and indifference, and a false understanding of "charity" and Christian freedom. It is also considered almost exclusively as something negative and is often equated with excommunication. It has, of course, negative aspects, but for Calvin it was essentially a positive measure, an aspect of "the cure of souls" and the preaching of the Word. "This care and this preaching are not two separate things, but two parts of one activity, the effective application of the Word, and discipline is a necessary appendage."[34] For without discipline the preaching of the Word often remains abstract and ineffectual. In Calvin's words, in order for doctrine not to remain idle (*otiosam*) it is necessary that "private admonitions, corrections, and other aids of this kind" be added to the preaching of doctrine. "Therefore discipline is like a bridle to restrain and tame those who rage against the doctrine of Christ; or like a spur to arouse those who are indifferent; and also sometimes like a father's rod to chastise mildly and with the gentleness of Christ's Spirit those who have more seriously lapsed" (*Inst.* IV.12.1).

Here it is clear that the purpose of discipline is not primarily punitive but pastoral and educational. Calvin's principal concern is the restoration of those who have erred and fallen away as well as the collective sanctification of the church.

Calvin specifically lists three aims of church discipline (*Inst.* IV.12.5). The prime aim is the glory of God and the honor of his name. Consequently, those who by their lives openly and continuously deny and disgrace Christ must be banned from celebrating the Lord's Supper and, if necessary, be expelled from the church. "For since the church itself is the body of Christ (Col. 1:24), it cannot be corrupted by such foul and decaying members without some disgrace falling upon its Head" (*Inst.* IV.12.5). Thus one of the main activities of discipline was the examination of those who wished to partake of the Lord's Supper. Both in Strasbourg and Geneva this was done by Calvin himself, together with the elders, although he regarded this as the main task of his newly formed consistory.[35]

The prevention of the profanation of the Lord's Supper was obviously a paramount concern of Calvin's. Some historians attribute this to a moralistic overscrupulousness, but most Calvin scholars conclude otherwise. They point out that among all the reformers none was more concerned than Calvin to restore again the conditions that prevailed in the church of the first three centuries. He recognized (as John Knox also did later) that "the Holy Supper of the Lord was the center of the religious life of the church, and the apex and crown of her worship. . . . discipline was the nerve of the early church, and excommunication was the nerve of discipline. . . . Calvin desired to reintroduce all these distinctive features of the church of the first three centuries—weekly communion, discipline, and excommunication exercised by the pastorate and the members."[36]

One of the great ironies of Calvinism is that in certain areas it reverted to the very practice which Calvin was opposing in the Roman Church, namely, the celebration of communion once or twice a year—or at most, as is the case in many Reformed/Presbyterian congregations, four times a year. Moreover, in some countries such as the Netherlands and Scotland the holiness of the Lord's table was taken so seriously that only a few old "sanctified" elders dared to partake of the sacrament. This represents a frightful perversion of Calvin's intention. There is, of course, always the danger of making the Lord's table a means of exclusion and division instead of forgiveness and unity. But the danger today in most Protestant churches is just the opposite, namely, to demean the sacrament to a meaningless rite offered indiscriminately to anyone. To do so is to "prostitute" the sacrament, avers Calvin.[37]

The second purpose of discipline is to protect the faithful members of the church from the influence of the wicked. "A little leaven leavens the whole lump," Calvin reminds us, in reference to the incident recorded in 1

Corinthians 5:6f. (*Inst.* IV.12.5). Here we see that the reformer is definitely concerned about the morality of the members of the church (contra Niesel, who asserts that "Church discipline does not exist in order to promote moral conduct in the church, or in order to attain purity of church life").[38]

The third and ultimate purpose is to bring to repentance those who have been disciplined or excommunicated. Thus "they who under gentler treatment would have become more stubborn so profit by the chastisement of their own evil as to be awakened when they feel the rod" (*Inst.* IV.12.5). In this matter, that is, excommunication, according to Bohatec,[39] there is a difference in approach between Calvin and Luther. For the latter regarded excommunication in a more final, official manner than Calvin, for whom excommunication was more a corrective, educational means than a permanent condemnation. Calvin advises us that "it is not our task to erase from the number of the elect those who have been expelled from the church, or to despair as if they were already lost. It is lawful to regard them as estranged from the church, and thus from Christ—but only for such a time as they remain separated" (*Inst.* IV.12.9; cf. IV.11.2). Moreover, note the following important distinction:

> Excommunication differs from anathema in that the latter, taking away all pardon, condemns and consigns a man to eternal destruction; the former, rather, punishes and chastens his moral conduct. And although excommunication also punishes the man, it does so in such a way that, by forewarning him of his future condemnation, it may call him back to salvation. But if that be obtained, reconciliation and restoration to communion await him. Moreover, anathema is very rarely or never used (*Inst.* IV.12.10).[40]

In short, the purpose of excommunication is twofold: "to lead the sinner to repentance and to remove bad examples from the midst, lest either Christ's name be maligned or others be provided to imitate them" (*Inst.* IV.12.8). Note again that excommunication (like all discipline) is basically a pastoral measure, not punishment.

VI. SOME PRACTICAL CONSIDERATIONS

Calvin also spells out some of the practical aspects of how discipline is to be exercised. The first and most important concerns the whole spirit in which discipline is carried out in the church. Despite Calvin's reputation for being severe and harsh—some of it deserved—in theory he is amazingly gentle and conciliatory. For although he likens discipline to a "bridle" and a "father's rod," he adds that we must "chastise mildly and with the gentleness of Christ's Spirit those who have more seriously lapsed" (*Inst.* IV.12.1). Again, although he wants to restore the early church's practice of discipline, he is critical of the early church for its "excessive severity."

Rather, it befits the church to judge with "a spirit of gentleness" (Gal. 6:1—
Inst. IV.12.8; cf. IV.12.11–13). Moreover, "the whole body of the church
should deal mildly with the lapsed and should not punish with extreme
rigor, but rather, according to Paul's injunction, confirm its love toward
them" (2 Cor. 2:8—*Inst.* IV.12.9). For "unless this gentleness is maintained
in both private and public censures, there is danger lest we soon slide down
from discipline to butchery" (*Inst.* IV.12.10).

Second, note that discipline should be a concern of and is to be exercised by the whole church, not by the minister alone. In fact, it is particularly the responsibility of the elders as delegated representatives of the
congregation.[41] Church discipline is "not to be administered by the decision of one man, but by a lawful assembly [*legitimum consessum*]" (*Inst.*
IV.11.5; cf. IV.3.8; IV.12.2), that is, "the assembly of the elders" (IV.11.6).
Here again Reformed and Lutheran practices differ, for "in Lutheranism
the power of excommunication was used by the minister *on behalf* of the
church, in private rather than in public, but in Calvinism, it was employed
publicly by the ministers and elders in the church."[42]

Third, Calvin distinguishes between three stages of discipline. The first
is private admonition. "Let pastors and elders be especially watchful to do
this, for their duty is not only to preach to the people, but to warn and exhort in every house, wherever they are not effective enough in general instruction" (*Inst.* IV.12.2). The second stage comes when such a person
"stubbornly rejects" or scorns such admonitions. Then that person must
be called before the assembly of elders and publicly warned. However, if
even this has no effect and the person "perseveres in his wickedness" we
must follow Christ's command and remove him from the believers' fellowship because he is "a despiser of the church" (Matt. 18:15, 17—*Inst.*
IV.12.2).

Recall, in the fourth place, that church discipline is not limited to the
laity, but there is also "a second part which applies particularly to the
clergy" (*Inst.* IV.12.22). Again Calvin finds precedent for this in the practice among the bishops in the early church. I am not sure how this should
be practiced today, but in any case ministers should heed Calvin's admonition that they should expect no more from their members than they
themselves show "by example and act. And it is truly fitting that the common people be ruled . . . by a gentler and laxer discipline, that the clergy
practice harsher censures among themselves and be far less indulgent
toward themselves than toward others" (ibid.).

It should be apparent that for Calvin a church cannot really be a church
which does not practice discipline. Without discipline, Calvin reminds us,
the preaching of the Word and instruction in doctrine have no real force
or authority, and the church will eventually become weak and ineffec-
tive.[43]

14

THE MAGISTRACY
AND CIVIL GOVERNMENT[1]
(Section 33)

This is a very unusual way to conclude a book on Christian doctrine. The last chapter in most systematic theologies and dogmatics is on eschatology, the doctrine of last things, which treats such topics as the return of Christ, the final judgment, the resurrection of the body, and a new heaven and a new earth. Calvin has no formal eschatology as such. He discusses such matters in other contexts such as that of the Apostles' Creed.

But this is further evidence that for Calvin one must not separate the sacred from the secular, the inner spiritual life from the public life of a citizen. Personal righteousness and civil justice must go hand in hand. When this is recognized, Calvin's magisterial final chapter of the *Institutes*, and its shorter counterpart in his first Catechism, should come as no surprise.

I. CALVIN'S HIGH VIEW OF
THE MAGISTRATE AND CIVIL GOVERNMENT

It is commonly recognized that Calvin was the great churchman of the sixteenth century. What is not so widely known is that the Genevan reformer was equally concerned about the political arena of life. Unlike Luther, for whom the state, though ordained of God, is primarily the work of God's left hand, that is, a remedy for sin, preventing disorder and anarchy;[2] and unlike the Anabaptists of the sixteenth century who considered politics "carnal" and a dirty business,[3] for Calvin, to be a government official (magistrate) is a singular honor comparable to that of being a minister of the gospel. Note how he begins this section in his Catechism:

> The Lord has not only testified that the office of magistrate is approved and acceptable to him, but he also sets out its dignity with the most honorable titles and marvelously commends it to us. And indeed he affirms the work of his wisdom: "that kings reign, that counsellors decree what is just, that the judges of the earth are august." And elsewhere he calls them "gods," since they carry out his business. Also in another passage they are said to "exercise judgment for God not for man." And Paul names "ruling" among God's gifts. But when he undertakes a longer

discussion of these matters, he very clearly teaches that their power is an ordination of God; further, that they are ministers of God . . . (sec. 33).

Likewise, the state, or political order, is to Calvin a very positive blessing. In the *Institutes* Calvin waxes eloquent on this theme. Civil government is a gift of God, a positive means toward realizing the kingdom of God on earth. Although Christ's spiritual kingdom and the civil or political order are two distinct realms (*Inst.* IV.20.1), the two are "not at variance" (*Inst.* IV.20.2) and are indispensable to each other. Civil government is as essential as bread, water, sun, and air and its place of honor far more excellent (*Inst.* IV.20). For "it provides that a public manifestation of religion may exist among Christians, and humanity be maintained among men" (ibid.).

This concern for civil justice and outward morality, so characteristic of Calvin, was manifest in his earliest writings. In the first (1536) edition of the *Institutes* the final chapter (chap. 6) is on Christian liberty.[4] Midway through the chapter, however, he turns to the "twofold government" (*duplex regimen*) under which people are placed.[5] The one government is spiritual, the other temporal—the former being supervised by ministers of the Word, the latter by civil magistrates. But in both cases Christ is the supreme ruler and the ultimate rule (*regula*) is the Word of God.

In the same year (1536) Calvin and Farel composed the Genevan Confession. The order of the twenty-one articles is similar to that of the topics in the *Institutes*. The last one, "Magistrates," begins in a manner similar to that of the Catechism: "We hold the supremacy and dominion of kings and princes, as also of other magistrates and officers, to be a holy thing and a good ordinance of God [cf. *Inst.* IV.20.31]. And since in performing their office they serve God and follow a Christian vocation [cf. *Inst.* IV.20.4] . . . we on our part also ought to accord them honor and reverence, to execute their commands, to bear the charges they impose upon us, so far as we are able without offence to God."[6] Calvin then describes rulers and magistrates as nothing less than "vicars and lieutenants of God [*vicaires et lieutenans de Dieu*][7] whom one cannot resist without resisting God himself." This terminology is also repeated in the 1559 *Institutes*, where magistrates are called "ministers[8] [*ministros*] of divine justice," "vicars" [*vicarios*] and "deputies" [*legatos*] of God (IV.20.6; cf. IV.20.22 where *legatos* is translated as "representatives," for some reason).

Omitting other writings of Calvin and the treatment of this subject in subsequent editions of the *Institutes*, we come now to the famous last chapter of the final edition of the *Institutes*, already cited several times above. This is the only systematic treatment of this subject to come out of the Reformation and is indeed "one of the most impressive parts of Calvin's classic."[9] Although this topic is now taken up at the very end of the *Institutes* (this was not the case in the second edition and in all following editions through 1554), it still logically follows the chapter on Christian freedom (III.19). Here Calvin discusses "inward integrity of the heart," that is, a good conscience, in response to God's law, whereas in IV.20 he discusses the matter of outward morality from the standpoint of the "true religion which is contained in God's Law."

II. THE TWOFOLD GOVERNMENT

In III.19.15 of the *Institutes* we find the same distinction as in IV.20.1, namely, that there is "a twofold government in man." The one is political, the other spiritual. Hence they have different types of rules and different types of laws. Calvin's concern in both chapters is to avoid the misuse of the freedom of the Christian in the first realm, issuing in licentiousness and anarchy in the second. "We are not to misapply to the political order the gospel teaching on spiritual freedom, as if Christians were less subject, as concerns outward government, to human laws, because their consciences have been set free in God's sight; as if they were released from all bodily servitude because they are free according to the spirit" (III.19.15).

The point to keep in mind at this juncture is that civil government is a "divinely established order" (IV.20.1) and that although the spheres of church and state must not be confused, yet ultimately both of them serve the same end. This is why this subject is so important for Calvin. He could not have imagined—and never would have countenanced—the modern notion of the state as a completely secular order with no responsibility to the church. The church, in turn, is responsible to the state. It may not be too apt to speak of "the marriage between church and state in Geneva,"[10] but the relationship, in any case, was an intimate one which "might roughly be described as of the nature of two intersecting circles."[11] On the one hand, the church claimed the cooperation of the state in carrying out its resolutions; on the other, the church pledged its assistance to the state in the performance of its task. In the sixteenth century—even in Geneva, which was unique in several respects—this relationship was often so intimate, if not confused, that it was often difficult to distinguish between the two.

Calvin conceived of the state as having basically three functions. In the Catechism these are stated succinctly in one sentence: The task of princes and magistrates "ought to be exerted to keep the public form of religion uncorrupted, to form the people's life by the best of the laws, and publicly and privately to look after the welfare and tranquility of the realm" (sec. 33). These responsibilities of civil leaders are developed at length in the *Institutes*: "Civil government has as its appointed end, so long as we live among men, to cherish and protect the outward worship of God, to defend sound doctrine of piety and the position of the church, to adjust our life to the society of men, to form our social behavior to civil righteousness, to reconcile us with one another, and to promote general peace and tranquility" (*Inst.* IV.20.2).

The tasks of civil government are spelled out in a similar fashion, but in different words, in the next section. Here its function is basically twofold: The first is to "prevent idolatry, sacrilege against God's name, blasphemies against his truth, and other public offenses against religion from arising and spreading among the people." Thus far the function of the state is to guarantee and support a "public manifestation of religion [*publica religionis facies*] among Christians . . ." (IV.20.3; note that it is assumed that all members of the republic are Christians).

The second function of civil government is to "maintain humanity among men." This is done by "preventing the public peace from being disturbed; it provides that each man may keep his property safe and sound; that men may carry blameless intercourse among themselves; that honesty and modesty may be preserved among men" (IV.20.3).

The second function will not be problematic, even to moderns living in a secularized state. It is the first function, however, which proves to be a problem for many heirs of Calvin, despite the fact that this same view is taught in the Belgic Confession and in the Westminster Confession.[12]

Though our times and our situation are quite different from Calvin's, the goal of his reform movement is still a worthy one, namely, to "establish the heavenly reign of God upon earth."[13] Though their particular functions differ, both the church and the state are chosen instruments of God toward realizing that end.

III. THE FOUNDATIONS OF GOVERNMENT

In his Catechism Calvin makes only a passing allusion to that which makes possible a well-ordered government, that is, justice and judgment (*iustitia et iudicio*). These are two basic qualities recommended by the prophet Jeremiah.[14] "Justice," according to Calvin, "is to receive into safekeeping, to embrace, to protect, vindicate, and free the innocent"; whereas "judgment is to withstand the boldness of the ungodly, to repress their violence, and to punish their misdeeds" (sec. 33).

In the *Institutes* Calvin cites other passages in addition to Jeremiah 22:3, particularly from Deuteronomy and the Psalms, which refer to the obligation of kings and rulers to execute justice and righteousness, defend the rights of the poor and the needy, and so forth. However, godly rulers can only effectively promote such civic righteousness when they are equally concerned about honoring God. In other words, the second table of the law (love of neighbor) always depends on the first (love of

God). For "no government can be happily established unless piety [i.e., the love and honor of God] is the first concern." Moreover, "those laws are preposterous which neglect God's right and provide only for men" (IV.20.9).[15]

Both tables of God's law then undergird a well-ordered society which is just and righteous. Just laws in turn must be based on God's law, although they are not identical with it. Such laws are the second key component in good government.

> Next to the magistracy in the civil state come the laws, stoutest sinews of the commonwealth, or, as Cicero, after Plato, calls them, the souls, without which the magistracy cannot stand, even as they themselves have no force apart from the magistracy. Accordingly, nothing truer could be said than that the law is a silent magistrate, the magistrate a living law (IV.20.14).

Calvin hastens to explain that the laws of a state are different from the Mosaic legislation which was designed specifically for God's chosen people. Hence it is "perilous and seditious" to think that a commonwealth cannot be ruled by "the common laws of nations" (IV.20.14). Accordingly, he rejects any notion of a theocracy based on Mosaic legislation. "For the Lord through the hand of Moses did not give that law to be proclaimed among all nations and to be in force everywhere; but when he had taken the Jewish nation into his safekeeping, defense, and protection, he also willed to be a lawgiver especially to it . . ." (IV.20.16).

Rulers are free to make laws as they see fit, so long as they ultimately conform to "the perpetual rule of love," namely, the Decalogue. Calvin adds the further qualification that they must promote true justice, "humanity and gentleness" so that people may "live together blamelessly and peaceably" (IV.20.15).

There is one other notion which is very important for Calvin in his description of a well-ordered state: equity (*aequitas*). Again and again he speaks of equity in conjunction with justice and love as a quality which must characterize the execution of the legal system. The magistrates, for example, must "exercise equity in the courts of justice" (IV.20.4). The constitution itself is "founded and rests" on equity. Constitutions, like civil laws, reflect local situations and circumstances and hence differ from place to place. This does not matter, however, as long as they "all equally press toward the same goal of equity" (IV.20.16).

It is clear that equity is an important concept for Calvin. What Calvin means by equity, however, is not easy to determine. In two brief paragraphs he comes close to defining it, but even here assumes that we understand what he means by the term. Note particularly its close relationship to natural law and the conscience:[16]

It is a fact that the law of God which we call the moral law is nothing else than a testimony of natural law and of that conscience which God has engraved upon the minds of men. Consequently, the entire scheme of this equity of which we are now speaking has been prescribed in it. Hence, this equity alone must be the goal and rule and limit of all laws.

Whatever laws shall be framed to that rule, directed to that goal, bound by that limit, there is no reason why we should disapprove of them, howsoever they may differ from the Jewish law, or among themselves (ibid.).

In this case the "rule" according to which everything is to be directed is not the law, but equity as the "goal, rule and limit of all laws." It is a natural, not a revealed, quality—like the consciousness of right and wrong—so Calvin can even speak of "natural equity" (IV.20.11). Nevertheless, "the care of equity and justice grows cold in the minds of many, unless due honor has been prepared for virtue" (IV.20.9). And in a remarkable passage in one of his commentaries, Calvin suggests that both justice and equity can be maintained only by the grace of God. "Kings," he points out, "can keep themselves within the bounds of justice and equity only by the grace of God; for when they are not governed by the Spirit of righteousness, proceeding from heaven, their government is converted into a system of tyranny."[17]

Josef Bohatec has made a study of this term and points out that Calvin sometimes equates love and equity, so that the essential content of equity is "brotherly love."[18] This is rather general, however, whereas Ford Lewis Battles provides the historical background which gives us a more precise understanding of this key notion. He points out that Aristotle made a distinction between equity and the letter of the law (*kata ton nomon dikaion*). "Equity endeavors to penetrate beneath the surface, the literal language of the law, the time-bound form in which the law was originally cast, to the spirit and intent of the original."[19]

According to Battles, Calvin employs this distinction several times in his earliest writing, his *Commentary on Seneca's De Clementia*. Here this principle gives flexibility to a judge in applying the law so that he may show clemency or compassion in pronouncing a sentence. Calvin later appeals to this principle in his discussion of law in the *Institutes* (II.2.13) and in his treatise on the Christian life in book III, where based on Titus 2:11–14 he concludes that the apostle "limits all actions of life to three parts: soberness, righteousness, and godliness." He then defines each briefly, explaining that "righteousness embraces all the duties of equity in order that to each one be rendered what is his own [cf. Rom. 13:7]" (III.7.3). So Battles concludes:

Equity, then, is the prime principle for Calvin in understanding true justice. The social justice sought, for example, by the civil rights movement, in direct conflict with unjust laws, if examined under the rule of equity, would demonstrate the superiority of *aequitas* over *summum jus*. It is this principle that should animate the framers of laws as well as the judges whose verdicts stand upon laws. It is upon this foundation that all human laws and their just application must rest.[20]

Thus, whereas the ultimate norm of all constitutions and laws is the eternal rule of love as summarized in the two tables of the law, the proper administration or application of such laws must be done with a sense of justice moderated by equity, that is, with consideration and compassion appropriate to each case.

IV. THE RESPONSIBILITY
OF THE PEOPLE

Calvin, following Cicero, considers civil government in terms of three categories: the magistrate, the laws, and the people. We come now to that last category. At first glance—if one reads only the Catechism and the *Institutes*—this seems to be a fairly simple matter. Here Calvin appears to be very conservative and to encourage the obedience of subjects regardless of how tyrannical or corrupt their rulers might be. Here is the view of the young Calvin in his 1538 Catechism:

> The duty of subjects is not only to honor and revere their leaders, but also with their prayers to commend their safety and prosperity to the Lord, to subject themselves voluntarily to their authority, to obey willingly their edicts and constitutions; not to slip out from under the burdens imposed by them, whether these be taxes or tributes or civil duties, and anything else of this sort. Not only should we behave obediently toward those leaders who perform their office uprightly and faithfully as they ought, but also it is fitting to endure those who insolently abuse their power, until freed from their yoke by a lawful order. For as a good prince is a proof of divine beneficence for the preservation of human welfare, so a bad and wicked ruler is his whip to chastise the people's transgressions. Yet this we must hold as a universal truth: that power is given to each by God, nor can they be resisted without our resisting what God has ordained (sec. 33).

The mature Calvin of the final edition of the *Institutes* takes the same position. Rulers are not only to be obeyed; they are to be honored and revered. "With hearts inclined to reverence their rulers, the subjects should prove their obedience toward them, whether by obeying their proclamations, or by paying taxes, or by undertaking public offices and burdens which pertain to the common defense, or by executing any other commands of theirs" (*Inst.* IV.20.23).

This may seem severe, and Calvin might be accused of political naïveté, but three important factors must be taken into consideration here.

The first and foremost is that Calvin takes this stand on the basis of his understanding of Scripture. Romans 13 is a key passage in this regard, particularly the first two verses: "Let every person be subject to the higher powers.... For he who resists authority resists what God has ordained."[21] Calvin finds further support for this position in passages such as Titus 3:1; 1 Peter 2:13–14; 1 Timothy 2:1–2 (in IV.30.23). Moreover, he finds in the Old Testament many cases where the Israelites are commanded to obey even wicked rulers. A prime example is Nebuchadnezzar. Calvin points to Jeremiah 27 and concludes: "We see how much obedience the Lord willed to be paid to that abominable and cruel tyrant for no other reason than that he possessed the kingship" (IV.20.27).

The second thing to keep in mind is that Calvin makes a distinction between the person and the office of the ruler. Calvin's ideal magistrate is "a father of his country," a "shepherd of his people, guardian of peace, protector of righteousness, and avenger of innocence" (IV.20.24); but Calvin is quite aware of the fact that most rulers fall far short of this ideal. He describes in considerable detail what the majority of rulers are like: lazy, greedy, corrupt, even guilty of "sheer robbery, plundering houses, raping virgins and matrons, and slaughtering the innocent" (IV.20.24).

But we must obey them, says Calvin, despite all their faults and vices, for the office or "the order itself is worthy of such honor and reverence" (IV.20.22). Again Calvin appeals to Romans 13. We should obey "not only because of wrath, but because of conscience" (v. 5). So once more Calvin's conclusion is a very conservative one: "The magistrate cannot be resisted without God being resisted at the same time" (IV.20.13). Obedience is due even to the unjust magistrate.

However, there is a loophole of a sort, and this is the third important factor. The last sentence cited above from the *Institutes* is virtually the same as the last sentence quoted earlier from the Catechism. Yet, Calvin immediately adds, "But in obeying rulers we are always to make one exception, that such obedience is never to lead us away from obedience to him, to whose decrees the commands of all kings ought to yield" (sec. 33).

And then Calvin concludes this section on the magistracy with the following brief paragraph:

> The Lord, therefore, is the King of kings, who, when he has opened his sacred mouth, must alone be heard, before all and above all men. Next to him we are subject to those men who are in authority over us, but only in him. If they command anything against him, let it go unesteemed. But let us prefer this as our maxim: "We must obey God rather than men" (Acts 5:29).

Thus, for Calvin, "all authority in the political arena is *derived* authority, given by God."[22] All rulers, "whoever they may be, have their authority solely from him" (*Inst.* IV.20–25). Here again Calvin takes his cue from the apostle Paul's understanding of the state. For in Romans 13:1, after urging "every person to be subject to the governing authorities," the apostle adds immediately: *"for there is no authority except from God . . ."* (emphasis added).[23] The following verses, however, urge submission to the authorities, and that raises the question whether resistance or rebellion is ever possible.

V. THE RIGHT OF RESISTANCE

As pointed out earlier (section 4), Calvin states emphatically that citizens must obey their rulers, whether they are good or bad. Even tyrannical governments are God-ordained. Wicked rulers represent God's judgment on a sinful people. Magistrates who "rule unjustly and incompetently have been raised up by God to punish the wickedness of the people" (*Inst.* IV.20.25). It is God's will to "govern the world in this manner," so "any who despise his power are therefore resisting God himself, since to despise the providence of God who is the author of civil government [*iuris politici*] is to wage war against him."[24]

Calvin's position appears clear and unequivocal. And yet in the very context of the passage just cited Calvin adds a concession; for "dictatorships and unjust authorities are not ordained by governments."[25] In his dedicatory letter to King Francis I of France in the final edition of the *Institutes* Calvin states what "is at stake" here: "how God's glory may be kept safe on earth, how God's truth may retain its place of honor, how Christ's kingdom may be kept in good repair among us."[26] But Calvin recognizes that rulers who seek to uphold such ideals are exceedingly rare. Tyrants, not God-fearing rulers, dominate.[27]

Does this, then, warrant a popular uprising against tyrants and unjust rulers? Are there conditions that justify a popular rebellion? The answer is no, at least insofar as the general populace is concerned. Calvin concedes that there is an "inborn feeling" (*ingenitus sensus*) in the minds of people "to hate and curse tyrants as much as to love and venerate lawful kings" (*Inst.* IV.20.24).

Even so, Calvin will only allow for the overthrow of tyrants and unjust rulers by holders of subordinate office such as elected or appointed magistrates. For individuals to do so would lead to anarchy, which for Calvin is worse than even the most oppressive government. For the worst tyranny is "more bearable than no order at all."[28] God will eventually dispose of such tyrants, but the means toward that end is not the people as a whole but their lawful representatives. "For, if the correction of unbridled despotism is the

Lord's to avenge, let us not at once think that it is entrusted to us, to whom no command has been given except to obey and suffer" (*Inst.* IV.20.31).

Actually, the populace as a whole can do more than simply "obey and suffer." They also have recourse to prayer. They can "implore the Lord's help, in whose hand are the hearts of kings and the changing of kingdoms [Prov. 21:1]" (IV.20.29). "They must also pray to God that he will bring good out of the evils of bad rulers."[29]

The proper instrument, however, for removing despotic rulers is the constituted magistracy. The classical passage in this regard comes near the end of the *Institutes* (IV.20.31):

> If there are now any magistrates of the people, appointed to restrain the willfulness of kings . . . , I am so far from forbidding them to withstand, in accordance with their duty, the fierce licentiousness of kings, that, if they wink at kings who violently fall upon and assault the lowly common folk, I declare that their dissimulation involves nefarious perfidy, because they dishonestly betray the freedom of the people, of which they know that they have been appointed protectors by God's ordinance.

This would seem to end the matter, but in some of his later commentaries[30] Calvin opened the door just a crack to suggest to some of his followers, including his disciple, the Scottish reformer John Knox, that under certain circumstances a popular uprising might be justified, for example, when rulers were deemed opponents of true religion.[31]

Moreover, Calvin's last word on this subject is that Christian citizens not only have the right but also the obligation to disobey rulers who would try to force them to do anything contrary to God's will. The means, however, is passive resistance, not armed rebellion. Accordingly, Calvin concludes his *Institutes* (IV.20.32) as he concluded his Catechism, with the reminder that "We must obey God rather than men" (Acts 5:29). Appealing to various biblical figures who resisted rulers or edicts which would have required them to disobey God, Calvin repeats, "The Lord, therefore, is the King of kings," and he elaborates more fully than in the Catechism:

> But in that obedience which we have shown to be due the authority of rulers, we are always to make this exception, indeed, to observe it as primary, that such obedience is never to lead us away from obedience to him, to whose will the desires of all kings ought to be subject, to whose decrees all their commands ought to yield, to whose majesty their scepters ought to be submitted. . . . If they command anything against him, let it go unesteemed. And here let us not be concerned about all that dignity which the magistrates possess; for no harm is done to it when it is humbled before that singular and truly supreme power of God. . . .

GOD BE PRAISED[32]

APPENDIX:
CALVIN, THEOLOGIAN
OF THE HOLY SPIRIT

I. INTRODUCTION: WHY THE LACUNA?

Over eighty years ago the Princeton Seminary theologian B. B. Warfield dubbed Calvin "the theologian of the Holy Spirit." "The doctrine of the Holy Spirit," he said, "is a gift from Calvin to the church."[1] This has been repeated and reaffirmed several times by subsequent Calvin scholars, particularly in our own time.[2] No one has denied this, as far as I know.

Hence it is a conundrum that so little has been written concerning Calvin's doctrine of the Holy Spirit, especially in the English-speaking world where there has been so much Calvin research over the last forty years. There are, however, two major studies of this theme, one in Dutch, the other in German. The former is by Simon van der Linde, *De Leer van den Heiligen Geest* (1943); the latter is by Werner Krusche, *Das Wirken des Heiligen Geistes nach Calvin* (1957); but since then we have had only a few essays on isolated themes. There is one exception, a lengthy essay by H. Quistorp in a collection of essays on the Holy Spirit, *De Spiritu Sancto:* "Calvin's Lehre vom Heiligen Geist."[3] As the title indicates, it is a comprehensive study, but it is somewhat rambling and lacks precise documentation. In contrast, the works of van der Linde and Krusche are careful, thoroughly researched studies, but each is marred by an overly zealous polemic: van der Linde against Karl Barth and Krusche against Emil Brunner and his disciples. Consequently, we still have need of a balanced treatment of this important subject utilizing the researches of the last thirty-five years.

The one topic related to the Holy Spirit which has received considerable attention is the relation of Word and Spirit, particularly the internal or secret testimony of the Spirit to the authority of Scripture.[4] Apart from that, however, Calvin's doctrine of the Holy Spirit has been given scant attention in Calvin studies, although it was the theme of the sixth colloquium of the North American Calvin Studies Society in 1987.[5] And a few years earlier, the British Calvin scholar Tony Lane published a paper on "John Calvin: The Witness of the Holy Spirit."[6] In standard studies of

Calvin's theology, however, one will not find a chapter on the Holy Spirit.[7] The main reasons for this lacuna are probably that (1) Calvin has only one brief chapter on the Holy Spirit per se in his *Institutes* (III.1); and (2) he relates the Holy Spirit to almost every doctrine he discusses.[8] Thus, to do justice to Calvin's doctrine of the Holy Spirit one must discuss his whole theology. This is such a formidable task that it is not surprising that no one has recently dared undertake it.

I hope to do so some day, *Deo volente*, but for now must settle for an overview of three themes in Calvin's doctrine of the Holy Spirit. Even with this limitation, however, I can only point out some of the distinctive aspects of his treatment of various themes, in particular the Spirit and the Trinity, the Spirit and the Word, and the Spirit and the Christian life. Time and space unfortunately do not permit a treatment of a specially fruitful area, that of the Spirit and the sacraments.

II. WHO IS THE HOLY SPIRIT?

On the surface, Calvin's answer to this question appears to be simple and traditional. In short, the Holy Spirit is the third person of the Trinity, equal in deity with the Father and the Son. The question, however, is what Calvin means by "person." This, in fact, is the critical question in any doctrine of the Trinity. The alternative is to speak of "modes of being" (Barth: *Seinsweisen*).[9] The danger with the word "persons" is that its meaning has changed, so that with our modern understanding we are in danger of falling into tritheism. As soon as one uses the word "mode," however, there is the suspicion of the ancient heresy of modalism.

Calvin was not satisfied with some of the traditional terminology, and he got into trouble early in his career for refusing to sign one of the creeds for this reason.[10] Eventually, however—in one of the last editions of the *Institutes*—he defines "person" as "a 'subsistence' in God's essence, which, while related to the others, is distinguished by an incommunicable quality" (*Inst.* I.13.6). This sounds very technical, but Calvin is thinking of Hebrews 1:3, where we read that Christ "bears the very stamp of his [God's] nature" (RSV/NIV: "the exact representation of his being"; NRSV: "the express imprint of God's very being").[11] Calvin then explains precisely what he means by these terms, but he really isn't interested in such technicalities. He complains about those people who "persistently quarrel over words" and concludes: "Say that in the one essence of God there is a trinity of persons; you will say in one word what Scripture states, and cut short empty talkativeness" (*Inst.* I.13.5).

Calvin's real concern here, as elsewhere, is not theological abstraction but practical Christian living. Note how he defines the Trinity in his first catechism (1538):

> When we name Father, Son, and Holy Spirit, we are not fashioning three Gods, but in the simplest unity of God, Scripture and the very experience of godliness [*pietatis*] disclose to us the Father, his Son, and the Spirit (Catechism, sec. 20).

What is distinctively Calvinian in this definition is his appeal not only to Scripture but also to "the experience of godliness." He makes a similar reference in his discussion of the divinity of the Spirit in the *Institutes:* "What Scripture attributes to him [the Holy Spirit] we ourselves learn by the sure experience of godliness" (*Inst.* I.13.14). Calvin frequently appeals to experience as a secondary sort of confirmation of Scripture, and in this case particularly godliness (or piety). "This practical knowledge [of the Trinity] is doubtless more certain and firmer than idle speculation" (*Inst.* I.13.13). Thus, for Calvin, "the doctrine of the Trinity did not stand out of relation to his religious consciousness but was a postulate of his profoundest religious emotions; was given, indeed, in his experience of salvation itself."[12]

In other words, for Calvin, the doctrine of the Trinity should not become a matter of speculation and debate but should be a source of strength and comfort for faith and practice. Consequently, when the question arises concerning the peculiar functions of each person of the Trinity he simply answers:

> To the Father is attributed the beginning of activity, and the fountain and wellspring of all things; to the Son, wisdom, counsel, and the ordered disposition of all things; but to the Spirit is assigned the power and efficacy of action (*Inst.* I.13.18).

III. THE SPIRIT AND THE WORD

As noted earlier, the relation of the Spirit to the Word in Calvin's theology has received considerable attention. What has been of special interest is one of Calvin's few original contributions in the history of Christian thought, that is, his notion of the internal, secret witness (*testimonium*) of the Spirit to the authority of the Bible.[13] Luther had alluded to this connection, but it was Calvin who first developed this idea of the internal witness into a distinctive doctrine. Almost every discussion of the authority of the Bible refers to Calvin at this point—and usually with approval, although two criticisms are occasionally made. The one is that Calvin's argument is too subjective; the other is that it is circular. I shall respond to both arguments shortly; but first, how precisely does Calvin establish the authority of Scripture?

First, consider the historical situation in which Calvin was operating. On the one hand, there were the Roman Catholics who maintained that the authority of Scripture was derived from the church. On the other hand, there were certain Anabaptists and radical "spiritualist" types who believed in private, special revelations of the Spirit.[14] Both were guilty, Calvin believed, of separating the Word from the Spirit.

Then there was also the problem of human sinfulness, which Calvin took very seriously. For if human beings by nature are spiritually blind and dead in sin, how can they receive God's revelation? And how will they be able to understand it and recognize it as God's revealed Word? The answer to all these questions is the Holy Spirit. Here is a fundamental statement that relates to all of these questions:

> The Word of God is like the sun, shining on all to whom it is proclaimed, but with no effect among the blind. Now all of us are blind by nature in this respect. Accordingly, it cannot penetrate in to our minds unless the Spirit, as inner teacher, through his illumination makes entry for it (*Inst.* III.2.34).

Then, concerning the dangers to the left and the right, that is, the radical Spiritualists and the Roman Catholics, Calvin affirms:

> The Spirit wills to be conjoined [*coniunctus*] with God's Word by an indissoluble bond [*individuo nexu*], and Christ professes this when he promises the Spirit to his church. . . . It is this inviolable decree of God and of the Holy Spirit which our foes are trying to set aside when they pretend that the church is ruled by the Spirit apart from the Word (*Inst.* IV.8.13).

This, for Calvin, is fundamental: the Word and Spirit belong inseparably together. We shall see later that he does allow for a special leading and guidance of the Spirit, but never in contradiction to the Word. To repeat his basic thesis in other words (but his own):

> For by a kind of mutual bond [*mutuo nexu*] the Lord has joined together the certainty of his Word and of his Spirit so that the perfect religion of the Word may abide in our minds when the Spirit, who causes us to contemplate God's face, shines; and that we in turn may embrace the Spirit with no fear of being deceived when we recognize him in his own image, namely, in the Word (*Inst.* I.9.3).

We have not yet come, however, to the oft-quoted passage that speaks of the "secret" and "inward testimony of the Spirit." Note carefully what Calvin is affirming here. The inner witness/testimony does not *prove* that the Bible is the Word of God; nor does it *establish* the authority of the Word. For the Scriptures are self-authenticating. They do not require some external proof. Rather, by the internal witness of the Spirit the authority of Scripture is *confirmed* and *authenticated* for the believer.[15] As Werner Krusche perceptively notes, for Calvin, "The objective basis for the certainty of Scripture [*Schriftgewissheit*] lies in the Scripture itself, not in the judgment of an external court."[16] No amount of argumentation will ever convince anyone that the Bible is the very Word of God. As Calvin puts it, "They who strive to build up firm faith in Scripture through disputation are doing things backward" (*Inst.* I.7.4).

Calvin's great concern is again a practical one. He is concerned about the assurance that believers need that they can really rely on the Bible as being true. "If we desire to provide in the best way for our consciences," he says in one of his classic statements, "we ought to seek our conviction in a higher place than human reasons, judgments, or conjectures, that is, in the secret testimony of the Holy Spirit" (ibid.).

A little later, in response to cynics ("despisers of God") who disparage Scripture, Calvin replies that he could easily refute all their objections. But, he adds,

> the testimony of the Spirit is more excellent than all reason. For as God alone is a fit witness to himself in his Word, so also the Word will not find acceptance in men's hearts before it is sealed by the inward testimony of the Spirit (ibid.).

Calvin is not averse to providing rational proofs "to establish the credibility of Scripture,"[17] but they are only of secondary value. Once one is convinced by the Spirit of the divine character of the Scriptures such arguments will be "useful aids"—but only if a firm foundation has already been laid![18] "For even if it [Scripture] wins reverence for itself by its own majesty, it seriously affects us only when it is sealed upon our hearts through the Spirit" (*Inst.* I.7.5).

This is only a sampling of the many places where Calvin appeals to the witness of the Holy Spirit in our hearts to give us the assurance that the Bible is truly the Word of God. For many theologians, this approach is classic and unsurpassed. But not everyone is so impressed. In the nineteenth century, the liberal German scholar David F. Strauss complained that this was "the Achilles' heel of the Protestant system." In our own time some fundamentalists as well as liberals maintain that this argumentation is too subjective. Others claim the reasoning is circular.[19]

In a sense the argument is circular. For how do we know the Bible is the Word of God? Answer: The Spirit tells us so. How do we know it is truly the Spirit who gives us this assurance? Answer: The Bible itself convinces us of this. Yet it should be noted that this kind of argumentation is no invention of the theologians! There are several passages in the New

Testament which suggest this approach: John 8:13ff.; 1 Corinthians 2:11; Romans 8:16; and 2 Corinthians 3:1–3, for example.[20]

Karl Barth acknowledges that this argument is indeed circular but, he says, it is a "logical circle."[21] Accordingly, we are not left in some kind of existential subjectivism. For in this approach the subjective (the Spirit) and the objective (the written Word) coalesce. As Otto Weber points out, what appears to be "objective" (the Bible), is "by its very essence also 'subjective'" (the persuasion of its divine origin). The testimony of the Spirit encounters us in the testimony of the biblical witnesses and thereby the "polarity of object and subject is overcome."[22] The result, in Calvin's words, "is a conviction that requires no reasons, a knowledge with which the best reason agrees—in which the mind reposes more securely and constantly than in any reasons" (*Inst.* I.7.5).

IV. THE HOLY SPIRIT
AND THE CHRISTIAN LIFE

Nowhere is Calvin more obviously the theologian of the Holy Spirit than in his understanding of the Christian life. As he points out in his discussion of the Christian life, "The Christian philosophy bids reason give way to, submit, and subject itself to, the Holy Spirit" (*Inst.* III.7.1). It should be noted at the same time that the concepts of God's gracious election and preservation are correlates, even if they are not always explicitly stated. For the Holy Spirit is the agent or power which effects God's sovereign grace in the life of the believer; and grace, in turn, is a manifestation of God's election. Unfortunately, the English language does not have a precise equivalent for the lovely German expression used so often by German theologians, especially Karl Barth: *Gottes Gnadenwahl* (God's gracious election—or election of grace). In any case, for Calvin, the working of the Holy Spirit in the life of the believer is an implementation of God's *Gnadenwahl*. For from beginning to end the Christian life is made possible by God's grace[23] as it is experienced by the presence and power of the Holy Spirit.[24]

I said earlier that Calvin had no special chapter on the Holy Spirit. This is not quite true, for in many ways the theme of books III and IV of the *Institutes* is the work of the Holy Spirit: in book III in relation to faith or regeneration, in book IV in relation to the church and sacraments. Space limitations prevent me from dealing with the latter subject. In book III, however, Calvin moves from the objective work of Christ on our behalf to the subjective appropriation of the benefits of Christ's redemptive work.[25] There is no explicit mention of the Holy Spirit here, but note the title of chapter 1 (of book III): "The Things Spoken Concerning Christ Profit Us by the Secret Working of the Spirit." This chapter contains, in brief, Calvin's doctrine of the Holy Spirit in relation to soteriology.

He begins with a foundational statement: "First, we must understand that as long as Christ remains outside of us, and we are separated from him, all that he has suffered and done for the salvation of the human race remains useless and of no value for us" (*Inst.* III.1.1). To use more technical terms, "Christ *extra nos* [outside of us] through the Spirit becomes Christ *in nobis* [in us]."[26] In Calvin's own words, we ought not "think of Christ, standing afar off," but "rather dwelling in us" (*Inst.* III.2.24). Thus there is an inseparable relation between Christology and pneumatology.[27] For Christ does not dwell in us or we in him apart from the Holy Spirit. For Christ "unites himself to us by the Spirit. By the grace and power of the same Spirit we are made his members, to keep us under himself and in turn to possesses him" (*Inst.* III.1.3).

To put it simply, the Spirit is the link or "the bond by which Christ effectually unites us to himself" (*Inst.* III.1.1).[28] Or, to use Kierkegaardian terminology, the Spirit is the agent or means by which the historical Christ becomes "contemporaneous" with us.

In this connection, Calvin also uses the same terminology he used in reference to the authority of Scripture, namely, "the testimony of the Spirit." Citing 1 John 5:7–8, Calvin concludes that the reference here to the testimony of the Spirit (along with the water and the blood) is "a testimony we feel engraved like a seal upon our hearts, with the result that it seals the cleansing and sacrifice of Christ" (ibid.).[29]

We should not conclude that this testimony of the Spirit is a different testimony from that of the witness to the divine origin of Scripture. Actually, there are four different facets to the one "testimony" of the Spirit: (1) the certainty of Scripture; (2) the certainty of salvation; (3) the certainty of our divine adoption; and (4) the certainty of the divine authority of the Word, which offers the promise of adoption.[30] Ultimately, however, there are not two or four distinct witnesses (*testimonia*) of the Spirit but one. As Krusche notes, "There are not two different witnesses [a witness of the Holy Spirit to Scripture and a separate witness to our adoption by God] but only one," although George Hendry distinguishes between a formal witness (the Scripture as the Word of God) and a material witness (the content of Scripture, the gospel).[31] However, Krusche goes on to affirm that

> Calvin has not separated the certainty of Scripture from the certainty of salvation as it happened in orthodoxy. The *testimonium* does not first convince us of the divine origin of Scripture apart from its content as promise, and then convince us of its content. Both belong inseparably together [beides fällt untrennbar in eins].[32]

Thus far we have considered the role of the Holy Spirit in relation to the general theme of soteriology. Now I would like to focus briefly on three specific aspects of the doctrine of salvation: faith, union with Christ, and the leading or guidance of the Spirit.

A. Faith

Calvin concludes his discussion of the work of the Spirit in chapter 1 of book III with the assertion: "Faith is the principal work of the Holy Spirit" (*Inst.* III.1.4). He makes this point several times in a monumental chapter on faith (chapter 2). For example, "the peculiar work" of the Spirit is faith (III.2.39). Here also we see the intimate connection between the Word, the witness of the Spirit, and faith. Faith is grounded in the Word,[33] particularly in the promise of God's grace in Jesus Christ.[34] But, again, God's gracious promises will neither be understood nor accepted without the aid of the Spirit. For they "cannot penetrate into our minds unless the Spirit, as the inner teacher, through his illumination makes entry for it" (III.2.35).

In this passage Calvin refers to the Word "penetrating our minds." It is important to recognize, however, that Calvin emphasizes the heart more than the head, the affections (*affectus*) more than the brain.[35] First, let us look at Calvin's most comprehensive definition of faith:

> We call it [faith] a firm and certain knowledge of God's benevolence toward us, founded upon the truth of the freely given promise in Christ, both revealed to our minds and sealed upon our hearts through the Holy Spirit (*Inst.* III.2.7).

Note particularly four things in this definition: (1) The object of faith is God's kindness toward us grounded in his promise in Christ. (2) Faith can simply be defined as knowledge.[36] (3) This knowledge, however, is not academic knowledge, for it is a matter of the head ("our minds") and the heart. (4) Finally, this existential knowledge, though our own act, is ultimately a gift of the Holy Spirit.

Calvin amplifies these points in later sections of this chapter. "It is clear," he says, "that faith is much higher than human understanding. And it will not be enough for the *mind* to be illumined by the Spirit of God unless the *heart* is also strengthened by his power" (III.2.33). "We cannot come to Christ unless we are drawn by the Spirit of God, so when we are drawn we are lifted up *in mind and heart* above our understanding" (III.2.34, emphasis added).

There are several other places where Calvin stresses that the knowledge of faith is a special kind of knowledge,[37] but one passage should suffice:

> It now remains to pour into the *heart* what the *mind* has absorbed. For the Word of God is not received by faith if it flits about in the top of the *brain*, but when it takes root in the depth of the *heart* that it may be an invincible defense to withstand and drive off all the stratagems of temptation. But if it is true that the mind's real *understanding* is illumination by the Spirit of God, then in such confirmation of the *heart* his power is much more clearly manifested, to the extent that the *heart's* distrust is

greater than the *mind's* blindness. It is harder for the *heart* to be furnished with assurance than for the *mind* to be endowed with thought. The Spirit accordingly serves as a seal, to seal up in our *hearts* those very promises the certainty of which it has previously impressed on our *minds;* and takes the place of a guarantee to confirm and establish them (III.2.36, emphasis added).

Once again we see Calvin's concern with assurance[38] and what a later generation would call "experiential religion." At times Calvin sounds more like a Wesleyan than a Calvinist! In any case, he does not intellectualize faith as some of his followers did in the next century. Moreover, faith, which is more a matter of the heart than the head, is for Calvin from beginning to end the work of the Holy Spirit.

B. Union with Christ[39]

Faith comes to its fullest expression for Calvin in the notion of the mystical union of the believer with Christ. Except for Calvin specialists, few people are aware of this facet of Calvin's thought. For when some scholars hear the phrase "mystical union," they immediately conclude that this represents some form of mysticism. But as Wilhelm Niesel points out, when Calvin uses this phrase, this "has nothing to do with the absorption of the pious mystic into the sphere of the divine being."[40] François Wendel agrees that when Calvin speaks of a union or communion with Christ he is not suggesting "any absorption into Christ, or any mystical identification that would diminish human personality in the slightest degree, or draw Christ down to us." Nevertheless, "the relationship with Christ is none the less the closest . . ."[41]

Therefore, note carefully the wording in this key passage where Calvin is responding to Osiander:

> I confess that we are deprived of this utterly incomparable good [Christ and his righteousness] until Christ is made ours. Therefore, that joining together of Head and members, that indwelling of Christ in our hearts—in short, that mystical union [*mystica unio*]—are accorded by us the highest degree of importance, so that Christ, having been made ours, makes us sharers with him in the gifts with which he has been endowed. We do not, therefore, contemplate him outside ourselves from afar in order that his righteousness may be imputed to us but because we put on Christ and are engrafted into his body—in short, because he deigns to make us one with him. For this reason, we glory that we have fellowship of righteousness with him (*Inst.* III.11.10).

There is no mention of the Holy Spirit in this passage, but as we have seen from earlier quotations, such a faith-union is only possible because of the work of the Holy Spirit. Calvin makes this explicit elsewhere: "We hold ourselves," he says, "to be united with Christ by the secret power of the Spirit" (III.11.5).[42]

In the *Institutes*, Calvin only speaks once of a "mystical union" with Christ, but he expresses the same idea elsewhere in slightly different words. For example, in his discussion of our partaking of Christ in the Lord's Supper he speaks of the "mystery of Christ's secret union [*arcanae unionis*] with the devout" (IV.17.1). Also, in this sacrament we "have a witness of our growth into one body with Christ such that whatever is his may be called ours" (IV.17.2). Again, there is no mention of the Holy Spirit in these passages, but that is presupposed. For, as he writes a little later, "Christ's flesh, separated from us by such a great distance, penetrates to us . . . [by] the secret power of the Holy Spirit" (IV.17.10).[43] Romans 8:9 is a key text for Calvin here, for this verse "teaches that the Spirit alone causes us to possess Christ completely and have him dwelling in us" (III.17.12).

Such mystical language may strike one as un-Reformed, but it is not peculiar to Calvin. Niesel finds similar passages in the Heidelberg Catechism and in his *Reformed Symbolics*,[44] where he calls union with Christ "the basic confession of the Reformed Churches."[45] This may be too strong an assertion, but there is no doubt that this is true for Calvin.[46] Moreover, for Calvin, the fruits of this mystical faith-union with Christ by the Holy Spirit are incalculable: regeneration, faith, justification, sanctification, and ultimately glorification.[47] "In Christ" we enjoy all of Christ's gracious gifts, for he is not "far off" but one with us.

C. The leading and guidance of the Spirit

Finally, there is one more aspect of Calvin's doctrine of the Holy Spirit which merits special attention—especially since this theme has been almost entirely missed in studies of Calvin's theology. I am referring to the leading and guidance of the Holy Spirit in the Christian life. Phrases like the following occur again and again: The Holy Spirit "governs," "guides," and "rules" the believer. Yet, for some inexplicable reason, this theme has been overlooked by almost all Calvin scholars.[48]

Here is a typical example of this usage: "The Lord by his Spirit *directs, bends,* and *governs* our heart and *reigns* in it as his possession. . . . It is obviously the privilege of the elect that, regenerated through the Spirit of God, they are *moved and governed by his leading*" (II.3.10, emphasis added). This passage is from the *Institutes*, but similar phrases can be found in all of Calvin's writings.[49] For example, in his Geneva Catechism, he writes: In repentance "we yield ourselves to be *ruled by the Spirit of God,* and bring all the actions of our life into obedience to the divine will."[50] And from a sermon on Ephesians 4:20–24: "Christ is given to us for our sanctification, in order that we should *be governed by his Spirit* (emphashis added)."[51]

Note that in this last quotation the context for being "governed by Christ's Spirit" was sanctification. Many of these references occur in relation to this aspect of the Christian life. In these cases the special role of the Holy Spirit is to implement and assist the life-long process of mortification and vivification—terms Calvin uses to describe conversion or repentance.

In other cases, however, these phrases refer to a special understanding of God's will and guidance in living out that will. Such guidance is never contrary to God's will as expressed in Scripture, but it does supplement and give concrete direction in following that will. The apostle Paul, for example, "did not teach anywhere except by the guidance [*manuducente*] of the Spirit. . . ."[52] Moreover, because he had such great responsibilities, "he needed the extraordinary direction [*singulari directione*] of the Spirit."[53]

We do not receive new revelations by such guidance of the Spirit, but it may mean new insights, deeper understanding, and specific direction for our lives.

This may sound dangerously subjective, but as in the case of our faith-union with Christ, the work of the Spirit is always grounded in the Word and related to Jesus Christ. This is true of Calvin's whole doctrine of the Holy Spirit.

My hope is that this survey of a few aspects of Calvin's doctrine of the Spirit does indeed confirm the thesis that Calvin is a theologian of the Holy Spirit. Focusing on this dimension of his theology reveals a personal, dynamic, and experiential side of the Genevan reformer that is often overlooked. This is also a dimension in our own faith and work that is often missing. Hence we can well emulate Calvin—and above all, God's Word—in seeking to be Spirit-filled and Spirit-led servants of Jesus Christ.

NOTES

CALVIN'S CATECHISM OF 1538

1. Catechismus, sive christianae religionis institutio.
2. Here I have substituted the translation of the French version (1537) for the Latin, which Battles translates literally as "any other fellowship than that of marriage."

1. INTRODUCTION

1. This was the approach taken originally by the promoters of the Consultation on Church Union.
2. Translation by Ford Lewis Battles: *John Calvin: Catechism, 1538*, originally privately published in Pittsburgh in 1972. I am quoting from the last edition of this translation given to me by Ford Battles a few days before he died, November 22, 1979.
3. Ibid., i, iii.
4. An English translation of the former is found in *The School of Faith: The Catechisms of the Reformed Church*. Translated and edited by T. F. Torrance (London: James Clarke, 1959); an English translation of the latter edition is available in *Calvin: Theological Treatises*, trans. by J.K.S. Reid, Library of Christian Classics, vol. XXII (Philadelphia: Westminster Press, 1954).
5. *The History and Character of Calvinism* (New York: Oxford Univ. Press, 1954), 140.
6. Op. cit., 9–10.
7. John Calvin, *Institution of the Christian Religion* [originally published at Basel, 1536], translated and annotated by Ford Lewis Battles (Atlanta: John Knox Press, 1975). Published by John Knox Press in 1975, and published in a new edition by Wm. B. Eerdmans Publishing Co. in 1986. In the preface to his translation of the 1538 Catechism Battles traces the development of Calvin's thought from the 1536 *Institutes* through the 1537–38 Catechisms to the 1539 *Institutes* (op. cit., x–xi).
8. In section 3, however, there is an exhortation to "search and trace God in his works" so that our minds will not be kept "in suspense with vain and empty speculations."
9. Cf. *Inst.* I.14.4: "Let us remember here, as in all religious doctrine, that we ought to hold to one rule of modesty and sobriety: not to speak, or guess, or even

to seek to know, concerning obscure matters anything except what has been imparted to us by God's Word. Furthermore, in the reading of Scripture we ought ceaselessly to endeavor to seek out and meditate upon those things which make for edification. Let us not indulge in curiosity or in the investigation of unprofitable things. And because the Lord willed to instruct us, not in fruitless questions, but in sound godliness, in the fear of his name, in true trust, and in the duties of holiness, let us be satisfied with this knowledge. For this reason, if we would be duly wise, we must leave those empty speculations which idle men have taught apart from God's Word concerning the nature, orders, and number of angels." How prophetic this last sentence is! For today we are being bombarded by New Age fanciful tales and speculations about angels and angelic encounters, most of which have little basis in Scripture. Calvin's remarks here, however, have a far wider relevance than simply speculation concerning angels.

10. No one has expressed this point more eloquently than John T. McNeill, editor of the Library of Christian Classics (LCC) edition of the *Institutes*, trans. by Ford Lewis Battles. Hence his Introduction to this edition is worth quoting at length: "One who takes up Calvin's masterpiece with the preconception that its author's mind is a kind of efficient factory turning out and assembling the parts of a neatly jointed structure of dogmatic logic will quickly find this assumption challenged and shattered. The discerning reader soon realizes that not the author's intellect alone but his whole spiritual and emotional being is enlisted in his work. Calvin might well have used the phrase later finely composed by Sir Philip Sidney, 'Look in thy heart, and write.' He well exemplifies the ancient adage, 'The heart makes the theologian.' He was not, we may say, a theologian by profession, but a deeply religious man who possessed a genius for orderly thinking and obeyed the impulse to write out the implications of his faith. He calls his book not a *summa theologiae* but a *summa pietatis*. The secret of his mental energy lies in his piety; its product is his theology, which is his piety described at length. His task is to expound (in the language of his original title) 'the whole sum of piety and whatever it is necessary to know in the doctrine of salvation.' Quite naturally, in the preface to his last Latin edition he affirms that in the labor of preparing it his sole object has been 'to benefit the church by maintaining the pure doctrine of godliness'" (Philadelphia: Westminster Press, 1960), li–lii.

11. The phrase, a knowledge which "rattles around the brain and does not touch the heart at all," is repeated with variations in the *Institutes* in regard to the knowledge of God the Creator in I.5.9, and in regard to true faith in III.2.36: "The Word of God is not received by faith if it flits about on top of the brain, but when it takes root in the depth of the heart." The key verbs "rattle around" and "flits about" are both translations of the same Latin verb *volutatur*.

12. In a letter to Farel, his friend and former colleague in Geneva (now a pastor in Neuchatel), Calvin writes from Strasbourg just prior to his return to Geneva. Farel had apparently warned him against returning to Geneva, and Calvin concedes that personally he would prefer to stay in Strasbourg. "But when I remember that I am not my own, I offer up my heart, presented as a sacrifice to the Lord." Letter no. 12 in *Letters of John Calvin*, selected from the Bonnet edition (Carlisle, Pa.: Banner of Truth Trust, 1980), 66.

13. In the Introduction to his *Analysis of the Institutes of the Christian Religion of John Calvin*, Ford Battles makes a similar observation concerning the *Institutes*: "Always before Calvin's eyes are the chapters of what we today call 'salvation

history,' a history which every Christian must experience for himself, however simply" (Grand Rapids: Baker Book House, 1980), 19. Cf. Brian Armstrong's thesis that the essential nature of Calvin's theology is simply for the spiritual purpose of providing for the nurture of the saints, "Duplex cognitio Dei, Or? The Problem and Relation of Structure, Form and Purpose in Calvin's Theology," in *Probing the Reformed Tradition: Historical Studies in Honor of Edward A. Dowey, Jr.,* ed. by Elsie Anne McKee and Brian C. Armstrong (Louisville, Ky.: Westminster/John Knox Press, 1989), 138.

2. THE KNOWLEDGE OF GOD AND TRUE RELIGION

1. The Westminster divines may be dependent on Calvin for at least part of this answer. For example, in his Commentary on Jeremiah 9:23 Calvin writes: "To know God is man's chief end, and justifies his existence."
2. The latter phrase may be a variation of Augustine's famous statement in his *Confessions* I.1: "You have made us for yourself, and our hearts are restless until they rest in you, O God."
3. This becomes the theme of a whole chapter in the discourse on the Christian life in book III: "Meditation on the Future Life" (chap. 9).
4. "There is within the human mind, and indeed by natural instinct, an awareness of divinity (*Divinitatis sensum; Inst.* I.3.1).
5. Cf. Commentary on Isaiah 46:8: "There is no person who does not have some seed of religion implanted in him by nature, but men choke it by their unbelief, or corrupt and debase it by their inventions."
6. In this context (*Inst.* I.4.2) Calvin is commenting on a passage in the Psalms which might seem to refute his thesis, viz., the fools who say in their hearts, "There is no God" (Ps. 14:1; 53:1). Later in book II, chapter 2, Calvin discusses at length another relevant passage, John 1:5: "The light shines in the darkness and the darkness did not overcome it." More about this in the next chapter, but here it is germane to note that in his commentary on this passage Calvin speaks again of "the seed of religion planted in all men . . . which still remains in corrupt nature."
7. According to Alexandre Ganoczy, "Calvin's plan for upholding 'true religion' is quite clear. Both the faithful individual and the community should obediently submit to the 'rules' of the Bible, return to and remain within its limits, content themselves with what is essential, and renounce all superfluous and superstitious extras in order to give themselves with fear and love to the worship of God in spirit and in truth." *The Young Calvin,* trans. David Foxgrover and Wade Provo (Philadelphia: Westminster Press, 1987), 207.
8. Ford Lewis Battles goes so far as to say that the word *pietas* is "untranslatable." Although he cites some of the familiar definitions of piety, Battles is convinced that the best way to understand what Calvin means by piety or godliness is to "define *pietas* in Calvin's own words and acts," (17). Hence the bulk of Battles's beautiful book on Calvin's piety consists of original sources, including fresh strophic translations of what Battles calls "the kernel of Calvin's faith," Calvin on the Christian life, and Calvin on prayer. *The Piety of John Calvin: An Anthology of the Spirituality of the Reformer,* trans. and ed. by Ford Lewis Battles, music ed. by Stanley Tagg (Grand Rapids: Baker Book House, 1978), 13. For a more historical-

theological analysis, see the magisterial study by the Roman Catholic theologian, Lucien Joseph Richard, *The Spirituality of John Calvin* (Atlanta: John Knox Press, 1974).

9. S. Y. Lee, "Calvin's Understanding of Pietas," unpublished seminar paper presented at the International Calvin Congress in Edinburgh, September, 1994, 1.

10. "I acknowledge that some grains of piety were always scattered throughout the whole world and there can be no doubt at all that God sowed, so to say, by the hand of philosophers and secular authors the noble statements that exist in their writings. But since that seed was defiled from the very root and since the corn which might have sprung from it (although it was neither good nor natural) was choked by a huge mass of errors, it is ridiculous for such harmful corruption to be compared to sowing." Comm. John 4:36.

11. The editors of the LCC edition add a footnote at this point. "It is a favorite emphasis in Calvin that *pietas*, piety, in which reverence and love of God are joined, is prerequisite to any true knowledge of God" (39n1).

12. The contrary is also true. That is, where there is no true knowledge of God, "no real piety remains in the world" (*Inst*. I.4.1). Again, a "confused knowledge of God differs from the piety from which religion takes its source, which is instilled in the breasts of believers only" (I.5.4). Cf. the title of chapter 9 of book I: "All the Principles of Piety Subverted by Fanatics, Who Substitute Revelations for Scripture" (Beveridge trans.).

13. "Love to God is here [in Ps. 18:1] laid down as constituting the principal part of true godliness; for there is no better way of serving God than to love him." Comm. Ps. 18:1.

14. Princes and other rulers must be "intent on having their piety, righteousness, and uprightness approved of God [cf. 2 Tim. 2:15]" (IX.20.10). A little later piety is identified with "the perpetual duties and precepts of love" (IV.20.15).

15. "Luke [in Acts 10:2] considers the fear of God and prayer as fruits of piety and the worship of God." Comm. Acts 10:2. "Godliness includes not only a good conscience towards men and reverence for God, but also faith and prayer." Comm. 1 Tim. 4:8.

16. The whole title page in English translation can be found in Battles's translation of the 1536 edition of the *Institutes* (Grand Rapids: H. H. Meeter Center for Calvin Studies and Wm. B. Eerdmans Publishing Co., 1975), iii.

17. LCC edition of the *Institutes*, 9.

18. John T. McNeill, Introduction to *John Calvin: On God and Political Duty* (New York: Liberal Arts Press, 1950/56), vii.

19. The same can be said of medieval Catholic piety or the so-called *devotio moderna* which flourished during the fifteenth and sixteenth centuries and which apparently influenced Calvin to some extent. The father of this movement was Gerhard Groote, "the evangelist of the North" (i.e., the Low Countries); its best known representative was Thomas à Kempis, usually regarded as the author of *The Imitation of Christ*. There is much in this movement that would have been congenial to Calvin, but not its individualism or anti-intellectualism, although Calvin also was opposed to a sterile scholastic intellectualism. However, Calvin would have been closer to the approach of the Brethren of the Common Life, who combined the contemplative with an active life. On this whole subject see Lucien Joseph Richard, *The Spirituality of John Calvin*, chaps. 1 and 6.

20. "Calvin's spirituality was a mystique of service. . . . Within the spirituality

of Calvin was a demand for greater earthly activity and a thrust toward the conquest of the world for the glory of God" (ibid., 177).

21. Comm. John 4:23.

22. Note that after enumerating each of these things which are revealed to us in the universe Calvin adds a brief explanatory phrase: God's power "which both framed this great mass and now sustains it . . . his mercy, which, to call us back to repentance tolerates our iniquities with great gentleness" (sec. 3). This long sentence is repeated almost verbatim in the *Institutes* I.5.1.

23. In the *Institutes* Calvin makes a distinction between the knowledge of God the Creator (book I) and the knowledge of God the Redeemer (books II–IV). Thus the whole of the *Institutes*, in a sense, is concerned with the knowledge of God. By the knowledge of God the Creator Calvin means the knowledge of God's creative activity and providence as he is revealed in nature and above all in Scripture. By the revelation of God the Redeemer Calvin means the revelation of God in Christ, the work of the Holy Spirit in appropriating the gift of salvation, and the church with its sacraments. These are the themes of books II, III, and IV of the *Institutes*.

24. There has also been a rather sharp debate about the question of the structure of the *Institutes* by an American and an English Calvin scholar who wrote books about the knowledge of God in Calvin's theology at the same time. For the former, see Edward A. Dowey, *The Knowledge of God in Calvin's Theology* (New York: Columbia Univ. Press, 1952; 3d ed., Wm. B. Eerdmans Publishing Co., 1995). For the latter, see T.H.L. Parker, *Calvin's Doctrine of the Knowledge of God*, rev. ed. (Grand Rapids: Wm. B. Eerdmans Publishing Co., 1959). Dowey has apparently had the last word on this subject. See his essay, "The Structure of Calvin's Thought as Influenced by the Twofold Knowledge of God," appended to the 3d ed. of his *Knowledge of God in Calvin's Theology*.

25. Calvin frequently refers to the creation as a theater of God's glory. Cf. *Institutes* I.6.2; I.14.20; II.6.1; and III.9.2. "This world is like a theater in which the Lord shows to us a striking spectacle of his glory." Comm. 1 Cor. 1:21.

26. "Knowledge of ourselves lies first in considering what we were given at creation and how generously God continues his favor toward us, in order to know how great our natural excellence would be if only it had remained unblemished" (*Inst.* II.1.1). On the question of whether Calvin in any sense teaches a natural theology, see David Steinmetz, *Calvin in Context*, chap. 2, "Calvin and the Natural Knowledge of God" (New York: Oxford Univ. Press, 1995).

27. Brian Armstrong finds in this hypothetical approach a fundamental clue to Calvin's theology. On the basis of this phrase—"*if* Adam had remained upright"— and similar hypothetical arguments in the *Institutes*, Armstrong concludes: "What is to be carefully noted at this point is that this pattern . . . is the one which will be followed throughout; that is to say, Calvin always develops what might have been if sin had not occurred, of what God has perfectly done, as over against that disruption and distortion which has been brought about by sin. "Duplex cognitio Dei, Or? The Problem and Relation of Scripture, Form and Purpose in Calvin's Theology," in *Probing the Reformed Tradition*, 143.

28. Romans 1:20b: "We must, therefore, make this distinction, that the manifestation of God by which he makes his glory known among his creatures is sufficiently clear as far as its own light is concerned. It is, however, inadequate on account of our blindness. But we are not so blind that we can plead ignorance without being convicted of perversity" (Comm. Rom. 1:20).

29. *Inst.* I.7.4–5. For a discussion of that subject see the following chapter, the excursus on the Word and the Spirit.

30. For Calvin's view of the inspiration and authority of Scripture, in addition to the standard works on Calvin by A. Mitchell Hunter, W. Niesel, and F. Wendel, see especially Dowey, *The Knowledge of God,* 37ff., 86–124; and Donald K. McKim, "Calvin's View of Scripture," in *Readings in Calvin's Theology,* ed. by D. K. McKim (Grand Rapids: Baker Book House, 1984).

31. In the next section in this chapter in the *Institutes* Calvin makes the same point in a slightly different way: "However fitting it may be for man seriously to turn his eyes to contemplate God's works, since he has been placed in this most glorious theater to be a spectator of them, it is fitting that he prick up his ears to the Word, the better to profit. And it is therefore no wonder that those who were born in darkness become more and more hardened in their insensibility; for there are very few who, to contain themselves within bounds, apply themselves teachably to God's Word, but they rather exult in their own vanity. Now, in order that true religion may shine upon us, we ought to hold that it must take its beginning from heavenly doctrine and that no one can get even the slightest taste of right and sound doctrine unless he be a pupil of Scripture. Hence, there also emerges the beginning of true understanding when we reverently embrace what it pleases God there to witness of himself" (I.6.2).

32. This sentence is repeated almost verbatim in the *Institutes* I.5.10.

33. It is quoted, for example, by theologians as diverse as Karl Barth and Emil Brunner, John Baillie and Paul Tillich, Otto Weber and Reinhold Niebuhr, Jürgen Moltmann and Alister McGrath, not to mention Calvin specialists.

34. The editors of the LCC edition of the *Institutes* point out in a footnote (36n.3) that Calvin's basic concept here finds precedents in Clement of Alexandria, Augustine, and Aquinas, although none of them states the matter quite the way Calvin does.

35. Already quoted in I.1.2. Cf. I.5.3, 10; II.8.1, 3; IV.17.40. In this last instance the context is the Lord's Supper. Here Calvin urges the believer to "descend into himself," not to discover his sinfulness, as in book I, but rather to "ponder with himself whether he rests with inward assurance of heart upon the salvation purchased by Christ"—and more!

36. LCC *Institutes,* 54n11. However, as I have pointed out in the above note, this is not always the case.

37. Comm. Amos 7:16. "So then, wherever the judgments of God come into our memory, . . . let us have the prudence to enter ourselves, and let each one look at his own person. For the judgments of God must not remain, as it were, buried without ever speaking of them, but each one must apply them to himself and to his particular use," sermon no. 111 on Job 31:1–4.

38. William J. Bouwsma, *John Calvin: A Sixteenth Century Portrait* (New York: Oxford Univ. Press, 1988), 178. The quotation is from the commentary on Galatians 6:4.

39. See chap. 8.

40. Edward Dowey prefers to speak of the true knowledge of God as "existential," reflecting the time in which his *The Knowledge of God in Calvin's Theology* was first written (1951—and under the supervision of Emil Brunner). More recently—again reflecting the Zeitgeist—this type of knowledge has been described as "relational." So Benjamin Reist, who goes so far as to claim that "for Calvin the only possible understanding of God and humanity is a relational one," *A Reading of*

Calvin's Institutes (Louisville, Ky.: Westminster/John Knox Press, 1991), 10. Similarly, T. A. Noble, an English scholar: "Of all the possible terms which might be used to refer to this central characteristic of our knowledge of God, the best, I think, is *relational*. Our knowledge of God takes place within a personal relationship established by God in his grace." "Our Knowledge of God according to John Calvin," in *The Evangelical Quarterly* 54, no. 1 (Jan.–March, 1982): 5. Earlier, T. F. Torrance characterized this knowledge as "intuitive" over against the "abstract" knowledge of the Ockhamists, i.e., "the knowledge of objective realities we gain through direct experience." Calvin and the Knowledge of God," in *The Christian Century* (27 May, 1964): 697.

41. For a more thorough and technical analysis of this aspect of Calvin's understanding of the knowledge of God see Richard A. Muller, *"Fides* and *Cognitio* in Relation to the Problem of Intellect and Will in the Theology of John Calvin," in *Calvin Theological Journal* 29, no. 2 (Nov. 1994). He, too, refers to Calvin's view of the knowledge of God as "existential" rather than "theoretical" (364–65).

42. Comm. Joel 3:17. In his commentary on Zechariah 2:9 Calvin defines the knowledge of faith as experiential in contrast to experimental knowledge (*scientia experimentalis*), so the meaning shifts from time to time. In this context he says: "There are two kinds of knowledge—the knowledge of faith [*scientia fidei*] and what they call experimental knowledge [*scientia experimentalis*]. The knowledge of faith is that by which the godly feel certain that God is true—that what he has promised is indubitable; and this knowledge at the same time penetrates beyond the world and goes far beyond the heavens, that it may know hidden things; for our salvation is concealed; things seen, says the apostle, are not hoped for [Rom. 8:24]. It is no wonder then that the Prophet says that the faithful shall know that Christ has been sent by the Father, that is, in reality or by experience" (Comm. Zech. 2:9). I am indebted for these quotations to Charles Partee. See further his discussion of this issue, "Calvin and Experience," in *Scottish Journal of Theology* 26, no. 2 (May 1972): esp. 174ff. Cf. Willem Balke, "The Word of God and Experientia according to Calvin," in *Calvinus Ecclesiae Doctor*, ed. W. H. Neuser (Kampen, Netherlands: J. H. Kok, 1980).

43. See his *Church Dogmatics* I, 1 (Edinburgh: T. & T. Clark, 1936), 19.

44. Comm. Jeremiah 7:33.

45. Comm. 1 John 2:3.

46. Comm. 1 Peter 1:21.

47. It may sound extravagant to describe this "Argument" as "famous," but it is at least widely known and highly regarded among many theologians and Calvin scholars such as K. Barth, Niesel, Dowey, Paul Lehmann, Wendel, Krusche, Parker, and Van der Kooi.

48. Comm. Genesis, "Argument," 63.

3. EXCURSUS:
THE AUTHORITY OF SCRIPTURE

1. F. L. Battles's translation. This Confession, perhaps written by both Calvin and Farel, is appended to the earlier Battles editions of the 1538 Catechism which were privately published in Pittsburgh and revised continually until his death.

These editions also contained the original Latin text and copious notes and annotations. The Genevan Confession is also available in vol. 22 of the Library of Christian Classics, *Calvin: Theological Treatises*.

2. Almost the same expression occurs in the *Institutes* I.6.3: "the rule of eternal truth."

3. This is a constant refrain of Calvin's.

4. For illustrations of this, see Donald K. McKim, *What Christians Believe About the Bible* (Nashville: Thomas Nelson, 1985).

5. In his discussion of creation and the angels in particular Calvin sees another illustration of divine accommodation. "To be sure, Moses, accommodating himself to the rudeness of the common folk, mentions in the history of creation no other works of God than those which show themselves to our own eyes" (*Inst.* I.14.3). In the Genesis creation account Calvin sees many illustrations of how Moses wrote "in a popular style which, without instruction, all ordinary persons, endued with common sense, are able to understand" (Comm. Genesis 1:16).

6. The seminal study of this subject is the essay by Ford Lewis Battles, "God Was Accommodating Himself to Human Capacity," which appeared first in *Interpretation* 31 (Jan. 1977), and is reprinted in *Readings in Calvin's Theology*. Earlier, Edward Dowey had dealt with this theme in his *The Knowledge of God in Calvin's Theology* (New York: Columbia Univ. Press, 1952). He begins his study with a subsection entitled "The Accommodated Character of All Knowledge of God," 3ff. A more recent treatment of this theme is given by David F. Wright, "Calvin's 'Accommodation' Revisited," in *Calvin as Exegete*, ed. by Peter De Klerk (Grand Rapids: Calvin Studies Society, 1995).

7. Calvin frequently speaks of Scripture as "the oracles of God," and instead of saying, "As Scripture says," he will say, "As the Holy Spirit says." At times he will even use dictation language. For example, in the *Institutes* he refers to various parts of the Old Testament canon as "composed under the Holy Spirit's dictation" (IV.8.6). A little later he refers to the apostles' contribution to the canon and comments, "Yet they were not to do this except from the Lord, that is, with Christ's Spirit as precursor in a certain measure dictating the words [*verba quodammodo dictante Christi spiritu*]" (*Inst.* IV.8.8). The qualification, "in a certain measure," is important. On the question of Calvin's view of inspiration see McKim, op. cit., 62–64. Ian Hamilton, a conservative critic of McKim and Jack Rogers's book which was written, in part, to defend the position of Fuller Seminary in the inerrancy controversy (*The Authority and Interpretation of the Bible: An Historical Approach* [1979]), agrees with them on at least this point, i.e., that Calvin does not teach a mechanical dictation theory. "Although on occasions . . . Calvin used the word 'dictation' in connection with the giving of Scripture, it is clear that he was not advocating a theory of mechanical dictation—a theory no reputable Reformed divine ever subscribed to; and a theory which has never been acceptable to evangelicals!" *Calvin's Doctrine of Scripture: A Contribution to the Debate* (Edinburgh: Rutherford House, 1984), 9.

8. See, for example, his commentary on Num. 25:9, 26; Matt. 10f.; 27:9; Acts 7:14, 16; and Rom. 10:6. For further illustrations, cf. Ronald S. Wallace, *Calvin's Doctrine of the Word and Sacrament* (Grand Rapids: Wm. B. Eerdmans Publishing Co., 1957), 111ff.

9. Comm. Hebrews 3:7.

10. Comm. 1 Corinthians 2:11.

11. Comm. Matthew 3:7.

12. A similar list is found in the Westminster Confession, chap. I.5.

13. Wilhelm Niesel is misleading, therefore, when he dismisses the whole argument of chap. 8 in a footnote saying these arguments "are not of great value" (*The Theology of Calvin*, 27n1). T.H.L. Parker takes the same line. Parker maintains that the "proofs" Calvin addresses in chap. 8 "are historically valueless today and theologically valueless in 1559." Then he takes a swipe at today's fundamentalists, which is hardly fair. "Some [proofs] are certainly more weighty than others; but strong or weak, they collectively constitute a blemish on Calvin's doctrine of the Word of God which has had for its progeny the busyness of fundamentalists to prove the truth of the Bible to the neglect of discovering and preaching the truth of the Bible." *Calvin's Doctrine of the Knowledge of God*, 74.

14. The finest treatment of this subject is by Bernard Ramm, *The Witness of the Spirit: An Essay on the Contemporary Relevance of the Internal Witness of the Holy Spirit* (Grand Rapids: Wm. B. Eerdmans Publishing Co., 1959). "It was Calvin who saw clearly the role of the Spirit as the witness *par excellence*, and taught that the Holy Spirit was the author of all witnessing," 72.

15. Werner Krusche, *Das Wirken des Heiligen Geistes nach Calvin* (Göttingen: Vandenhoeck & Ruprecht, 1957), 206.

16. A striking example is Thomas Watson, the venerable Puritan divine, in his "best seller," *A Body of Divinity* (originally published in 1692; reprint by Banner of Truth Trust, 1965). This outline of theology is ostensibly based on the Westminster Shorter Catechism, but in his chapter, "The Scriptures" he gives "seven cogent arguments" (many the same as Calvin's) "which may evince it [the Scriptures] to be the Word of God," 27. What is remarkable is that he never comes to the internal witness of the Spirit as the ultimate confirmation that the Bible is the Word of God.

17. *Church Dogmatics* I, 2, 536. On this question see the perceptive discussion of Klaas Runia, *Karl Barth's Doctrine of Scripture* (Grand Rapids: Wm. B. Eerdmans Publishing Co., 1962), 15ff.

18. The phrase comes from Werner Krusche, *Das Wirken*, 210.

19. *Church Dogmatics* I, 2, 537.

20. Runia, 8.

21. Barth, op. cit., 535.

22. "All the objections on circularity of reasoning fail to see that the divinity perceived is resident in Scripture, and not in some sort of psychic aura of divinity which we experience as the Spirit persuades us." Ramm, op. cit., 108.

23. *The Foundations of Dogmatics*, vol. 1 (Grand Rapids: Wm. B. Eerdmans Publishing Co., 1981), 244.

24. Ibid., 245.

25. Ramm, op. cit., 107.

26. "The Spirit is like a seal by which the truth of God is testified to us." Comm. 1 John 2:27. "It should, therefore, be clear that the function of the internal testimony is, after all, what the term 'internal' implies, namely, an operation in our minds [better, "hearts," I.J.H.] directed to the persuasion, assurance and conviction appropriate to what Scripture intrinsically is," John Murray, *Calvin on Scripture and Divine Sovereignty* (Grand Rapids: Baker Book House, 1960), 49.

27. Paul J. Achtemeier, *The Inspiration of Scripture: Problems and Proposals* (Philadelphia: Westminster Press, 1980), 138.

4. OUR PLIGHT APART FROM GOD

1. Calvin speaks frequently of human depravity, but never, as far as I know, uses the phrase "total depravity." Two examples: "Man's whole nature is so imbued with depravity that of himself he possesses no ability to act aright." "Necessity of Reforming the Church," in *Calvin: Theological Treatises,* ed. J.K.S. Reid (Philadelphia: Westminster Press, 1954) 198. "The Holy Spirit teaches us in Scripture that our mind is smitten with so much blindness that the affections of the heart are so depraved and perverted, that our whole nature is so vitiated that we can do nothing but sin, until he forms a new will within us," Comm. 1 Peter, Dedication, in Torrance ed., 223–24. It is not inaccurate, however, in reference to Calvin's anthropology, to speak of "total perversity," as does T. F. Torrance in *Calvin's Doctrine of Man* (London: Lutterworth Press, 1949). He uses this phrase as the title of chaps. 7 and 8. One will also not find the phrase "total depravity" in two later Reformed Confessions—the Canons of Dort (1618–19) and the Westminster Confession (1646)—although they also have an equally radical view of sin. For a fuller discussion of this issue, see my book, *On Being Reformed: Distinctive Characteristics and Common Misunderstandings.* 2d ed. (New York: Reformed Church Press, 1988), chap. 7.

2. Luther could speak of "the whore of reason" in some contexts, but this is not the whole picture. For a balanced study see Brian Gerrish, *The Grace of Reason: A Study in the Theology of Luther* (Oxford: Clarendon Press, 1962)

3. As Heiko Oberman has pointed out in a recent essay, "there is no such thing as 'humanism' or 'Reformation,' at least not in the singular. And we know that if these monoliths existed, Calvin would not have sought to occupy a 'middle position'! Yet Renaissance scholarship, particularly in the United States, reaching from Quirinius Breen (1896–1975) to William Bouwsma, has developed a consensus which affirms, articulates, and delineates the humanistic dimension in Calvin's work." "The Pursuit of Happiness: Calvin between Humanism and Reformation," in *Humanity and Divinity in Renaissance and Reformation: Essays in Honor of Charles Trinkaus* (Leiden: E. J. Brill, 1993), 253–54.

4. This is the English translation of the French version of the Catechism (*Instruction in Faith*). Battles's translation of the Latin is "deprived of all God's benefits."

5. "Flesh" here is used in the Pauline sense, meaning that part of human nature which is opposed to God. See, e.g., Rom. 7:5; 8:3, 6; Gal. 2:20; 5:16.

6. Cf. Rom. 7:14b: "but I am of the flesh sold into slavery under sin" (NRSV); and John 8:34; 2 Peter 2:19. In his comments on Rom. 7:14 Calvin describes the *totality* of sin, but does not use the phrase "total depravity." "We are so completely driven by the power of sin that our whole mind, our whole heart, and all our actions are inclined to sin." Then Calvin makes a crucial distinction: "Compulsion I always exclude, for we sin of our own free will. It would not be sin if it were not voluntary. We are, however, so addicted to sin that we can do nothing of our own accord but sin." Comm. Romans 7:14.

7. One can find similar negative judgments in Calvin's later writings. A few examples: From the *Institutes:* "Only Damnable Things Come Forth from Man's Corrupt Nature" (the title of chapter 3 of book II). "We are so vitiated and perverted in every part of our nature that by this corruption we stand justly condemned and

convicted before God . . . (II.1.8). From the commentaries: Adam, "by falling from the Lord, in himself be corrupted, vitiated, depraved, and ruined our nature. . . . We have all sinned, therefore, because we are imbued with natural corruption, and for this reason are wicked and perverse," Comm. Romans 5:12. From the sermons: "What remains in men? Now, notwithstanding their bravery, they are only vermin and rottenness," sermon 94 on Job (25:1–6); Nixon trans., 151.

8. Calvin gratefully acknowledges that a related distinction comes from Augustine, viz., "that the natural gifts were corrupted in man through sin; but that his supernatural gifts were stripped from him" (*Inst.* II.2.12). Among the natural gifts are reason, understanding, and the will. Here in particular one must read Calvin's statements in context, for he can say, on the one hand, "Human understanding possesses some power of perception, since it is by nature captivated by the love of truth"; but, on the other hand, add the cautionary note: "Yet this longing for truth, such as it is, languishes before it enters upon its race because it soon falls into vanity" (ibid.).

9. It is God's "peculiar office to illuminate our minds, so that we may comprehend heavenly mysteries. For although we are naturally endued with the greatest acuteness [*summo acumine*], which is also God's gift, yet we may call it a limited endowment since it does not reach to the heavens" Comm. Daniel 2:30.

10. "Now the discovery or systematic transmission of the arts, or the inner and more excellent knowledge of them, which is characteristic of few, is not a sufficient proof of common discernment. Yet, because it is bestowed indiscriminately upon pious and impious, it is rightly counted among natural gifts." *Inst.* II.2.14.

11. Calvin does not use this expression but refers in this connection to "the general grace of God" (*generalem Dei gratiam* [*Inst.* II.2.17]). See further nn. 63 and 64 appended to this section in the LCC edition of the *Institutes*.

12. Will Durant, *The Reformation* (New York: Simon & Schuster, 1957), 165.

13. "Shall we count anything praiseworthy or noble without recognizing at the same time that it comes from God? Let us be ashamed of such ingratitude" (*Inst.* II.2.15).

14. Calvin's actual adversaries in this matter were in all likelihood the Anabaptists, who tended to be world-denying. "Many of Calvin's statements about the Christian's participation in the natural world were, once again, directed against the perfectionist and separatist arguments of the Anabaptists. Against these 'new Donatists' Calvin rejected any isolationism that condemned human participation in society." Susan E. Schreiner, *The Theater of His Glory: Nature and Natural Order in the Thought of John Calvin* (Durham, N.C.: Labyrinth Press, 1991), 92. These remarks are also applicable to Calvin's high view of civil government and the Christian's obligation to become involved in it. Cf. chap. 16. Cf. the thorough study of Calvin's relation to the Anabaptists by the Dutch scholar, Willem Balke: *Calvin and the Anabaptist Radicals* (Grand Rapids: Wm. B. Eerdmans Publishing Co., 1981).

15. This cannot be said, however, of Heinrich Bullinger, Zwingli's successor in Zurich and the author of the Second Helvetic Confession (1566). Following Calvin, he distinguishes between humanity's capabilities on the horizontal as over against the vertical realms. In the latter realm "Man not yet regenerate has no free will for good, no strength to perform what is good." Here Bullinger cites such passages as 1 Cor. 2:14; 2 Cor. 3:5; John 8:34; and Rom. 8:7. However, in regard to earthly things, "fallen man is not entirely lacking in understanding." This is particularly

true of the arts, where "God commands us to cultivate our natural talents, and meanwhile adds both gifts and success." But even in this realm of common grace "we make no progress in all the arts without God's blessing," chap. 9, in the *Book of Confessions*, Presbyterian Church (U.S.A.), 5.045–6.

16. It may appear that undue space is given to this subject, given the slight attention paid to it in the Catechism. However, as various Calvin scholars have noted, this is a fundamental doctrine for Calvin and thus requires more than passing consideration. T. F. Torrance, in his pioneering work on Calvin's anthropology, comments: "Calvin's doctrine of the *imago dei* in man sums up the whole of this relation between man and God." *Calvin's Doctrine of Man* (London: Lutterworth, 1949/52), 59. Cf. Brian Gerrish, "The notion of the divine image in Calvin's theology has far greater significance than its modest entrance [in the *Institutes*] suggests; for the way in which Calvin interprets it opens up, better than anything else, the heart of his understanding of man and his place in the world. Further, it constitutes an important link with other parts of the system." "The Mirror of God's Goodness: A Key Metaphor in Calvin's View of Man," in *Readings in Calvin's Theology*, 110.

17. Calvin complains about those scholars who make fine distinctions between "image" and "likeness" in Genesis 1:26. He rightly observes that " 'likeness' has been added by way of explanation," for "we know," he adds, "that repetitions were common among the Hebrews, in which they express the same thing twice" (*Inst.* I.15.3). He reiterates this view in his commentary on Genesis 1:26 and complains that Augustine, among others, "speculates with excessive refinement for the purpose of fabricating a Trinity in man."

18. "Although the primary seat of the divine image was in the mind and heart, or in the soul and its powers, yet there was no part of man, not even the body itself, in which some sparks did not glow" (*Inst.* I.15.3). On the question as to what extent the body also reflects the image of God, see Potter Engel, 42–47.

19. Comm. Ephesians 4:24.

20. For the proponents of the two views, again see Mary Potter Engel, *John Calvin's Perspectival Anthropology* (Atlanta: Scholars Press, 1988), 48–50. She resolves the question by using her perspectival approach. "From the perspective of God the image is seen as a supernatural gift, from the perspective of humankind, a natural endowment" 50.

21. The French is equally strong: "this resemblance to God having been *effaced* in us," *Instruction in Faith*, 21 (emphasis added).

22. Comm. Romans 5:12.

23. Comm. Ephesians 4:24. "The purpose of the gospel is the restoration in us of the image of God which had been cancelled by sin [*inducta fuerat per peccatum*] ..." (Comm. 2 Cor. 3:18).

24. The phrase is Wendel's, 185. Note also the wording of this comment on Genesis 1:26: "Although some obscure lineaments of that image [which was originally found in Adam] are found remaining in us; yet they are so vitiated and maimed that *they may be said* to be destroyed" (Comm. Gen. 1:18, emphasis added). Note well: Calvin does not say here that they actually are destroyed.

25. Comm. Daniel 2:22.

26. Calvin defines the soul quite differently in his commentary on the Psalms. In his essay, " 'An Anatomy of All Parts of the Soul': Insights into Calvin's Spirituality from His Psalms Commentary," James A. De Jong points out that "Key passages in the commentary itself show that for Calvin the soul is the living core of

the believer's subjective feelings, attitudes, responses, and convictions. His term of preference is 'affections' . . . and is closer to what is meant by the heart." *Calvinus Sacrae Scripturae Professor: Calvin as Confessor of Holy Scripture*, ed. Wilhelm H. Neuser (Grand Rapids: Wm. B. Eerdmans Publishing Co., 1994), 4–5. Cf. Comm. Psalm 34:2.

27. *John Calvin: Treatises against the Anabaptists and the Libertines*, trans. Benjamin Wirt Farley (Grand Rapids: Baker Book House, 1982), 236–37.

28. Cf. sec. 2 of this chapter and the *Institutes* II.2.12–16. Recall that all of these gifts are derived from the Spirit of God.

29. See Stauffer's *Dieu, la creation et providence dans la predication de Calvin* (Berne: Peter Lang, 1978), 201. For the positions of David Cairns, Niesel, Torrance, Dowey, and Gerrish, see Mary Potter Engel, 38, 67n68, 71–72 n95.

30. T. A. Noble distinguishes between the wider and narrower *imago dei*. The former "refers to the 'natural gifts,' the attributes of the soul—reason and will—without which man would cease to be man and would be reduced to an animal." The latter "refers to the 'supernatural gifts' which are the function of a living intelligent response to the Word of God." "Our Knowledge of God according to John Calvin," in *The Evangelical Quarterly*, 54, no. 1 (Jan.-March 1982): 8.

31. In addition to the *Institutes* I.15.3, cited earlier, cf. Calvin's commentary on Genesis 1:26: "The chief seat of the divine image was in his [Adam's] mind and heart, where it was preeminent; yet there was no part of him in which some signs of it did not shine forth." With the latter phrase Calvin also includes the body, for he explains: "In the mind perfect intelligence flourished and reigned . . . and all the senses were prepared and molded for due obedience to reason; and in the body there was a suitable correspondence with this internal order."

32. *The Nature and Destiny of Man*, vol. 1 (New York: Charles Scribner's Sons, 1947), 159.

33. Comm. Genesis 1:26. It is strange, and perhaps not a mere oversight, that neither Torrance nor Potter Engel in their extensive treatments of the *imago dei* and the profuse citations from the *Institutes*, commentaries, and sermons, quotes or refers to the important passage from the *Institutes* III.7.6, or to this passage from the commentary on Genesis 9:6.

34. This "solution" has some affinity with Potter Engel's perspectival approach, but she applies it in too doctrinaire a fashion and as a result makes questionable assertions like this: "We have already shown that Calvin believes all the natural gifts to be totally lost along with the spiritual gifts, since they count for nothing in the judgment of God the redeemer" (op. cit., 59).

35. "Even in his early debate with Emil Brunner, Karl Barth agreed that 'even as a sinner, man is a man and not a tortoise.' Calvin could not have said it better. The inherently active nature of the human being manifests itself not only in sin but in the activities, judgments, and contributions which men and women carry out in their natural societal lives," Schreiner, 70.

36. Although the soul is not man, yet it is not absurd for man, in respect to his soul, to be called God's image. . . . The proper seat of his [man's] image is in the soul" (*Inst.* I.1.53). Cf. Comm. Genesis 2:7: "Three gradations are to be noted in the creation of man: that his dead body was formed out of the dust of the earth; that it was endowed with a soul, whence it would receive vital motion, and that on this soul God engraved his own image, to which immortality is annexed." For historical background and a more detailed discussion of Calvin's view of the soul and

the immortality of the soul in particular, see Schreiner, 60ff., and her conclusions on 72; and Potter Engel, 44ff. and chapter 5. As Potter Engel points out, "Calvin's view of the immortality of the soul is complex, for he both denies and affirms immortality according to the context in which he is speaking" (ibid., 152–53). In any case, "immortality is for Calvin not an inborn characteristic of the human soul but of the image of God (annexed!) crafted into the soul, but soon exposed in all its fragility" (Oberman, 269).

37. This is the thesis of Torrance's book, but he goes too far in denying the substantial aspects of the image, 39, 51. Here Potter Engel is more balanced. Cf. Brian Gerrish: "To sum up: In Calvin's view the image of God in man denotes not an endowment only but also a relationship." "The Mirror of God's Goodness," 115.

38. Oberman, 265. I think Oberman modernizes Calvin too much, however, in the comment which follows the sentence just quoted, namely, "This paradigm shift can best be captured by the formula 'from ontology to psychology,' " ibid.

39. "The *imago dei* is not just some one thing in man but refers to his total relation with God and concerns the totality of his being. . . . It is essential to man as God made him and is constitutive of his whole person. . . . It is not therefore external to him, nor is it something super-added. It is absolutely essential to true human nature." Torrance, 86.

40. Comm. John 1:18.

41. Comm. Genesis 1:26.

42. Torrance, in particular, emphasizes the significance of the mirror image in understanding Calvin's view of the image of God. "There is no doubt that Calvin *always* thinks of the *imago* in terms of a mirror," (36, emphasis added; the word "frequently" could best be substituted for "always").

43. Comm. Eph. 4:24. "Just as our Lord Jesus is the second Adam, so he must be like a pattern [*patron*] to us, and we must be fashioned after him and his image that we may be like him" (sermon on Eph. 4:23–26).

44. Calvin often refers to this text in his discussion of our being renewed in the image of God. Concerning this text he comments: "Observe that the purpose of the Gospel is the restoration in us of the image of God which had been cancelled by sin, and that this restoration is progressive and goes on during our whole life because God makes his glory to shine in us little by little." Comm. 2 Cor. 3:18.

45. I have taken up this question anew and examined it from both a historical and theological perspective in a forthcoming book, *Sovereign Grace and Human Freedom. How They Coalesce* (Grand Rapids: Wm. B. Eerdmans Publishing Co., 1998).

46. Augustine discusses this issue in several treatises. Cf. his *Grace and Free Will* and *The Spirit and the Letter* (412). An earlier work, *On Free Will*, written about 395, does not express Augustine's eventual position.

47. Luther's famous controversial treatise, *De servo arbitrio* (*The Bondage of the Will*) was written in 1525 in response to an attack by Erasmus. Both treatises are available in *Luther and Erasmus: Free Will and Salvation*, ed. Gordon Rupp and Philip Watson, Library of Christian Classics (Philadelphia: Westminster Press, 1969).

48. This is Calvin's translation which corresponds to the RSV. The NRSV reads: "I am of the flesh, sold into slavery under sin."

49. Comm. Romans 7:14. "Calvin is willing to affirm that the will is free in the sense that we have wills which are not coerced but self-determined, choosing voluntarily, of their own accord." A.N.S. Lane, "Introduction" to the new translation

of Calvin on *The Bondage and Liberation of the Will,* trans. G. E. Davies and ed. Lane (Grand Rapids: Baker Book House, 1996), xix.

50. Comm. Romans 7:15. Note that in the first statement Calvin speaks of sinning with the *mind* but in the second with the *soul.* Earlier, in the quotation from the commentary on Romans 7:14, Calvin said that "our whole *mind,* our whole *heart,* and all our actions are inclined to sin." This is another illustration of Calvin's lack of precision in dealing with human psychology. Mind, heart, and soul all refer to the self, that inner core of our being. However, in the *Institutes,* I.15.7, Calvin says that the soul "consists of two faculties, understanding and will," but the understanding is "the leader and governor of the soul," whereas the will "is always mindful of the bidding of the understanding and in its own desires awaits the judgment of the understanding."

51. Calvin cites not only Origen, among the church fathers, but also Chrysostom, one of his favorites, as among those who wrote "obscurely" on this issue. The same is true of Bernard of Clairvaux, whom Calvin admired. The only exception is Augustine, who is quoted favorably by Peter Lombard and Thomas Aquinas, who, however, then proceed to develop their ideas in a confused fashion. See the *Institutes* II.2.4–5.

52. This, at least, is Calvin's interpretation of Lombard in the *Institutes* II.26. Cf. 264n36, LCC *Institutes.*

53. Calvin apologizes for seeming to quibble here about words, but he asks, "But how few men are there who when they hear of free will attributed to man do not immediately conceive him to be master of his own mind and will, able of his own power to turn himself toward either good or evil?" (*Inst.* II.2.7).

54. *De servo arbitrio* (CO 6:279), as quoted in A.N.S. Lane, "Did Calvin Believe in Freewill?" in *Vox Evangelica* 12 (1981): 79. This is the most thorough study of this subject in English and should be consulted if one wants to investigate this question further. A summary and analysis of Pighius's position is found in the published dissertation by L. F. Schulze, *Calvin's Reply to Pighius* (Potchefstroom, South Africa: Pro-Rege Press, 1971). For the complete text of this work, see the new translation by G. E. Davies and ed. by A.N.S. Lane (cited in n.50).

55. Ibid.

56. Luther had made a similar distinction in his debate with Erasmus on the will. See 295n10 in LCC *Institutes.* Recall that earlier in his Catechism Calvin had rejected the notion of "violent necessity," and in his Romans Commentary he further distinguished between our natural, i.e., necessary, inclination to sin, which is voluntary, and compulsion or a "forced restraint" which corresponds to the "violent necessity" referred to in the Catechism. It is interesting that all of these documents come from the same period: the Catechism in 1538, the Romans commentary and second edition of the *Institutes* (which is repeated in the final edition) in 1539, and the responses to Pighius in 1542 (published in February 1543, by which time Pighius had died). Pighius's attack was based on the 1539 *Institutes,* so Calvin's defense represents a clarification of some of the views expressed there.

57. This is G. C. Berkouwer's summary of Calvin's position in *Man: The Image of God* (Grand Rapids: Wm. B. Eerdmans Publishing Co.), 319n13.

58. *The Nature and Destiny of Man,* vol. 1, 255, 262–63.

59. Ibid., 263. Despite some differences, Niebuhr finds Calvin's position more balanced and biblical than Luther's. "Luther seems to heighten the Augustinian

doctrine in the interest of greater consistency but at the price of imperiling one element of the paradox, the element of human responsibility" (ibid., 244).

60. *The Doctrine of the Holy Spirit* (Richmond, Va.: John Knox Press, 1964)), 71. He then quotes the passage from the *Institutes* II.7.2 where Calvin belittles Lombard's understanding of free will and asks, "What purpose is served by labeling with a proud name such a slight thing?"

61. "The Doctrine of the Will" in *Institutes of the Christian Religion: Essays on Calvin and the Reformation in Honor of Ford Lewis Battles,* ed. by B. A. Gerrish in collaboration with Robert Benedetto (Pittsburgh: Pickwick Press, 1981), 53.

62. In *Vox Evangelica,* 80.

63. "Calvin's primary theological concern in this whole discussion is to give God the glory. . . . Calvin is especially concerned to reject all theological strategems that seem to divide the work of salvation, attributing some to God and some to man." Everything is from God. However, in the conversion of the will, "God moves the will in such a way that respects the integrity of the will as will and in such a way that the works of the converted will are truly the works of the will as well as the work of God" (Leith, 57). Cf. *Institutes* II.5.5.

64. Comm. Ezekiel 11:20, Foxgrover and Martin trans. Cf. *Institutes* II.5.15: "Any mixture of the power of free will that men strive to mingle with God's grace is nothing but a corruption of grace. . . . Even if there is something good in the will, it comes from the prompting of the Spirit."

65. The corresponding discussions in the *Institutes* are found in chaps. 1 and 2 of book II. However, here he makes an additional point. True self-knowledge should include not only a knowledge of our sinful state but also of our original state, i.e., "What we were given at creation and how generously God continues his favor toward us in order to know how great our natural excellence would be if only it had remained unblemished" (II.1.1).

66. "To know the true flavor of Christ, each of us must carefully examine ourselves, and each must know himself condemned until he is vindicated by Christ." Comm. Isaiah 53:6.

67. The translation of the French edition reads: "consciously enters our hearts."

68. Comm. Romans 11:19.

69. From a knowledge of "our miserable condition after Adam's fall . . . arise abhorrence and displeasure with ourselves, as well as true humility; and thence is kindled a new zeal to seek God, in whom each of us may recover those good things which we have utterly and completely lost" (*Inst.* II.1.1). Cf. II.2.10.

70 . In a very different context—the discussion of justification and works—Calvin uses the same metaphor in quite a different way. "If one seeks the first cause that opens for the saints the door to God's kingdom . . . at once we answer: Because the Lord by his own mercy has adopted them once for all . . . (*Inst.* III.17.6).

71. Sermon on Job, no. 80, cited in the LCC *Institutes,* 269n50. The editors add: "Calvin, like the monastic and Scholastic moralists, regards pride as the chief of vices, and humility as the pre-eminent virtue."

72. "When we rise up toward God, that assurance of ourselves vanishes in a flash and dies" (*Inst.* III.12.2).

73. "The right knowledge of God is a wisdom which far exceeds what can be comprehended by human understanding, and therefore no one can attain it except by a secret revelation of the Spirit." Comm. Hebrews 8:11. "Light shines in darkness until the Spirit opens the eyes of the blind." Comm. 1 Cor. 2:11.

74. Occasionally, instead of referring to the law to serve this purpose, Calvin will urge us to "lift up our minds to God's judgment seat," so that we measure our righteousness not "by our own small measure," but according to the "heavenly Judge as he is depicted for us in Scripture" (*Inst*. III.12.1).

75. For Calvin, this is the first use of the law, for Luther the second, i.e., to make us so aware of our helplessness that we will turn to God for grace and forgiveness in Jesus Christ. This use of the law is the theme of sec. 11: "The Law is a Preparation to Come to Christ." For Calvin, however, the principal use or function of the law is as a norm and guide for the believer. On the uses of the law, see chapter 5.

5. THE LAW OF GOD AND THE CHRISTIAN LIFE

1. For the unregenerate "the law is like a mirror. In it we contemplate our weakness, then the iniquity arising from this, and finally the curse coming from both—just as a mirror shows us the spots on our face" (*Inst*. II.7.7). Calvin then cites Romans 3:20: "Through the law comes knowledge of sin"; Romans 5:20: "Law slipped in to increase the trespass"; and 2 Cor. 3:7: "and thus it is 'the dispensation of death' that brings wrath" (Rom. 4:15). It should be kept in mind that this is only the first use of the law.

2. For a fuller discussion of the uses of the law, see my book, *Calvin's Concept of the Law* (Allison Park, Pa.: Pickwick Publications, 1992), chap. 5. Chapter 4, "Law and Gospel," is also relevant to this discussion.

3. Calvin discusses in various contexts how it is that the law of love in Deuteronomy and the law (*torah*) in which the psalmist rejoices in Psalm 119 becomes a law of sin and death for the apostle Paul. One solution is that the law which brings a curse and death is the "bare law [*nuda lex*] in a narrow sense," which is not "clothed with the covenant of free adoption" (*Inst*. II.7.2). Another way of putting it is that "as long as Christ is included in the law, the sun shines through the mist of the clouds so that men have enough light for their use, but where Christ is separated from the law, there is nothing left but darkness or rather a false appearance of light that dazzles instead of assisting men's eyes." Comm. 2 Corinthians 4:3.

4. There are various ways of dividing the Ten Commandments into two tables. The Roman Catholic and Lutheran Churches traditionally have placed three commandments in the first table and seven in the second. This is done by dividing the tenth commandment into two parts and combining the first and second commandments. Josephus divided them evenly into five each. Calvin's approach (4–6) is that generally accepted by Jewish and most Protestant traditions. See *Institutes* II.8.12 and nn. 16–21 on 378–79 in the LCC (McNeill-Battles) edition.

5. In the *Institutes* II.8.51–55 and his *Harmony of the Last Four Books of Moses*, Calvin treats at length the significance of Jesus' summary of the law.

6. *The Book of Concord*, trans. and ed. Theodore G. Tappert (Philadelphia: Fortress Press, 1959), 359–61, 407. Echoes of this last statement are found in Calvin's Geneva Catechism, Q. 230, and in the Heidelberg Catechism, Q. 91.

7. See especially Werner Elert, *Law and Gospel* (Philadelphia: Fortress Press, Facet Books, 1967); and Gerhard Ebeling, *Word and Faith* (Philadelphia: Fortress Press, 1963).

8. *The Doctrine of Creation*, III, 4 (Edinburgh: T. & T. Clark, 1961), 324ff.

9. See his commentaries on 2 Cor. 3:16, 17 and Rom. 10:4.

10. Georgia Harkness, *John Calvin, the Man and His Ethics* (Nashville: Abingdon Press, 1958), 63.

11. Ibid., 113.

12. This is the criticism of Paul Wernle, one-time professor of theology at Basel University, in his book, *Der Evangelische Glaube*, Band III (Tübingen: J.C.B. Mohr, 1919).

13. *Ethics in a Christian Context* (New York: Harper & Row, 1963) 78.

14. Calvin expresses the same idea somewhat differently in the *Institutes*. "God first shows himself to be the one who has the right to command and to whom obedience is due. Then, in order not to seem to constrain men by necessity alone, he also attracts them with sweetness by declaring himself God of the church" (II.8.14). On the spiritual captivity of which the bondage in Egypt is a type Calvin waxes eloquent in the *Institutes* II.8.15. He concludes this section with these lovely lines: "There is no one, I say, who ought not to be captivated to embrace the Lawgiver, in the observance of whose commandments he is taught to take especial delight; from whose kindness he expects both an abundance of all good things and the glory of immortal life; by whose marvelous power and mercy he knows himself freed from the jaws of death."

15. Cf. *Institutes* II.8.28–30. Paul K. Jewett, in his book *The Lord's Day*, faults Calvin (and Luther) for not "appreciating the unity of redemptive history, the continuation of the sabbatical division of time in the New Testament church" (Grand Rapids: Wm. B. Eerdmans Publishing Co., 1971), 105. Here Calvin is charged not with a legalistic sabbatarianism, but just the opposite, viz., taking an approach that is governed more by expediency than theological presuppositions!

16. Comm. Jeremiah 9:15.

17. Comm. Isaiah 8:20.

18. See *Institutes* II.8.5; Geneva Catechism, Qs. 130–32.

19. Zurich: Zwingli Verlag, 1965, 130ff., 143ff.

20. Ibid., 101.

21. Emil Brunner, *The Christian Doctrine of Creation and Redemption*. Dogmatics, vol. 2 (Philadelphia: Westminster Press, 1952), 219.

22. Emil Brunner, *The Christian Doctrine of the Church, Faith, and the Consummation*. Dogmatics, vol. 3 (Philadelphia: Westminster Press, 1962), 301.

23. The substance of this section appeared earlier in my essay "Christ, the Law, and the Christian," in *Reformatio Perennis: Essays on Calvin and the Reformation in Honor of Ford Lewis Battles*, ed. Brian Gerrish (Pittsburgh: Pickwick Press, 1981), 11–26, and reprinted in *Readings in Calvin's Theology*, ed. Donald McKim 179–91.

24. *Prädestination und Verantwortlichkeit bei Calvin* (Darmstadt: Wissenschaftliche Buchgesellschaft, 1968—a reproduction of the 1st ed. of 1937), 103.

25. Comm. Acts 7:30; cf. Comm. John 1:11 and 5:38.

26. Comm. 2 Corinthians 3:17.

27. Comm. Romans 10:4; *Institutes* II.7.2.

28. Comm. Romans 10:4.

29. Calvin discusses these two aspects of repentance in the *Institutes* III.3.5–9. Cf. the similar understanding in the Heidelberg Catechism, Q. 88.

30. Comm. Ephesians 4:22–3; cf. *Institutes* III.7.10.

31. There is another dimension of Calvin's treatment of the law which cannot be dealt with here, viz., the role of the Holy Spirit in providing guidance in special situations where it is difficult to discern the will of God. I discuss this briefly in the last chapter of my book, *Calvin's Concept of the Law*, 282f.; and in greater length in an essay, "Governed and Guided by the Spirit: A Key Issue in Calvin's Doctrine of the Holy Spirit," in *Reformiertes Erbe. Festschrift für Gottfried W. Locher*, Band 2, hrsg. von Heiko Oberman, Ernst Saxer et al. (Zurich: TVZ, 1993).

6. CHRISTIAN FREEDOM

1. On the uses of the law in Calvin's theology, see chap. 6 and my book, *Calvin's Concept of the Law*, chap. 5. Concerning the third use in particular, Jane Dempsey Douglass comments, "Despite the care with which Calvin frames his statements, through the years he has repeatedly been called a 'legalist,' usually in a pejorative fashion, by Protestants who do not understand his third use of the law." *Women, Freedom, and Calvin* (Philadelphia: Westminster Press, 1985), 109.
2. Comm. Acts 5:31.
3. Luther's classic treatment of his subject is his 1520 treatise "The Freedom of a Christian." There are many translations, but see specifically that of W. A. Lambert, revised by Harold J. Grimm in *Luther's Works*, vol. 31, *Career of the Reformer*, part I, ed. by Harold J. Grimm (Philadelphia: Muhlenberg Press, 1957). Herein are found Luther's famous theses: "A Christian is perfectly free lord of all subject to none. A Christian is a perfectly dutiful servant of all, subject to all" (344).
4. As the title of this section indicates, the emphasis here is on any reguations or traditions, civil or ecclesiastical, which "bind consciences," or undercut our freedom in Christ.
5. *Der evangelische Glaube nach den Hauptschriften der Reformatoren*, vol. 3, *Calvin* (Tübingen, J.C.B. Mohr [Paul Siebeck], 1919), 131.
6. *A Reading of Calvin's Institutes* (Louisville, Ky.: Westminster/John Knox Press, 1991), 67.
7. Ibid., 69. Reist then comments, "In that so much is made of 'spirituality' these days, it is important to insist that freedom, deliverance from the troubled conscience, and the continual, daily receiving of God's benefits—all of these animate Calvin's remarkable understanding of prayer."
8. Dempsey Douglass, 23.
9. Comm. Romans 6:15.
10. Comm. Romans 2:2. Cf. Comm. Galatians 4:4.
11. Cf. Comm. Romans 8:15.
12. Comm. Galatians 4:4.
13. Comm. Colossians 2:14. Cf. *Institutes* II.7.17.
14. Comm. Hebrews 9:15. On the question of the freedom of conscience in relation to the law in Calvin, see the recent study by Randall C. Zachman, *The Assurance of Faith: Conscience in the Theology of Martin Luther and John Calvin* (Minneapolis: Fortress Press, 1993), 224–43.
15. "Even though the law contributes nothing to the grace of justification, it is functionally related to the grace of sanctification. Therefore, although the conscience is freed from the law with regard to its justification before God, it is not

freed with regard to its sanctification, for the law still exhorts and teaches believers to be conformed to the goal of their calling." Zachman, 225.

16. Comm. John 14:22.

17. Wilhelm Niesel, *The Gospel and the Churches* (Philadelphia: Westminster Press, 1962), 221. The British edition has the title *Reformed Symbolics*.

18. C.F.H. Henry, *Christian Personal Ethics* (Grand Rapids: Wm. B. Eerdmans Publishing Co., 1957), 362.

19. Comm. 1 Peter 2:16.

20. Ibid. Cf. *Institutes* III.17.1.

21. Comm. Galatians 5:1.

22. Hendrikus Berkhof, *Christian Faith*, rev. ed. (Grand Rapids: Wm. B. Eerdmans Publishing Co., 1986), 462. Berkhof later refers to such passages as Galatians 5; Rom. 6:15–23; 1 Cor. 10:23f., which point to the unity of freedom and love, and then adds in Rom. 14:13; 1 Cor. 8:1–13; and 10:25–33, "Paul warns against using freedom in such a way that it is no longer a channel for love but an obstacle" (463).

23. Comm. Galatians 5:1.

24. Comm. Galatians 5:13. Concerning the latter phrase in Galatians 5:13— "but through love"—Calvin concludes: "In a word, if we serve one another through love, we shall always have regard to edification; so that we shall not grow wanton, but use the grace of God to his honor and the salvation of our neighbors."

25. *Calvin's Doctrine of the Christian Life* (Grand Rapids: Wm. B. Eerdmans Publishing Co., 1959), 311. I am indebted to Wallace for several references in his fine discussion of this subject, 308ff.

26. Comm. 1 Corinthians 10:29. Calvin goes on to explain that the "meaning here is a narrower one, since the soul of a believer looks only to the judgment seat of God, and not to any human authority, and rejoices in the blessing of freedom procured for it by Christ, it is under obligation to no individuals, or bound to no conditions of time or place."

27. Zachman, 230.

28. Comm. 1 Corinthians 8:11. Cf. Comm. 1 Corinthians 8:7.

29. Ibid.

30. Comm. Psalm 40:7. A dimension of freedom I have not dealt with here is the relation of freedom and order in Calvin's theology. Here Jane Dempsey Douglass has a helpful chapter in her book on *Women, Freedom, and Calvin:* "Freedom in God's Order." She concludes the chapter with this observation: "Political order and ecclesiastical order derive from God's gift to humanity of the power to govern, and they represent realms where humanity is free to adapt and transform tradition to carry out God's purposes in a changing world. Both kinds of order are informed by the ongoing lively activity of the Holy Spirit, who is moving human order in the direction of the freedom of the kingdom of God" (40). Cf. the earlier study of this theme by M. Eugene Osterhaven, "John Calvin: Order and the Holy Spirit," chap. 14 in *The Faith of the Church: A Reformed Perspective on Its Historical Development* (Grand Rapids: Wm. B. Eerdmans Publishing Co., 1982).

31. Comm. Galatians 5:18.

32. Comm. Acts 15:10.

33. Comm. John 15:10.

34. Comm. Jeremiah 30:9. "Christian freedom is not the antithesis of authority, but consists rather in the Lordship of Christ so that the will of the Lord becomes

one with our wills." Wilhelm Kolfhaus, *Vom christlichen Leben nach Calvin* (Neu-kirchen Kr. Moers: Buchhandlung des Erziehungsvereins, 1949), 139.

7. ELECTION AND PREDESTINATION

1. The terms "election" and "predestination" here connote basically the same thing, although election frequently has a more corporate connotation. Hence we speak of the election of Israel and the predestination of individuals. Election is often viewed as a manifestation of the eternal decree whereas predestination is often identified with foreordination. Some theologians, such as Rudolf Otto, have distinguished sharply between the two concepts, but generally they are used as synonyms.

2. In the first edition of the *Institutes* predestination was not treated as a separate doctrine and was mentioned only in passing in two places. Therefore, the Catechism represents a significant advance in his thinking about this subject. In the later editions of the *Institutes* up to the final (1559) edition Calvin discussed the doctrine together with the providence of God—and in his discussion of preaching. In the last edition of the *Institutes*, however, Calvin discusses predestination in the context of soteriology, i.e., after faith, justification, and prayer. Most Calvin scholars regard this as a very significant shift. Here see particularly the fine discussion of François Wendel, *Calvin: Origins and Development of His Religious Thought* (New York: Harper & Row, 1963), 263ff.

3. Ibid., 266–67.

4. See Deut. 7:7–8; 10:14–15; John 15:16, 19; 17:9, 20, 21; Rom. 8:28–30, chaps. 9–11; Eph. 1:3–6; 1 Peter 2:2.

5. This is good scriptural terminology; see Matt. 15:14; Rom. 2:18–21, 9:18; 2 Cor. 3:14; Rev. 3:17.

6. Two of the best studies of this subject from a Reformed perspective are by G. C. Berkouwer, *Divine Election* (Grand Rapids: Wm. B. Eerdmans Publishing Co., 1960; and Paul K. Jewett, *Election and Predestination* (Grand Rapids: Wm. B. Eerdmans Publishing Co., 1985). See especially chap. 1, "A Historical Overview." On Calvin, in particular, Edward Dowey is very good. See his *The Knowledge of God in Calvin's Theology*, 211–19, 239ff.

7. As was done by Alexander Schweizer, *Die Protestantische Centraldogmen*, vol. 2 (Zurich: Orell, Fesli, 1854).

8. Late in his career, because of vicious attacks on his doctrine of predestination, Calvin defended his position in a book, *De aeterna Predestinatione Dei*, which was published in 1552. This is available in English tranlation by J.K.S. Reid: *Concerning the Eternal Predestination of God* (London: James Clarke, 1961; repr., Louisville, Ky.: Westminster John Knox Press, 1997).

9. Calvin warns the curious that "when they inquire into predestination, they are penetrating into the secret precincts of divine wisdom. If anyone with carefree assurance breaks into this place, he will not succeed in satisfying his curiosity and he will enter a labyrinth from which he can find no exit" (*Inst.* III.21.1).

10. Berkouwer, 213–14. Cf. Francis Davidson, a conservative Scottish theolo-

gian, in his Tyndale Monograph, *Pauline Predestination* (London: Tyndale House, 1946), 32ff.; and Jewett, 81ff. Calvin's view however, still has some defenders. Cf. John Piper, *The Justification of God: An Exegetical and Theological Study of Romans 9:1–23* (Grand Rapids: Baker Book House, 1983). In this exhaustive study of this passage Piper points out that exegetes can generally be divided into those who interpret Romans 9:6–13 as referring primarily to the destinies of nations or to the individual and eternal predestination of individuals. He cites a number of modern scholars—and not all of them conservative Calvinists by any means—who support the latter position, e.g., distinguished German scholars such as E. Dinkler, V. Luz, O. Michel, and Ernst Käsemann, who in his highly regarded *Commentary on Romans,* writes in reference to 9:12–13, "The presence of a strong concept of predestination [in these verses] cannot be denied,—although only here does Paul present double predestination." But then he adds, referring to Herman Ridderbos, "Certainly Paul has no speculative interest in pre-temporal predestination" (Grand Rapids: Wm. B. Eerdmans Publishing Co., 1980), 265. For a popular defense of Calvin's—and the traditional Reformed doctrine of predestination—see R. C. Sproul, *Chosen by God* (Wheaton, Ill.: Tyndale House, 1986).

11. *The Epistle to the Romans.* Moffatt Commentary (New York: Harper, 1932), 157–58.

12. *Romans.* The Torch Bible Commentaries (London: SCM Press, 1955), 92.

13. Half of vol. 1 is devoted to the theology of Paul (New York: Charles Scribner's Sons, 1951).

14. See *Church Dogmatics* II, 2, *The Doctrine of God* (Edinburgh: T. & T. Clark, 1957), 123ff., 162ff. One of the best critiques of Barth's position is by G. C. Berkouwer in his *The Triumph of Grace in the Theology of Karl Barth* (Grand Rapids: Wm. B. Eerdmans Publishing Co., 1956), 89–122. A whole book is devoted to this question in Barth's theology by Donald Bloesch, *Jesus Is Victor: Karl Barth's Doctrine of Salvation* (Nashville: Abingdon Press, 1976). A more sympathetic but not uncritical evaluation is given by Otto Weber, *Foundations of Dogmatics,* vol. 2 (Grand Rapids: Wm. B. Eerdmans Publishing Co., 1983), 435ff. Weber devotes four chapters to the theme of "God's Gracious Election" (*Gottes Gnadenwahl*), the latter term being very popular in German theology. *Gnadenwahl* could also be translated as "election of grace."

15. Cf. *Institutes* III.21.1: "Human curiosity renders the discussion of predestination, already somewhat difficult of itself, very confusing and even dangerous."

16. In his scriptural defense of this doctrine in the *Institutes* this passage (Eph. 1:4–9) is discussed at length (III.25.1–2) and prior to Romans 9—11.

17. Calvin uses the same metaphor in his sermon on Ephesians 1:3–4 but in a slightly different way. "God must have had before him his pattern and mirror in which to see us, that is to say, he must have first looked on our Lord Jesus Christ before he could choose us and call us." The Second Sermon, *John Calvin's Sermons on Ephesians,* revision of Arthur Golding's translation (Carlisle, Pa.: Banner of Truth Trust, 1973), 33.

18. *Concerning the Eternal Predestination of God,* 126.

19. Ibid., 127. These three images are repeated on 113 and that of a mirror on 50. Paul Jacobs, the German Reformed theologian, on the basis of this and other evidence, simply concludes that for Calvin, "Christ is election itself," *Prädestina-*

tion und Verantwortlichkeit bei Calvin (Neukirchen: Neukirchener Verlag, 1937), 77.

20. From his Introduction to *Concerning the Eternal Predestination of God*, 39.

21. Using Aristotelian categories, Calvin sees in Ephesians 1:5–7 four causes of our salvation: "The *efficient cause* is the good pleasure of the will of God; the *material cause is Christ;* and the *final cause* is the praise of his grace." Later he designates "the preaching of the gospel, by which the goodness of God flows out to us," as the *formal cause*, Comm. Eph. 1:5, 8 (emphasis added).

22. Ibid., 40. For a similar criticism of Calvin and recommendation of Barth's view as a happy alternative, see the lengthy article on predestination by T.H.L. Parker in *A Dictionary of Christian Theology*, ed. Alan Richardson (Philadelphia: Westminster Press, 1969), 268–72.

23. In the *Institutes*, however, this verse is not cited once! Instead he refers to the parable of the wedding banquet in Matthew 22 and especially the phrase "Many are called but few are chosen" (22:14). Calvin interprets as a general or outward call, not the special or inner call here by "which believers ought to reckon their election" (*Inst*. III.24.8). In the Catechism Calvin does not mention the matter of calling.

24. *Eternal Predestination*, 70.

25. Comm. John 6:40.

26. Comm. Daniel 12:1. God "declares his election when he regenerates his elect by his Holy Spirit, and thus inscribes them with a certain mark, while they prove the reality of this sonship by the whole course of their lives, and confirm their own adoption" (ibid.).

27. "Salvation is [God's] work, not ours; it is of grace—all of grace. This is the truth we confess in the doctrine of election . . . ," Jewett, 139.

28. Timothy George, *Theology of the Reformers* (Nashville: Broadman Press, 1988), 234. George then points out that "during the Great Awakening of the eighteenth century, George Whitefield, a Calvinist, won far more people to Christ than his Arminian friend, John Wesley."

29. *Calvin: On the Christian Faith*, edited and with an introduction by John T. McNeill (Indianapolis and New York: Liberal Arts Press, 1957), xxviii. A further observation of McNeill's is very apropos: "Wherever Calvin calls our attention to the sphere of duty, the motives on which the Christian's service rests come to expression in clear and sufficient terms—gratitude for the undeserved gift of grace, and love for our fellow men, who, however unworthy, yet bear upon them the image of God." Ibid., xxvii.

30. Ibid.

31. Although this difficult doctrine is ultimately best dealt with in a doxological fashion, as I have done here, this does not resolve the tensions inherent in this doctrine. "To *confess* the truth is not to *explain* it," Jewett, 108. However, Berkouwer also concludes with an important insight: "The knowledge of the electing God is not the outcome of rational considerations, but it is found only when man walks in the way of this truth," 329.

In the doctrines of election and human responsibility we are confronted with an insoluble mystery. We must do our best to understand them and do justice to all the scriptural data, but eventually we may have to learn to live with paradox. However, I have attempted to resolve this paradox in a forthcoming book, *Sovereign Grace and Human Freedom: How They Coalesce.*

8. FAITH

1. The image of knowledge "rattling around in the brain" is virtually repeated later in the *Institutes:* "The Word of God is not received by faith if it flits about in the top of the brain, but when it takes root in the depth of the heart . . . "(III.2.36).

2. Here, as so often in Calvin's theology, the Holy Spirit plays a crucial role, particularly that of illuminating and sealing the knowledge which the mind has received. "It is clear that faith is much higher than human understanding. It will not be enough for the mind to be illumined by the Spirit of God unless the heart is also strengthened and supported by his power" (*Inst.* III.2.33). "It now remains to pour into the heart itself what the mind has absorbed. The Spirit accordingly serves as a seal, to seal up in our hearts those very promises the certainty of which it has previously impressed upon our minds" (III.2.36). Cf. chap. 15, "Calvin, Theologian of the Holy Spirit."

3. In reference to the phrase "I have believed" in John 6:69, Calvin comments, "The word *believe* is put first because the obedience of faith is the beginning of true understanding; or rather, faith is itself truly the eye of the mind. But at once knowledge is added which distinguishes faith from erroneous and false opinions. . . . Knowledge is joined to faith because we have a sure and undoubted conviction of God's truth, not in the same way sciences are apprehended, but when the Spirit seals it in our hearts." Comm. John 6:69.

4. Comm. Romans 10:10. "If the personality is conceived of as a mysterious unity, knowing must be reconceived as a function of the whole, above all involving its 'center,' the heart. Unlike philosophical knowledge, a knowledge of the heart is not coldly objective but suffused with feeling." William J. Bouwsma, *John Calvin: A Sixteenth Century Portrait* (New York: Oxford Univ. Press, 1988), 157. Cf. 131–33. In Calvin's own words, "We must note that faith is not simple assent of the mind to what we are taught, but we must also bring the heart and the affections." Sermon 20 in *The Deity of Christ*, on 2 Thess. 1:6–10, CO 52: 226.

5. "Our knowledge of God's benevolence is pivotal, in that without our knowledge of that goodness we should never cast ourselves upon him." Victor A. Shepherd, *The Nature and Function of Faith in the Theology of John Calvin* (Macon, Ga.: Mercer Univ. Press, 1983), 11. Cf. Dowey, *The Knowledge of God in Calvin's Theology*, chap. 4.

6. Christ may be the proper object of faith, but Calvin loves to dwell particularly on the *promises* of God's mercy which culminate in Christ. In sec. 14 of the Catechism there are three references to God's promises. Here Calvin has in mind the definition of faith in Hebrews 11:1 when he says, "While the Lord bestows his mercy upon us through the promise of his gospel, if we surely and unhesitatingly have confidence in the Promiser, we are said to grasp his Word by faith" (ibid.).

7. Faith is not only an understanding and conviction of God's gracious will toward us in Christ made possible by the illumination of the Holy Spirit, but it is also "a *pledge* which establishes in our *hearts* the assurance of divine truth, and a *seal* whereby our *hearts* will be sealed unto the day of the Lord" (Catechism, sec. 15, emphasis added). Note that here and in the passage just cited from the *Institutes* there is a frequent linking of the sealing of the heart by the Holy Spirit with assurance. This is the subjective ground for the assurance of faith.

8. Comm. John 3:33.
9. Comm. Acts 17:11.
10. Despite his candid confessions about the struggle of faith and doubt, Calvin's great emphasis is on the assurance or certainty of faith. "The commencement of faith is knowledge; the completion of it is a firm and fixed persuasion [*persuasio*] which admits no opposing doubts. Both . . . are works of the Spirit," Comm. Eph. 1:13. After discussing this issue in the *Institutes*, Calvin adds, "We conclude that the knowledge of faith consists in assurance [*certitudo*] rather than in comprehension" (III.2.14). As Dowey points out, "Faith without certainty," for Calvin, "is no faith at all" (181). Yet Bouwsma gives the impression that Calvin was an anxiety-ridden figure who rarely experienced the assurance about which he spoke so frequently. Here, I am convinced, Bouwsma errs and is guilty of psychological overkill. See Bouwsma's *John Calvin*, chap. 2, "Calvin's Anxiety."
11. Calvin only uses this precise expression once in the *Institutes* and in the Catechism not at all. But this intimate spiritual union with Christ is expressed vividly in his discussion of the Lord's Supper in the *Institutes* IV.17.1, 8–12 and in almost the same way in III.2.24: "Christ is not outside us but dwells within us. Not only does he cleave to us by an invisible bond of fellowship, but with a wonderful communion (*societas*) day by day, he grows more and more into one body with us, until he becomes completely one with us." Calvin scholars caution against confusing Calvin's notion of mystical union with certain types of mysticism. François Wendel warns that "in the technical sense of the term" Calvin's doctrine is not "a mystical union." *Calvin: Origins and Developments of His Religious Thought* (New York: Harper & Row, 1963), 237. Wilhelm Niesel also points out that Calvin nowhere teaches "the absorption of the pious mystic into the sphere of the divine being," *The Theology of Calvin*, 126. Cf. the recent study of this theme by Dennis E. Tamburello, *Union with Christ: John Calvin and the Mysticism of St. Bernard*, Columbia Series in Reformed Theology (Louisville, Ky,: Westminster John Knox Press, 1994).
12. See Küng's *Justification: The Doctrine of Karl Barth and a Catholic Reflection* (New York: Thomas Nelson & Sons, 1964).
13. After justification (sec. 16) and sanctification (sec. 17), however, Calvin treats "repentance and regeneration" (sec. 18), a most unusual sequence. In a traditional *ordo salutis* (plan of salvation), regeneration would *precede* faith, justification, and sanctification. More about this later.
14. Cf. Shepherd's discussion of justification in *The Nature and Function of Faith*, chap. 2, "Justification and Faith"; and John H. Leith, *John Calvin's Doctrine of the Christian Life* (Louisville, Ky.: Westminster/John Knox Press, 1989), chap. 2, "The Christian Life in Relation to Justification by Faith Alone."
15. The key forensic word is "reckoned" ("credited," NAB).
16. The word "imputation" is also crucial, for it is the opposite of the reformers' understanding of the Roman Catholic view of "*imbued*" (Catechism, sec. 16) and Osiander's notion of "essential righteousness" (*Inst.* III.11.5). "The logical consequence of the doctrine of the imputation of the righteousness of Christ is that never, not even after the remission of our sins, are we really righteous," Wendel, 259.
17. This is not the end of the matter as far as Calvin is concerned. The next chapter in the *Institutes* (III.14) is entitled "The Beginning of Justification and Its

Continual Progress." It may sound strange to speak of "progress" in justification since it is usually considered a once-for-all act. Calvin here, however, is largely arguing against the Roman Catholic expansion of the doctrine of justification to include the merit of good works. He continues this polemic in chap. 15.

18. "Calvin never tires of referring to 1 Corinthians 1:30: he whom the Christian 'puts on' is put on in the totality of his [Christ's] reality," Shepherd, 35.

19. This was one of the charges of the Council of Trent, which met 1545–63.

20. Wendel, 260. Wendel mentions that this idea was first introduced in the 1543 edition of the *Institutes*. However, it is also found in incipient form in the 1538 Catechism. Note how Calvin concludes sec. 19: "To sum up, we must conclude that fellowship with Christ has such great power because on its account we are not only freely reckoned righteous, but our works are also imputed to us as righteousness, and will be recompensed with an everlasting reward."

21. "We must always remember that God 'accepts' believers by reason of works only because he is their source and graciously by way of adding to his liberality deigns also to show 'acceptance' toward the good works he has himself bestowed" (*Inst.* III.17.5).

22. Wendel even maintains that "Calvin makes no special distinction between the two terms, i.e., regeneration and sanctification" (242n31). He then refers to a passage in Calvin's commentary on 1 Corinthians 1:2 which reads: "The word 'sanctification' denotes separation. This takes place in us when, by the Spirit, we are born again into newness of life. . . ."

23. Hendrikus Berkhof, in his *Doctrine of the Holy Spirit*, 68–70, points out that whereas the New Testament uses a wide variety of terms to describe the new life in Christ—election, calling, repentance, faith, etc.—systematic theology generally limits this variety to two or three comprehensive concepts such as justification and sanctification.

24. In the *Institutes* the approach appears to be different, for the title of chap. 3 (of book III) is "Our Regeneration by Faith: Repentance." But immediately Calvin proceeds to discuss regeneration in terms of repentance. Note also that this chapter follows the one on faith, where in later dogmatics it would precede it.

25. The first of his 95 theses reads: "When our Lord and Master Jesus Christ said, 'Repent' [Matt. 4:17], he willed the entire life of believers to be one of repentance [*poenitentia*]." *Luther's Works*, vol. 31, *Career of the Reformer* I, ed. Harold J. Grimm (Philadelphia: Muhlenberg Press, 1957), 25.

26. The latter phrase is only found in the French (1537) edition of the Catechism. Calvin's definition of repentance in the *Institutes* is similar. "It is the true turning of our life to God, a turning that arises from a pure and earnest fear of him; and it consists in the mortification of our flesh and of the old man, and in the vivification of the Spirit" (III.3.5).

27. The same understanding of repentance or conversion is also found in the Heidelberg Catechism, Qs. 88–90.

28. In his commentaries Calvin defines regeneration in a variety of ways, depending on the context. The main difference is that what Calvin attributes to *repentance* in the *Institutes* he refers to *regeneration* in the commentaries, thus confirming the contention that there is little, if any, difference between the two in his thinking. For example, in his commentary on Colossians 3:10 he defines *regeneration*

as "putting off the old man and putting on the new." There is an interesting variation in his commentary on Ephesians 4:22: Paul, Calvin says, here "demands from a Christian man *repentance or newness of life,* which he places in denial of ourselves and the *regeneration of the Holy Spirit"* (emphasis added).

29. Note that in sec. 18 of the Catechism and thus far in this chapter (III.3) of the *Institutes* dealing with regeneration, repentance, and conversion Calvin has not used the word most commonly employed to describe this process, viz., sanctification. However, recall that sec. 18 is entitled, "Through Faith We are Sanctified unto Obedience to the Law." Later in the *Institutes* (III.3.14) Calvin suddenly starts speaking of sanctification in connection with the role of the Spirit in the Christian life. Here he is refuting what he considers to be certain Anabaptists of his day who believed that the gift of the Spirit resulted in a form of Christian perfection. Calvin responds that even though we have received the Spirit of sanctification, we are "far removed from perfection and must move steadily forward, and though entangled in vices, daily fight against them."

30. *Church Dogmatics* IV, 3, Second Half (Edinburgh: T. & T. Clark, 1962), 913f.

31. Cf. the discussion, based largely on the commentaries, "Our Christian life and warfare are maintained by hope" in Ronald Wallace, *Calvin's Doctrine of the Christian Life,* 317ff.

9. "I BELIEVE IN GOD"

1. Similarly in the *Institutes* II.16.18: "I call it the Apostles' Creed without concerning myself in the least as to its authorship. . . . I have no doubt that at the very beginning of the church, in the apostolic age, it was received as a public confession by the consent of all—wherever it originated."

2. See the helpful volume of this genre by Wilhelm Niesel, *The Gospel and the Churches: A Comparison of Catholicism, Orthodoxy and Protestantism* (Philadelphia: Westminster Press, 1962). The British edition, published in Edinburgh by Oliver & Boyd, has the title *Reformed Symbolics).*

3. See Dowey, *The Knowledge of God in Calvin's Theology,* chap. 2, and the Preface to the second edition of this book (New York: Columbia Univ. Press, 1965; 3d ed., Wm. B. Eerdmans Publishing Co., 1995).

4. The first editions of both Dowey's and Parker's books appeared in 1952. Parker sharply contested Dowey's thesis in the American edition of his book (Grand Rapids: Wm. B. Eerdmans Publishing Co., 1959).

5. Will Durant, *The Reformation* (New York: Simon & Schuster, 1957), 490. Elsewhere in this volume he makes an equally venomous judgment about the *Institutes* as a whole: It is "the most eloquent, fervent, lucid, logical, influential, and terrible work in all the literature of the religious revolution (ibid., 490).

6. Harold J. Grimm, *The Reformation Era 1500–1560* (New York: Macmillan & Co., rev. ed. 1965), 352.

7. " . . . although the name 'God' is also common to the Son, it is sometimes applied to the Father par excellence because he is the fountainhead and beginning of deity—and this is done to denote the simple unity of essence" (*Inst* I.13.23).

8. See, e.g., Leonard Hodgson, *The Doctrine of the Trinity* (London: Nisbet, 1943), 165ff. "Of the three (St. Augustine, St. Thomas, and Calvin) . . . Calvin has

suffered the least from the inevitable contradiction between the evidence and the idea of unity," 175. Cf. T. F. Torrance, "Calvin's Doctrine of the Trinity," *Calvin Theological Journal* 25, no. 2 (Nov. 1990): 168–70.

9. "Calvin's Doctrine of the Trinity," in *Calvin and Augustine* (Philadelphia: Presbyterian and Reformed, 1956) 195.

10. On the role of the Spirit's guidance in the believer's experience see my essay, "Governed and Guided by the Spirit: A Key Issue in Calvin's Doctrine of the Holy Spirit," in *Reformiertes Erbe*. Festschrift für Gottfried W. Locher zu seinem 80. Geburtstag, Band 2, hrsg. von H. A. Oberman, Ernst Saxer et al. (Zurich: Theologischer Verlag, 1993).

11. See Barth's *Church Dogmatics* II, 1, *The Doctrine of God* (Edinburgh: T. & T. Clark, 1957).

12. *Church Dogmatics* II, 2, *The Doctrine of God* (Edinburgh: T. & T. Clark, 1957), 15ff., 32ff., 188ff. The first half of this volume is devoted to election.

13. Ibid., 145ff., 451ff.

14. So, e.g., even François Wendel, *Calvin,* 127–29, who cites A. Ritschl, W. Walker, and R. Seeberg in this connection, but he allows that E. Doumergue, A. Lecerf, and others find no connection at all. However, the German scholar Karl Reuter sides with Wendel, Ritschl, et al.: "Calvin has gained a Reformed knowledge of salvation, but his doctrine of God exhibits displays of nominalistic disturbances." *Das Grundverständnis der Theologie Calvins* (Neukirchen: Neukirchener Verlag, 1963), 154. The tide is now turning, however, as J. T. McNeill, F. L. Battles, and T. F. Torrance all deny any negative influence here. (See notes in the LCC *Institutes,* 214 and 950). Alexandre Ganoczy, the eminent Roman Catholic Calvin scholar, totally rejects the Reuter thesis and the view that the young Calvin was influenced by the Scottish theologian John Major. See Ganoczy's *The Young Calvin,* trans. David Foxgrover and Wade Provo (Philadelphia: Westminster Press, 1987), 174ff. For a more recent discussion of this subject see Heiko Oberman, *The Dawn of the Reformation* (Grand Rapids: Wm. B. Eerdmans Publishing Co., 1986, 1992), 253–5.

15. See Wendel, 128.

16. See Torrance, *Theology in Reconstruction,* (Grand Rapids: Wm. B. Eerdmans Publishing Co.), 78ff., 188ff., and *Space, Time and Incarnation,* (New York: Oxford Univ. Press, 1969), 27ff., 64f., 86f.

17. Also, in regard to the common view that Calvin one-sidedly emphasized God's transcendence over his immanence, the conclusion of Christopher B. Kaiser is important. "Theologically Calvin balanced the divine attributes of transcendence and personality, or sovereignty and love." *The Doctrine of God* (Westchester, Ill.: Crossway Books, 1982), 100.

18. So the editors of the McNeill-Battles edition of the *Institutes,* 121n1.

19. Op. cit., 206. Cf. Calvin's Commentary on Psalm 130:7: "The foundation upon which he [the psalmist] would have all the godly to rest is the mercy of God, the source from which redemption springs. . . . From this mercy, as from a fountain, the prophet derives redemption; for there is no other course which moves God to manifest himself as the redeemer of his people but his mercy."

20. Garret Wilterdink, *Tyrant or Father? A Study of Calvin's Doctrine of God;* vol. 1 (Bristol, Ind.: Wyndham Hall Press, 1985), 3.

21. Vol. ii, 909. Cf. Wilterdink's essay, "The Fatherhood of God," *Reformed Review* 30, no. 1 (autumn 1976).

22. "Calvin's Doctrine of God," in *Able Ministers of the New Testament* (London: A. G. Hasler & Co., 1965), 7.

10. "AND IN JESUS CHRIST"

1. The first edition of this important work appeared in 1938. Unfortunately, it was not translated into English until 1956, although Niesel made a few revisions for this edition. The next year, however, a considerably revised version appeared in German (Munich: Chr. Kaiser Verlag, 1957), but this has never been translated into English. More recently Alexandre Ganoczy has reaffirmed the Christocentric character of Calvin's theology. In a chapter entitled "Major Constructive Principles of Calvin's Thought," he writes: "Christ is the only Mediator. This is the central dogmatic affirmation of Calvin's theology from its opening statements. Therefore we may qualify this theology as essentially Christ-centered." *The Young Calvin*, 190.

2. For documentation and a further discussion of this point see the last chapter of this *Introduction*, sec. 2.

3. *The Theology of Calvin* (Philadelphia: Westminster Press, 1956; Grand Rapids: Baker Book House, 1980), 26ff.

4. Comm. John 5:39; cf. Comm. 2 Cor. 3:16.

5. In the treatment of the Apostles' Creed in the Catechism, secs. ii–v, and in the *Institutes* chaps. 12–17. Since three chapters each are devoted to the person and the work of Christ, it is inexplicable that Niesel devotes a whole chapter to the first three chapters on the person of Christ and completely ignores the three chapters dealing with the work of Christ. In the revised German edition he adds one brief section on the work of the mediator, but it is too little, too late.

6. On this development see John F. Jansen, *Calvin's Doctrine of the Work of Christ* (London: James Clarke, 1956), chap. 2; Karl Barth, *Church Dogmatics* IV, 3, 13ff.; Otto Weber, *Foundations of Dogmatics*, vol. 2, 172ff.

7. See, for example: Louis Berkhof, *Systematic Theology* (Grand Rapids: Wm. B. Eerdmans Publishing Co., 1941), 356ff., 406ff.; Karl Barth, *Church Dogmatics* IV, 3 (Edinburgh: T. & T. Clark, 1961), 5f., 13ff.; Emil Brunner, *The Christian Doctrine of Creation and Redemption*, Dogmatics, vol. 2 (Philadelphia: Westminster Press, 1952), 275ff.; Otto Weber, *Foundations of Dogmatics*, vol. 2 (Grand Rapids: Wm. B. Eerdmans Publishing Co., 1983), 169ff.; Regin Prenter, *Creation and Redemption* (Philadelphia: Fortress Press, 1967), 318ff.; Helmut Thielicke, *The Evangelical Faith*, vol. 2 (Grand Rapids: Wm. B. Eerdmans Publishing Co., 1977), chaps. 24–30. Hendrikus Berkhof defends the idea and says "it can be a useful distinction," but warns against the temptation to "artificial divisions." *Christian Faith*, rev. ed. (Grand Rapids: Wm. B. Eerdmans Publishing Co., 1986), 300.

8. This translation is based on the 1541 French edition and is found in *The School of Faith: The Catechisms of the Reformed Church*, trans. and ed. by T. F. Torrance (London: James Clarke, 1959), 11–12. A translation of the 1545 Latin edition is available in the Library of Christian Classics, vol. 22, *Calvin: Theological Treatises*.

9. The usual ordering is prophet, priest, and king. Here it is prophet, king, and priest, whereas in the Geneva Catechism it is king, priest, and prophet. Apparently the order was not important for Calvin. Re: this question see Weber, 173.

10. Weber, 174.

11. Cf. a similar passage in the *Institutes* in reference to Christ's kingship: "Such is the nature of his rule, that he shares with us all that he has received from the Father. Now he arms and equips us with his power, adorns us with his beauty and magnificence, enriches us with his wealth" (*Inst.* II.15.4).

12. Robert A. Peterson, in his solid study, *Calvin's Doctrine of the Atonement* (Phillipsburg, N.J.: Presbyterian and Reformed Publishing Co., 1983), points out that chap. 15 in book II of the *Institutes,* which treats the threefold office of Christ, forms a transition between chaps. 12–14, which deal with the person of Christ, and chaps. 16–17, which discuss his work. This, says Peterson, "is Calvin's way of telling his readers not to separate the person and work of Christ. To speak of Christ's person apart from his work is to fall into the perverse speculation of Osiander" (39).

13. Ibid., 1. As Donald Bloesch points out, "Calvin saw Christ not simply as an instrument of salvation but as its Author and Executor. . . . Perhaps one can say that for Calvin, Christ brought to realization and fulfillment a redemption that had already been determined in the eternal counsel of God." *Essentials of Evangelical Theology,* vol. 1 (San Francisco: Harper & Row, 1978), 154.

14. New York: Macmillan, 1951/1969. The British edition (SPCK) came out in 1931.

15. Ibid, 37. Aulén also maintains that this view is found in the Western Fathers, 39.

16. See, e.g., Hastings Rashdall, *The Idea of the Atonement in Christian Theology* (London: Macmillan & Co., 1925), 398ff.; L. W. Grensted, *A Short History of the Atonement* (Manchester: Manchester Univ. Press, 1920), 209ff. Grensted finds a basic unity in the approach of Luther and Calvin, both of whom, he affirms, follow the Anselmic method, but they substitute the justice of God for Anselm's requirement of the satisfaction of God's honor. Hence Grensted labels the Reformers' approach to the atonement the "penal theory."

17. On Anselm's theory of the atonement and a comparison of his view with Calvin's, see Robert H. Culpepper, *Interpreting the Atonement* (Grand Rapids: Wm. B. Eerdmans Publishing Co., 1966) 81ff., 10f.

18. On this question see Culpepper, 95f. Cf. Ronald Wallace, who finds three motifs or pictures that run through Luther's portrayal of the atonement: "Christ in our conflicts, Christ offering an exchange with us, Christ bearing and overcoming the wrath of God for us." *The Atoning Death of Christ* (Westchester, Ill.: Crossway Books, 1981), 77.

19. A dissertation has been written to demonstrate this, viz., *With the Spirit's Sword* by Charles A. M. Hall. The subtitle: *The Drama of Spiritual Warfare in the Theology of John Calvin* (Zurich: EVZ Verlag, 1968). John F. Jansen had pointed out the prominent place the *Christus Victor* motif has in Calvin's theology. He asserts that "the regal conquest of Christ over the devil, death, and sin . . . is Calvin's most recurrent theme . . . in any discussion of the reign of Christ." *Calvin's Doctrine of the Work of Christ* (London: James Clarke, 1956), 88. This may be true in the context of Christ's kingly office, but when Calvin discusses the priestly office of Christ the sacrificial/satisfaction motifs dominate.

20. For further references see Hall, 97ff., and Jansen, 88–89.

21. *The Oracles of God* (London: Lutterworth, 1947), 87ff.

22. This is the thesis of Paul van Buren's dissertation, *Christ in Our Place: The*

Substitutionary Character of Calvin's Doctrine of Reconciliation (Edinburgh: Oliver & Boyd, 1957).

23. WA 31:434. Cited in Wallace, 78.

24. Peterson, 87.

25. For example, Robert Paul observes that "even when Calvin appears to be setting forth the penal theory at its hardest, it is within the setting of sacrifice because this is the setting which is biblical." *The Atonement and the Sacraments* (London: Hodder & Stoughton, 1961), 103.

26. *Interpreting the Atonement*, 102.

27. The observant reader will notice that I have skipped over the intervening phrase in the Apostles' Creed, "He descended into hell," which Calvin discusses very briefly in the Catechism in the latter part of sec. 20, iv, and at considerable length in the *Institutes* (II.16.8–12). I have done so largely because of space limitations. Calvin's position is not unique here (see Battles's note 23 on p. 515 of the LCC *Institutes*), but it does represent a deviation from the traditional, literal view held by Aquinas, Luther, and the Council of Trent. Calvin interprets this phrase symbolically to mean the hellish torments Christ endured on the cross on our behalf. For here he was "afflicted by God and felt the dread and severity of divine judgment . . ." (Catechism, sec. 20, iv). In the *Institutes* Calvin stresses the "wonderful consolation" this doctrine provides us (II.16.10). For this is "our wisdom," Calvin explains, "duly to feel how much our salvation cost the Son of God" (II.16.12).

28. Comm. Galatians 6:14.

29. This does not mean, however, that when the context calls for it, Calvin does not spell out all the implications of the resurrection and its relevance for our faith. See the fairly lengthy discussions of Calvin on the resurrection in van Buren, chap. 6, "Resurrection and Ascension"; and Ronald Wallace, chap. 3, "Participation in the Resurrection and Glory of Christ."

30. Cited in the LCC edition of the *Institutes*, 520n34.

31. Comm. Philippians 3:10 (emphasis added).

32. *Calvin: Commentaries*, trans. and ed. by Joseph Haroutunian in collaboration with Louise Pettibone Smith. Library of Christian Classics, vol. 23 (Philadelphia: Westminster Press, 1958), 45. Yet the significance of this aspect of the work of Christ is virtually ignored by such eminent Calvin scholars as W. Niesel and F. Wendel.

33. See Anthony Hoekema, *The Bible and the Future* (Grand Rapids: Wm. B. Eerdmans Publishing Co., 1979), 1ff.

34. See Thomas F. Torrance, *Kingdom and Church* (Edinburgh: Oliver & Boyd, 1956), 153ff.; and especially the studies by his younger brother, James B. Torrance, "The Priesthood of Jesus," in *Essays in Christology for Karl Barth*, ed. T.H.L. Parker (London: Lutterworth Press, 1956) 169ff.; "The vicarious Humanity and Priesthood of Christ in the Theology of John Calvin," in *Calvinus Ecclesiae Doctor*, ed W. H. Neuser (Kampen: J. H. Kok, 1979). Cf. Wallace, *Calvin's Doctrine of the Christian Life*, 8ff.

35. It is hardly a coincidence that the Heidelberg Catechism also lists three benefits to be derived from Christ's ascension (Q. & A. 49)—and they are virtually the same as Calvin's, although the Catechism accents the sending of the Spirit at Pentecost more explicitly than Calvin.

36. Haroutunian, 45–6. He then comments, "Hence, there is no image so alive in Calvin's mind as that of the Son seated next to the Father."

37. Cf. Colossians 3:4: "When Christ, our life, shall appear . . ."Calvin remarks: "A beautiful consolation, that the coming of Christ will be the manifestation of our life." Comm. Col. 3:4.

38. Comm. Isaiah 62:11.

39. Comm. James 5:8.

11. PRAYER

1. LCC edition of the *Institutes*. For a thorough discussion of Calvin's view of prayer, see Wallace, *Calvin's Doctrine of the Christian Life*, part 5, chap. 3.

2. This paragraph is repeated almost verbatim in the *Institutes* III.20.1.

3. Comm. Psalm 25:8.

4. Calvin's preface to commentary on the Psalms, CO 31:17, (p. xxxvii in the Edinburgh edition). Cf. Wallace, *Calvin's Doctrine of the Christian Life*, 276 ff. He entitles this subsection, "Prayer must be controlled, formed and inspired by the Word."

5. An echo of this formulation is found in the Heidelberg Catechism, Q. 116, where prayer is called "the chief part of gratitude." Elsewhere Calvin speaks of thanksgiving as "the chief exercise of godliness." Comm. Psalm 50:23.

6. *The Soul of Prayer* (London: Independent Press, 1916/1949), 11.

7. *The Theology of Calvin*, 156.

8. For a critical analysis of Calvin's treatment of the Lord's Prayer, tracing its development from the earliest catechisms, his commentary, and the 1536 *Institutes* to the final edition, see Elsie Anne McKee, "John Calvin's Teaching on the Lord's Prayer," in *The Lord's Prayer: Perspectives for Reclaiming Christian Prayer*, ed. Daniel L. Migliore (Grand Rapids: Wm. B. Eerdmans Publishing Co., 1993), 88ff. The emphasis is mine. What she says about the first three petitions appears to be true of Calvin's treatment of the prayer as a whole, viz., that though "there are a number of changes over time, between the 1530s and the 1550s . . . these changes are primarily substitutions which do not alter the basic meaning" (97).

9. Other sources for Calvin's exposition of the Lord's Prayer are the Geneva Catechism (Qs. 255–95) and his *Commentary on the Harmony of the Synoptic Gospels*.

10. In his *Commentary on the Harmony of the Gospels* Calvin points out a parallel between the Lord's Prayer and the Decalogue. "As God's Law is divided into two tables, the first containing the claims of devotion, the second of charity, so in prayers Christ tells us to consider and search out in one part the glory of God, and then allows us in another part to think of ourselves." Comm. Matthew 6:9.

11. "We have the heart of God [*cor Dei*] as soon as we have placed before him the name of his son." Comm. John 16:26.

12. In the following seven sections in the *Institutes* Calvin critiques the Roman Catholic belief in the intercession of the departed saints.

13. Ronald Wallace cites other passages from the *Institutes*, III.20.34, and the commentaries to make the following points:

(1). We should not be rash in speaking in our prayers but wait for the Spirit to "instruct us how to pray aright" (*Inst*. III 20:34).

(2). Since our prayers should be a result of the moving of the Spirit, we should therefore pray for the *increase* of the Spirit, rather than the coming of the Spirit," op. cit., 287; cf. Comm. Acts 1:14.

(3). It is also the Spirit "who inspires our prayers with the ardour and earnestness which are also important characteristics of Christian prayer" (ibid.) Cf. Comm. Rom. 8:27.

14. "Let the Christian man, then, conform his prayers to this rule in order that they may be in common and embrace all who are his brothers in Christ, not only those whom he at present sees as such but all men who dwell on earth" (*Inst.* IV.17.38). In reference to this passage Elsie McKee comments, "Note that Calvin includes all people who dwell on earth—unexpected in someone who is usually identified primarily with predestination!" (op.cit., 97).

15. The quotation is from the new translation by A. W. Morrison of the Commentary on Matthew, Mark, and Luke, vol. 1 in the Torrance edition (Grand Rapids: Wm. B. Eerdmans Publishing Co., 1972), 208.

16. This text is cited in all of Calvin's treatments of this petition.

17. Op. cit., 293–94.

18. Most of these prayers are appended to the original version of the Geneva Catechism, but are not included in the version found in *Calvin: Theological Treatises* of the Library of Christian Classics. They are included, however, in A. Mitchell Hunter's *Teaching of Calvin* (London: James Clarke, 2d ed., 1950), 215–21. These and a few other prayers are also included in *John Calvin: The Christian Life*, ed. John H. Leith (San Francisco: Harper & Row, 1984), 78–82. Most of these prayers are taken from the larger collection in *Calvin's Tracts and Treatises*, vol. 2, trans. and ed. by Henry Beveridge (Grand Rapids: Wm. B. Eerdmans Publishing Co., 1958).

19. This and the following passages are all taken from the prayers found in Hunter, 215–21.

20. On the guidance and leading of the Spirit in Calvin's theology see my essay, "Governed and Guided by the Spirit—A Key Issue in Calvin's Doctrine of the Holy Spirit," in *Das Reformierte Erbe*, Teil 2, Festschrift for Gottfried Locher, ed. Heiko Oberman, Ernst Saxer, et al. (Zurich: Zwingli Verlag, 1993).

21. A representative selection of these prayers and a brief selection from the exposition they follow are found in *Calvin's Devotions and Prayers of John Calvin*, compiled by Charles E. Edwards (Grand Rapids: Baker Book House, 1954).

22. These two phrases follow respectively the exposition of Amos 8:11–12 (the 66th lecture on the Minor Prophets) and Obadiah 1:12–21 (lecture 71).

23. These prayers are all taken from the new Rutherford House translation of Calvin's Commentary on Ezekiel, chaps. 1–12, by D. Foxgrover and D. Martin (Grand Rapids: Wm. B. Eerdmans Publishing Co., 1994). These were to be Calvin's last biblical expositions. In fact, he could not complete them and only got through chapter 20. He completed this lecture on February 2, 1564, and then was forced to remain at home, largely confined to his bed. He died May 27, 1564.

24. Comm. on Ezekiel 3:21ff., lecture 11, 110. In contrast to all the formal general prayers, these prayers all begin simply with "Almighty God. . . ."

25. Comm. on Ezekiel 4:5ff., lecture 14, 137.

26. Comm. on Ezekiel 8:15ff., lecture 23, 217.

27. Comm. on Ezekiel 10:6ff., lecture 26, 244.

28. The title of chap. 9 of book III, which forms the climax of his discourse on the Christian life (chaps. 6–10). The final chapter of this discourse is entitled "How We Must Use the Present Life and Its Helps." What I have called a "discourse" came to be known after the 1550 edition of the *Institutes* as "The Little Book on the Christian Life," and in this form was published separately. It was very popular in

an earlier period and is available in English as *Golden Book of the Christian Life* (Grand Rapids: Baker Book House, 1952).

12. BAPTISM AND THE LORD'S SUPPER

1. *The Protestant Tradition* (Cambridge University Press, 1960), 145.

2. See Brunner's Dogmatics, vol. 3, *The Christian Doctrine of the Church, Faith, and the Consummation* (Philadelphia: Westminster Press, 1960), 19.

3. Only the adjectives describing the nature of the preaching and the administration of the sacraments differ. Instead of "purely preached," the Augsburg Confession has "where the gospel is rightly preached" and where the sacraments are "rightly administered." One other difference—one rarely noticed—is Calvin's slight amplification in the next section. Here he says that we have a church "where the preaching of the gospel is *reverently heard* and the sacraments are *not neglected*" (IV.1.10., emphasis added).

4. Cf. the book by that title by Joseph McLelland. The subtitle is: *An Exposition of the Sacramental Theology of Peter Martyr Vermigli* (Edinburgh: Oliver & Boyd, 1957). Peter Martyr was an Italian reformer who came under the influence of Zwingli and Bucer. He had to flee Italy in 1542; he became Regius Professor of Divinity at Oxford and ended his career in Strasbourg.

5. Cf. the title of the chapter on prayer in the *Institutes* III.20 where prayer is described as "the chief *exercise* of faith."

6. Cf. the definition in the Geneva Catechism, Q. 310: A sacrament is "an outward attestation of the grace of God which, by a visible sign, represents spiritual things to imprint the promises of God *more firmly* in our hearts, and to make us *more sure* of them" (emphasis added). In the 1538 Catechism Calvin says that the sacraments make us "more aware" of the Lord's special provision "for our slender capacity" (sec. 26).

7. See his unfinished *Fragment*, published as IV, 4 of the *Church Dogmatics* (Edinburgh: T. & T. Clark, 1969), 102ff.

8. This sentence is repeated with slight variations in the *Institutes* IV.4.3, although here Calvin cautions his readers against thinking that the Word by itself is inadequate. "Properly speaking," he notes, sacraments are "not so much needed to confirm his sacred Word as to establish us in faith in it. For God's truth is of itself firm and sure enough, and it cannot receive better confirmation from any other source than from itself."

9. For other references to the crucial role of the Holy Spirit in relation to the sacraments, see *Institutes* IV.14.8, 10, 11, 22.

10. "Antidote to the Council of Trent," canon IV, in Calvin's *Tracts and Treatises*, vol. 3, *In Defense of the Reformed Faith*, ed. T. F. Torrance (Grand Rapids: Wm. B. Eerdmans Publishing Co., 1958), 174.

11. On faith as "the principal work of the Holy Spirit," see the *Institutes* III.1.4.

12. *Defensio sanae et orthodoxae doctrinae de sacramentis,* CO 9:17; cited in Wendel, 318.

13. On the covenant, see M. Eugene Osterhaven, "Calvin on the Covenant," chap. 5 in *Readings in Calvin's Theology*, ed. Donald K. McKim (Grand Rapids: Baker Book House, 1984).

14. See Wendel, 323–24.

15. "If it please him, why may the Lord not shine with a tiny spark at the present time on those whom he will illumine in the future with the full splendor of his light . . . ?" *Inst.* IV.16.19.

16. Comm. Matthew 9:14.

17. "Although faith is required of those who are grown up, yet this is falsely transferred to infants whose condition is quite different." Comm. Acts 8:37.

18. Cf. further, the *Institutes* IV.16.3, 19, 32.

19. "The permanent effect of baptism [for Calvin] is that it is a sign of the unfailing promise of God offered and never withdrawn. It is there to be received by faith whenever the mind awakens to the Word under the action of the Spirit, whether this occurs at nine or ninety." Jill Raitt, "Three Inter-Related Principles in Calvin's Unique Doctrine of Infant Baptism," *Sixteenth Century Journal*, 11, no.1 (spring 1980): 57.

20. A major difference revolves around their respective views of the nature of Christ's ascended body and the question of the *communicatio idiomatum*. This, in turn, has implications for their differing interpretations of the nature of Christ's presence in the Supper. Concerning the issue, see *Institutes* IV.17.30 and David Willis, *Calvin's Catholic Christology* (Leiden: E. J. Brill, 1966).

21. The key word here is "communication" (*communicatio*), which has a far richer significance in Latin than in common English parlance. Calvin uses the same word a few lines later in the Catechism when he points out that despite Christ's absence from us, "no distance can prevent his [Christ's] power from feeding his believers on himself, and bringing it about that they still enjoy ever present communication with him. . . ." This term occurs with relatively less frequency in the *Institutes*, where Calvin uses more graphic language to indicate how Christ is experienced in the Supper. However, see IV.17.20, where there is a broader reference to "that secret communication by which we grow into one with Christ." Cf. IV.17.38. The term is also used several times in Calvin's *Short Treatise on the Lord's Supper*, (composed in 1540 shortly after the Catechism). Here he declares that "to deny the true communication of Jesus Christ to be offered us in the Supper is to render this holy sacrament frivolous and useless." *Calvin: Theological Treatises*, Library of Christian Classics, vol. 22, ed. J.K.S. Reid (Philadelphia: Westminster Press, 1954), 146.

22. Re the latter, see *Institutes* IV.17.1 and p. 1359n1; IV.17.20 and n.67; and IV.17.26–29 and notes appended to those sections.

23. Later in the *Institutes* Calvin warns about people like Westphal who teach that there is a "mixture or transfusion of Christ's flesh with our soul." Calvin feels this danger is avoided and yet a vital truth maintained if we believe that "from the substance of his flesh Christ breathes life into our souls—indeed pours forth his very life into us—even though Christ's flesh itself does not enter into us" (IV.17.32). This is a crucial distinction.

24. Brian Gerrish concludes his study of Calvin's eucharistic doctrine, *Grace and Gratitude* (Minneapolis: Fortress Press, 1993) with the following paragraph (on p.190): "It is not at all surprising that stalwart Reformed divines have sometimes been not merely puzzled but offended by Calvin's talk about the communication of Christ's life-giving flesh. They may choose to reject it as a perilous intrusion into Reformed theology and insist that Christ's body is life-giving only because it was crucified. But in so doing they should note that Calvin's view of the

Lord's Supper was bound up with a total conception of what it means to be saved and of how the historical deed of Christ reaches out to the present. It is impossible to read Calvin's ideas on Baptism and the Eucharist in their own historical context and not to notice that they were developed in part as a warning against what he took to be another peril: a mentality that reduces sacred signs to mere reminders, communion with Christ to beliefs about Christ, and the living body of the church to an association of likeminded individuals. Only a careful study of later Reformed history can show which has turned out to be the greater of the two perils. But this much, I think, can fairly be said in conclusion: even if the Calvinists have the greatest difficulty in expressing what exactly that something *more* is that they experience in the holy banquet, ecumenical theology will always have need of them to throw their weight on Calvin's side of the Reformed boat."

25. See, e.g., Hermann Sasse, *This Is My Body: Luther's Contention for the Real Presence in the Sacrament of the Altar* (Minneapolis: Augsburg Press, 1959); and the recent Lutheran *Christian Dogmatics,* vol. 2, ed. Carl Braaten and Robert Jenson (Philadelphia: Fortress Press, 1984), 357ff. However, even a friendly interpreter like Brian Gerrish finds "ambiguities" in Calvin's language which allow for differing interpretations, op. cit., 2–14.

26. *Short Treatise,* 147.

27. Here see chapter 11, the Excursus on Luther and Calvin on the person of Christ.

28. The version cited in the text is from a tradition of Latin edition (1545) by J.K.S. Reid in *Calvin: Theological Treatises,* 137. The earlier French version is more concise: We are able to partake of Christ's substance, though he is in heaven, "by the incomprehensible power of his Spirit, who conjoins things separated by a distance."

29. Comm. 1 Cor. 11:24. This translation is by John W. Fraser in the Torrance edition of Calvin's New Testament Commentaries (Grand Rapids: Wm. B. Eerdmans Publishing Co., 1960), 247.

30. Comm. 1 Cor. 11:24, 246.

31. "Calvin appears at times to be inconsistent in his statements about the Supper. He can in one place deny that Christ 'descends to the earth in the Supper' . . . and yet in other places he speaks freely about Christ as descending through the Supper. His meaning depends on the context and the course taken by the argument which has led up to the making of the statement." Ronald S. Wallace, *Calvin's Doctrine of Word and Sacraments* (Edinburgh: Oliver & Boyd, 1953), 208.

32. Despite such modesty, Calvin is still convinced that his view is true and is "confident" that his views "will be approved by godly hearts" (*Inst.* IV.17.7).

33. This does not mean that we should take refuge in pious ignorance or poor theology. As Kilian McDonnell rightly points out in regard to comments like these, "Calvin knew a mystery when he saw one and he knew that the mystery was beyond man's measuring. . . . But the insistence on the element of mystery is no reason for foregoing an explanation: 'Knowledge of this great mystery is most necessary and, in proportion to its importance, demands an accurate exposition' " (*Inst.* IV.17.1). *John Calvin, the Church, and the Eucharist* (Princeton, N.J.: Princeton Univ. Press, 1967), 207.

34. This phrase is found in the Wittenberg Concord.

35. WA xxvi, 292, cited by Wilhelm Niesel in *The Gospel and the Churches: A Comparison of Catholicism, Orthodoxy and Protestantism* (Philadelphia: Westminster

Press, 1962), 276. This position is found in the Schmalcaldic Articles, one of the Lutheran Confessions: "Of the Sacrament of the Altar we hold that bread and wine in the Supper are the true body and blood of Christ, and are given and received not only by the godly, but also by wicked Christians" (III, vi). Niesel's comparison of the Reformed and Lutheran views (275–83) is helpful.

36. "I am horrified at the absurd notion that Christ gives himself to unbelievers to be eaten in a lifeless form, as it were." Comm. 1 Cor. 11:27.

37. Op. cit., 272. On the alleged objectivism of Luther and the subjectivism of Calvin, cf. Otto Weber, *Foundations of Dogmatics* vol. 2 (Grand Rapids: Wm. B. Eerdmans Publishing Co., 1983). He concludes: "We would have to judge that it is impossible to deal with the question of the 'mode of the presence' in the Supper under the alternative of 'subject and object,' or under the alternative of 'spiritual and physical.'" (634).

38. "Whatever changes there may have been over the years in Calvin's sacramental theology, he does not seem to have wavered on this cardinal point: the holy banquet is a sign and pledge of union with Christ," Gerrish, 133.

39. See the *Institutes* IV.17.44–50, where Calvin traces the history of this unhappy development and the practice of giving laity only "one kind," i.e., the bread. Cf. n.39 on page 1421 of the LCC edition.

40. This is repeated in an amplified form in the *Institutes,* IV.17.32, but here instead of assuring us of the *"immortality of our flesh,"* he says the sacrament "brings an undoubted assurance of *eternal life* to our minds (emphasis added).

41. *Short Treatise,* 145.

42. Ibid., 148.

43. Ibid., 149.

44. In the *Institutes* Calvin lists various *purposes* of the sacrament which generally correspond to the *benefits* listed in the "Short Treatise on the Lord's Supper." See particularly IV.17.2, 37, 38. Elsewhere he points out that just as "bread nourishes, sustains, and keeps the life of our body, so Christ's body is the only food to invigorate and enliven the soul." And just as the benefits of wine "are to nourish, refresh, strengthen, and gladden" the body, so does the blood of Christ to our souls (IV.17.3).

45. Calvin says much the same, albeit much more briefly, in his "Short Treatise": "Since then it is a remedy which God has given us to assist our frailty, to fortify our faith, to augment our charity, and to further us in all sanctity of life, so far from making us abstain, we ought the more to make use of it, the more we feel oppressed by the disease," 152.

13. THE NATURE AND MARKS OF THE CHURCH

1. Augustine and Luther also speak of the church in this way. Cf. LCC *Institutes,* 1016n10; Wendel, *Calvin,* 294.

2. Wilhelm Niesel insists that Calvin's treatment of the notion of the invisible church "moves on strictly biblical lines." *The Theology of Calvin,* 192.

3. *The Misunderstanding of the Church* (Philadelphia: Westminster Press, 1953), 17.

4. See Geneva Catechism, Q. 100, and *Inst.* IV.1.3.

5. K. L. Schmidt, in his article on the Church in Kittel's *Theologisches Wörterbuch*

zum Neuen Testament, concludes: "If Luther distinguished—above all in his polemic against Rome—between the Church invisible and the Church visible, he was not thereby subscribing to the Platonism of those who came after him," E.T. in *Bible Key Words,* translated and edited by J. R. Coates, 67. Similarly Karl Barth: "The Reformers guarded themselves carefully against the idea that by the Church they meant only a *'civitas platonica,'* the pure idea of a Christian community [*Gemeinde*], and therefore only an invisible church." *Church Dogmatics* IV, 1, 653.

6. Whereas at the beginning of IV.1.2 Calvin says that this article of the Creed "refers not only to the visible church (our present topic), but also to God's elect," at the beginning of the next section concerning the communion of saints he says that this article "also applies *to some extent* to the outward church [*ad externam queque ecclesiam pertinet*]."

7. Jan R. Weerda, *Nach Gottes Wort reformierte Kirche* (Munich: Chr. Kaiser Verlag, 1964), 119.

8. Another way of distinguishing between the empirical church and the church known to God alone is to speak of the essence of the church in contrast to its form. So Hans Küng, who hastens to add that in regard to the church "essence and form cannot be separated." But they are also not identical. *The Church* (New York: Sheed & Ward, 1967), 5. Later Küng affirms that "The reformers, and before them, Wyclif and Hus, were basically right to oppose the idea that the church was simply the all too visible institution of the medieval church with its spiritual and political empire" (34).

9. *Christ and Ourselves* (New York: Harper & Row, 1965), 24–25.

10. *The Protestant Tradition* (Cambridge: Cambridge Univ. Press, 1960), 146f. A fuller analysis of this development is given by Alexandre Ganoczy, *Calvin, Théologien de L'église et du ministère* (Paris: Les Editions du Cerf, 1964), 184ff. He basically agrees with Whale's analysis (which he does not know) that in the first edition of the *Institutes* the stress is almost exclusively on the church as a spiritual reality with no visible form, whereas in the last edition the visible church as well as the invisible has become the object of faith.

11. Ibid., 152–53.

12. Ibid., 161.

13. A. Dakin, *Calvinism* (London: Duckworth, 1940/1949), 105. Joseph C. McLelland concurs: "The idea of an 'invisible' church known only to God did not play the large part in Calvin's thought that critics have supposed." *The Reformation and Its Significance for Today* (Philadelphia: Westminster Press, 1957), 41–42.

14. Geddes MacGregor, *Corpus Christi: The Nature of the Church according to the Reformed Tradition* (Philadelphia: Westminster Press, 1958), 57. Cf. Calvin's discussion of the ministry in the *Institutes* IV.3.1–3.

15. Cf. the excellent discussion of the Lordship of Christ and all this implies for the church by the Roman Catholic scholar, Kilian McDonnell, *John Calvin, the Church and the Eucharist* (Princeton: Princeton Univ. Press, 1967), 169–76.

16. Comm. Galatians 5:1.

17. This definition of the two marks of the church is taken over almost verbatim from the Augsburg Confession, the first Protestant (Lutheran) Confession (1530). But Calvin makes one significant addition, viz., the *hearing* of the Word (also repeated in IV.1.10). This is often overlooked. Moreover, just as the Word must be truly heard, so must the sacraments be faithfully received in order for the church to exist, and in both cases it is the correlation of Word and Spirit that makes possible any efficacy here. Cf. Comm. Isaiah 35:4 and *Inst.* IV.14.9.

18. "It is not, therefore, by the quality of its members, which could only give occasion for a subjective judgment, but by the presence of the means of grace instituted by Christ, that the Church is constituted and can be objectively judged," Wendel, 297. Cf. Calvin's attacks on sectarian groups such as the Cathari Donatists and the Anabaptists, which required a certain quality of life corresponding to the gospel (IV.1.3). Calvin was no less concerned about holy living—witness his stress on sanctification and church discipline—but he refused to make this a mark of the church.

19. Otto Weber points out that Calvin (and later Calvinism), by appealing basically to the consensus of the ancient church concerning fundamental doctrines, and by his own flexibility in regard to precisely what must be believed, was more "catholic" than Lutheran. "Die Einheit der Kirche bei Calvin," in *Calvin Studien 1959* (Neukirchen: Neukirchener Verlag, 1959), 141. Cf. my essay, "Calvinus Oecumenicus: Calvin's Vision of the Unity and Catholicity of the Church," *Reformed Review* 44, no. 2 (winter, 1990).

20. "In regard to the one God and his true and legitimate worship, the corruption of human nature, free salvation, the mode of obtaining justification, the office and power of Christ, repentance and its exercises, faith which, relying on the promises of the gospel, gives us assurance of salvation, prayer to God, and other leading articles, the same doctrine is preached by both. We call on one God the Father, trusting to the same Mediator; the same Spirit of adoption is the earnest of our future inheritance. Christ has reconciled us all by the same sacrifice. In that righteousness which he has purchased for us, our minds are at peace, and we glory in the same head. It is strange if Christ, whom we preach as our peace, and who, removing the ground of disagreement, appeased to us our Father in heaven, do not also cause us mutually to cultivate brotherly peace on earth." Calvin, *Tracts and Treatises*, vol. 2, 251. W. F. Dankbaar affirms that "One could hardly describe better the basis of ecumenical unity . . . ." *Calvin, Sein Weg und Sein Werk* (Neukirchen: Neukirchener Verlag, 1959), 182.

21. Comm. Micah 2:2.

22. McDonnell, 173.

23. Comm. Acts 20:21f.

24. Comm. Jeremiah 33:17.

25. One must not confuse here the enforcement of the civil laws of Geneva that regulated the private lives of citizens and the regulations of the church. There was often overlapping, but Calvin, as we shall see, tried very hard to distinguish these two realms.

26. Cf. James Mackinnon, *Calvin and the Reformation* (London: Longmans, Green, & Co., 1936), 59f; and François Wendel, *Calvin* (New York: Harper & Row, 1963), 52ff., 72–74.

27. Even in Strasbourg, however, the civil authorities were reluctant to give the church the freedom it sought under Bucer's leadership. Cf. Wendel, 60.

28. Cf. the Ordinances of 1541 in the *Library of Christian Classics*, vol. 22, *Calvin: Theological Treatises*, 58ff.

29. Op. cit., 74.

30. Cf. IV.1.10–12 where Calvin deals more explicitly with the marks and authority of the church.

31. So, e.g., J. T. McNeill, *The History and Character of Calvinism* (New York: Oxford Univ. Press, 1954), 214; and W. Nijenhuis, *Calvinus Oecumenicus* (The Hague: Martinus Nijhoff, 1959), 278, 313. Jan Weerda suggests that discipline did not be-

come a mark of the church because Calvin regarded it as enclosed in the proclamation of the Word and the administration of the sacraments. "For according to its proper meaning it is an application of the 'authority of the Word of God which requires neither authority nor carrying out [*Handanlegung*].' " "Ordnung zur Lehre," in *Calvin Studien 1959*, ed. Jürgen Moltmann (Neukirchen: Neukirchener Verlag, 1960), 168. Cf. R. N. Caswell, "Calvin and Church Discipline" in *John Calvin*, Courtenay Studies in the Reformation I, ed. G. E. Duffield (Grand Rapids: Wm. B. Eerdmans Publishing Co., 1966), 211.

32. A similar statement is found in Calvin's Reply to Cardinal Sadolet. "To hang together, the body of the church must be bound together by discipline as with sinews." E.T. in LCC, vol. 22, 245.

33. See John Kennedy, *Presbyterian Authority and Discipline* (Edinburgh: Saint Andrew Press, 1960). The fundamental cause, he feels, "is the loss by the Scottish church of the authority of the Word of God" (317ff.). This would apply to other churches as well.

34. Caswell, 211. Cf. Comm. on Matthew 15:18 (E.T., *Harmony of the Evangelists*, vol. 2, 358). In this Calvin was following the precedent set forth by Bucer in his *De Vera Animarum Cura* (Concerning the True Care of Souls). J. T. McNeill in *A History of the Cure of Souls* (New York: Harper, 1951/1965), 177f., gives a brief analysis of this work.

35. Cf. Caswell, 217–18.

36. T. M. Lindsay, *History of the Reformation*, vol. 2 (Edinburgh: T. & T. Clark, 1907/1956), 109–10. "The sacrifice of the Mass had been the symbol and heart of Romanism; the Lord's Supper was to be the same in the Reformed Church," Joseph C. McLelland, *The Reformation and Its Significance for Today* (Philadelphia: Westminster Press, 1962), 42.

37. From a Letter (CO 10:207) cited in Caswell, 216.

38. *The Theology of Calvin*, 198.

39. *Calvin's Lehre von Staat und Kirche* (Breslau: M. & H. Marcus, 1937/1961), 550–51.

40. Excommunication, as well, is to be used "only in necessity [*in necessitate*]," (*Inst.* IV.11.5).

41. For modern applications of this point, cf. Eugene Heideman, *Reformed Bishops and Catholic Elders* (Grand Rapids: Wm. B. Eerdmans Publishing Co., 1970), 122–32; and MacGregor, *Corpus Christi*, 216–18.

42. Wilhelm Pauck, *The Heritage of the Reformation* (Glencoe, Ill.: Free Press, rev. ed., 1961), 132–33.

43. "For doctrine obtains force and authority where the minister not only explains to all together what they owe to Christ, but also has the right and means to require that it be kept by those whom he has observed as either disrespectful or languid toward his teaching" (*Inst.* IV.12.2).

14. THE MAGISTRACY AND CIVIL GOVERNMENT

1. For the title of this chapter I am combining the simple title of sec. 33 of the Catechism, viz., "Magistracy" (*De magistratu*), with that of the final chapter (IV.20) of the *Institutes*, "Civil Government" (*De politica administratione*). Wilhelm Niesel,

in the second German edition of his theology of Calvin, points out that the German translation—"Das weltliche Regiment," like the English—is not a literal translation of the Latin original but reflects Calvin's own usage in the opening sentences of this chapter as well as the French translation of 1561, "Du gouvernement civil." *Die Theologie Calvins,* 2. neubearbeitete Auflage (Munich: Chr. Kaiser Verlag, 1957).

2. For Luther's approach to the state see William A. Mueller, *Church and State in Luther and Calvin* (Nashville: Broadman Press, 1954; New York: Doubleday & Co., Anchor Books, 1965), part 1, chap. 2: "Luther and Secular Authority"; and John Tonkin, *The Church and the Secular Order in Reformation Thought* (New York: Columbia Univ. Press, 1971), chap. 2.

3. For the Anabaptist view of church and state see Timothy George, *Theology of the Reformers* (Nashville: Broadman Press, 1988), 286–87, 303–4. George's discussion is largely based on Menno Simons's writings. According to George, "The Anabaptists did not deny that the magistrates were ordained of God to maintain law and order. They pledged obedience to civil authority in every area which did not violate the requirements of their faith" (286). One of those areas of conflict was that of bearing arms.

4. *Opera Selecta,* vol. 1, 223f.

5. Ibid., vol. 1, p. 258. The identical phrase appears in the final edition of the *Institutes,* IV.20.1.

6. I am quoting from the version of the Genevan Confession in *Calvin: Theological Treatises,* ed. J.K.S. Reid, Library of Christian Classics, vol. 22 (Philadelphia: Westminster Press, 1954), 32.

7. *Opera Selecta* I, 425.

8. "Ministers" is the only term used to describe the magistrate in the Catechism.

9. See John T. Mc Neill's Introduction to the LCC edition of the *Institutes,* lxv and following.

10. So Philip Hughes in his Introduction to *The Register of the Company of the Pastors in the Time of Calvin* (Grand Rapids: Wm. B. Eerdmans Publishing Co., 1966), 91.

11. A. Mitchell Hunter, *The Teaching of Calvin* (London: James Clarke, 2d rev. ed., 1950), 194.

12. In the Belgic Confession (1561) the office of the magistracy is "not only to have regard unto and watch for the welfare of the civil state, but also that they protect the sacred ministry, and thus may remove and prevent all idolatry and false worship, that the kingdom of the antichrist may be destroyed and the kingdom of Christ promoted" (Article 36). This statement has been dropped from the recent Christian Reformed version found in their *Ecumenical Creeds and Reformed Confessions* (Grand Rapids: CRC Publications, 1979). Their Synod of 1958 proposed a substitute statement, which is found on p. 83 of the above booklet.

The Westminster Confession of Faith (1648) warns against civil magistrates interfering "in matters of faith," but then states: "Yet, as nursing mothers, it is the duty of civil magistrates to protect the church of our common Lord, without giving the preference to any denomination of Christians above the rest . . . (chap. 23, 3).

13. Letter to Nicholas Radziwill of Poland. *Letters of John Calvin,* vol. 3, in *Calvin's Selected Works,* ed. John Beveridge and Jules Bonnet, vol. 6 in Baker Book House edition (1983), 135. For an illuminating discussion of politics in Calvin's correspondence, see John T. McNeill, "John Calvin on Civil Government," in

Calvinism and the Political Order, ed. John L. Hunt (Philadelphia: Westminster Press, 1965), 24–29.

14. In the Latin edition of the Catechism Calvin merely mentions "the prophet," but in the French edition Calvin refers specifically to Jeremiah 22:1–9. The two qualities Calvin mentions are cited in Jeremiah 22:3: "Thus says the Lord: Do *justice* and *righteousness . . .*" (emphasis added).

15. David Little, after discussing some of these passages, concludes: "The framework for proper order is provided by the consistent maintenance of the Reformed faith. There is no true order without the honor of God." *Religion, Order, and Law: A Study in Pre-Revolutionary England* (New York: Harper & Row, 1969), 55.

16. On the complicated matter of the relationship between the conscience, natural law, and the order of nature, see Dowey, *The Knowledge of God in Calvin's Theology,* 66–72.

17. Comm. Psalm 72:4. Moreover, "none of the kings of earth can frame or defend good order, except so far as he shall be assisted by the same Spirit." Comm. Matthew 12:18.

18. *Calvin und das Recht* (Feudingen: Buchdruckerei, 1934), 39–48.

19. "Notes on John Calvin, Justitia, and the Old Testament Law," originally published in *Essays Presented to Markus Barth on His 65th Birthday,* ed. Dikran Y. Hadidian. Reprinted in Ford Lewis Battles, *Interpreting John Calvin,* ed. Robert Benedetto (Grand Rapids: Baker Book House, 1996), 313.

20. Ibid., 314–15. Battles goes on to say: "But these remarks do not exhaust Calvin's use of *equity.* The sublimest task to which it is put in his system is the harmonization of the Decalogue and the Sermon on the Mount through *epieikeia.* Calvin penetrates to the intent of the lawgiver of the Decalogue, an intent implicit in the Old Testament law but made explicit in Jesus' reading of the commandments."

21. This is the translation as found in the LCC *Institutes* IV.20.23. The NRSV translation reads: "Let every person be subject to the governing authorities. . . . Therefore whoever resists authority resists what God has appointed. . . ."

22. Anna Case-Winters, "Theological Affirmations and Political Arrangements: Two Way Traffic," in *Calvin and the State,* ed. Peter De Klerk (Grand Rapids: Calvin Studies Society, 1993), 69.

23. In his commentary on Romans 13:1 Calvin stresses the obedience that subjects owe their rulers, but in his commentary on Daniel, Calvin emphasizes more the limits of rulers. For references see Niesel, 240–41.

24. Comm. Romans 13:1.

25. Ibid.

26. LCC edition, 11. Similar statements are found in the *Institutes* IV.20.29 and 31. On the basis of such passages John T. McNeill concludes: "Where the glory of God is not the end of government there is no legitimate sovereignty, but usurpation. The Kingship of Christ is over all earthly dominion." *John Calvin: On God and Political Duty* (New York: Liberal Arts Press, 1950, 1956), xiii. This Introduction is reprinted in *Readings in Calvin's Theology,* ed. Donald K. McKim (Grand Rapids: Baker Book House, 1984), chap. 15.

27. Calvin provides a vivid description of the all-too-typical ruler in the *Institutes* IV.20.24: "But it is the example of nearly all ages that some princes are careless about all those things to which they ought to have given heed, and, far from all care, lazily take their pleasure. Others, intent upon their own business, put up

for sale laws, privileges, judgments, and letters of favor. Others drain the common people of their money, and afterward lavish it on insane largesse. Still others exercise sheer robbery, plundering houses, raping virgins and matrons, and slaughtering the innocent."

28. CO 53: 131, quoted by Niesel, 242.

29. Sermon on 1 Timothy 2:2, in Niesel, ibid.

30. See, e.g., his comments on the oft-cited passage Acts 5:29: "God sets men over us with power in such a way that he keeps his own authority unimpaired. Therefore we must do the will of those who rule over us *to the extent that the authority of God is not violated*" (emphasis added). A prime example for Calvin is Daniel. Concerning his refusal to obey Darius, Calvin comments: "When earthly princes rise up against God, "We absolutely ought to defy them rather than obey them whenever they are so restive and wish to despoil God of his rights, and, as it were, draw him down from heaven." Comm. Daniel 6:22.

31. On this point see the extensive note on pages 1518–19 of the LCC *Institutes*.

32. This is the way Calvin concludes the *Institutes*.

APPENDIX:
CALVIN, THEOLOGIAN OF THE HOLY SPIRIT

1. "John Calvin the Theologian," in *Calvin and Augustine* (Philadelphia: Presbyterian and Reformed Publishing Co., 1956), 484–85.

2. See especially Simon van der Linde, *De Leer van den Heiligen Geest* (Wageningen: H. Veenman & Zonen, 1943), 2; and Werner Krusche, *Das Wirken des Heiligen Geistes nach Calvin* (Göttingen: Vandenhoeck & Ruprecht, 1957), 12.

3. Edited by J. de Graf for the Stipendium Bernardinum (Utrecht: Drukkerij V/H Hemink & Zoon, 1964), 109–50.

4. See Bernard Ramm, *The Witness of the Spirit: An Essay on the Contemporary Relevance of the Internal Witness of the Holy Spirit* (Grand Rapids: Wm. B. Eerdmans Publishing Co., 1960); and H. Jackson Forstman, *Word and Spirit: Calvin's Doctrine of Biblical Authority* (Stanford, Calif.: Stanford Univ. Press, 1962). This theme was also given serious attention by earlier Reformed theologians such as B. B. Warfield (see n.1) and Abraham Kuyper in his monumental study, *The Work of the Holy Spirit* (1900 and many reprints). There are also several fine essays on this subject, the latest being "Word and Spirit in Calvin" by Richard C. Gamble in the collection of papers given at the sixth colloquium of the Calvin Studies Society, *Calvin and the Holy Spirit*, ed. Peter De Klerk (Grand Rapids: Calvin Studies Society, 1989).

5. See n.4. Other essays included in that volume are: "The Saving Work of the Holy Spirit in Calvin" by Jelle Faber; "Spiritus Creator: The Use and Abuse of Calvin's Cosmic Pneumatology" by John Bolt; "'Extra Nos' and 'in Nobis' by Calvin in a Pneumatological Light" by Willem van't Spijker; "The Role of the Holy Spirit in Calvin's Teaching on the Ministry" by Brian Armstrong; and "What Is the Meaning of These Gifts?" by Leonard Sweetman, Jr.

6. In "Faith and Ferment," papers read at the 1982 Westminster Conference in London. Lane focuses on two aspects of Calvin's doctrine of the Holy Spirit: the witness of the Spirit to the Word and the witness of the Spirit to salvation.

7. This is even true of the comprehensive collection of essays edited by Donald

K. McKim, *Readings in Calvin's Theology*. This volume has 18 chapters by different Calvin scholars, including topics such as "True Piety according to Calvin" and "Eschatology and History"—but nothing on the role of the Holy Spirit in Calvin's theology.

8. The one exception might be Calvin's doctrine of creation. There are a few scattered references to the role of the Spirit in this realm, but they are not as prominent as elsewhere. Despite the impressive title, this becomes apparent in John Bolt's essay, "Spiritus Creator: The Use and Abuse of Calvin's Cosmic Pneumatology," in *Calvin and the Holy Spirit*, 17–33. Cf. Krusche, op. cit., Kap. II, "Der Heilige Geist und der Kosmos." This is by far the shortest chapter in the book.

9. See *Church Dogmatics* I, 1 (Edinburgh: T. & T. Clark, 2d ed., 1975), 359f. (German ed. *Kirchliche Dogmatik* I., 1, 379f.). It is noteworthy that even a traditional Calvinist such as Louis Berkhof can define the Trinity using this terminology. The persons of the Trinity, he rightly observes, "are not three persons in the ordinary sense of the word; they are not three individuals, but rather three *modes or forms of being* in which the Divine Being exists," *Summary of Christian Doctrine* (Grand Rapids: Wm. B. Eerdmans Publishing Co., 1938/1975), 42. (Emphasis added.)

10. In disputes with Pierre Caroli in 1537 and 1540, Calvin, for some reason, refused to declare his acceptance of the Nicene and Athanasian Creeds, even though he had no substantial objections to their content. See François Wendel, *Calvin: Sources and Development of His Thought* (New York: Harper & Row, 1963), 54–5.

11. See *Institutes* I.13.2.

12. B. B. Warfield, "Calvin's Doctrine of the Trinity," in *Calvin and Augustine*, 195.

13. Much of the material in this section was covered earlier in chap. 3, the Excursus on "The Authority of Scripture." It is repeated here because the focus is now more on the Holy Spirit than on the Bible.

14. See Richard Gamble's essay, "Word and Spirit in Calvin," in *Calvin and the Holy Spirit*, 75ff. Here Gamble focuses on Calvin's theological method as being a continued polemic against Anabaptists and Spiritualists, on the one hand, and Roman Catholics, on the other. Here he is following the thesis of Ford Lewis Battles's paper given at the first international Calvin Congress in Amsterdam in 1978, "Calculus Fidei," later published in *Calvinus Ecclesiae Doctor* (Kampen: J. H. Kok, 1980), 85–110.

15. "The authority of Scripture is authenticated by the inner witness of the Holy Spirit. The reverence which the Church gives to the Scripture is due primarily to the influence of the Holy Spirit in giving inward testimony to the believer that this word is the Word of God," Ronald S. Wallace, *Calvin's Doctrine of the Word and Sacrament* (Edinburgh: Oliver & Boyd, 1953), 101–2.

16. *Das Wirken*, op. cit., 206. Cf. Klaas Runia: "If the Bible is the Word of God, it can only provide its own proof." *Karl Barth's Doctrine of the Word of God* (Grand Rapids: Wm. B. Eerdmans Publishing Co., 1962), 8.

17. Part of the title of book I, chap. 8.

18. *Institutes* I.8.1, 81–2. "The testimony of the Holy Spirit does not render apologetic arguments useless; it merely puts them firmly in their place," Lane, 3.

19. Cf. Otto Weber, *Foundations of Dogmatics*, vol. 1 (Grand Rapids: Wm. B. Eerdmans Publishing Co., 1981), 242–45.

20. Cf. the discussions of the biblical basis of the internal witness of the Spirit in Ramm, *The Witness of the Spirit*, chap. 3; and Runia, *Karl Barth's Doctrine of Scripture*, chap. 1.

21. *Church Dogmatics* I, 2 (Edinburgh: T. & T. Clark, 1956), 535.

22. *Foundations* I, 244.

23. "We shall never be fully persuaded, as we ought to be, that our salvation flows from the wellspring of God's free mercy until we come to know his eternal election, which illuminates God's grace: that he does not indiscriminately adopt all unto the hope of salvation but gives to some what he denies to others" (*Institutes* III.21.1).

24. "The doctrine of election [for Calvin] is the doctrine of utter trust and repose in the sheer grace of God that precedes and envelops all, but the doctrine of the Spirit is the doctrine of the passage of God's mighty creative power from God to man, thrusting him out into the world to do the will of God as a servant of Christ the King. . . ," T. F. Torrance, Preface to William F. Keesecker, ed., *A Calvin Treasury* (London: SCM Press, 1963), xiii.

25. The title of book III reads: "The Ways in Which We Receive the Grace of Christ: What Benefits Come to Us from It, and What Effects Follow."

26. Willem van't Spijker, "'Extra Nos' and 'In Nobis' by Calvin in a Pneumatological Light," in *Calvin and the Holy Spirit*, 44.

27. This is also true of Calvin's sacramentology. For example, in his doctrine of the Lord's Supper, where Calvin insists that the glorified humanity of Christ is localized, so to speak, in heaven, and is yet partaken of by us in the celebration of the Lord's Supper, it is "the Spirit [who] truly unites things separated in space" (*Inst.* IV.17.10).

28. Cf. *Inst.* IV.17.12, p. 1373: "The bond [*vinculum*] of this connection [between the risen Christ and the believer] is the Spirit of Christ, with whom we are joined in unity, and is like a channel [*canalis*] through which all that Christ himself is and has is conveyed to us. . . . On this account, Scripture, in speaking of our participation in Christ, relates its whole power to the Spirit."

29. Cf. the Geneva Catechism, Q. 91. After referring to 1 Peter 1:19 in Q. 90, Calvin responds: "The Holy Spirit, while he dwells in our hearts, makes us feel the virtue of our Lord Jesus [Rom. 5:5]. For he enlightens us to know his benefits; he seals and imprints them in our souls, and makes room for them in us [Eph. 1:3]. He regenerates us and makes us new creatures, so that through him we receive all the blessings and gifts which are offered to us in Jesus Christ." (Translation based on the French edition and included in the T. F. Torrance collection of Reformed Catechisms in *The School of Faith* [London: James Clarke, 1959], 19.

30. I am indebted to Krusche, *Das Wirken*, 263, for these distinctions.

31. *The Holy Spirit in Christian Theology*, 77, cited in Ramm, 100.

32. Op. cit., 217–18. (Translation by Ramm, 100. Cf. his further discussion of this issue involving B. B. Warfield and A. Kuyper.)

33. *Institutes* III.2.6: "Take away the Word and no faith will remain."

34. *Institutes* III.2.7.

35. After defining faith as an "assent" to God's promises in Scripture, he goes on to explain that this assent "is more of the heart than of the brain, and more of the disposition [*affectus*—translated as "affections" by Allen] than of the understanding." *Institutes* III.2.8.

36. In the famous definition of faith (Q. 21) in the Heidelberg Catechism, faith consists of knowledge *and* trust. However, knowledge in this case is more abstract, i.e., less existential, than in Calvin.

37. Cf. *Institutes* III.2.8, 14, and throughout sec. 36.

38. Calvin's emphasis on certainty and assurance runs completely counter to one of the theses of William Bouwsma's brilliant but one-sided book, *John Calvin*, viz., that Calvin was an anxiety-ridden, doubt-filled believer (New York: Oxford Univ. Press, 1988), chap. 2.

39. The most recent and complete study of this theme in English is by Dennis E. Tamburello, *Union with Christ:. John Calvin and the Mysticism of St. Bernard* (Louisville, Ky.: Westminster John Knox Press, 1994).

40. *The Theology of Calvin* (Philadelphia: Westminster Press, 1956), 126.

41. *Calvin: Origins and Development of His Religious Thought*, 235. Wendel cites a number of passages from Calvin's sermons and commentaries where Calvin comes dangerously close to a substantial union of the believer with Christ, but he became more cautious after 1550 because of his conflict with Osiander and his mystical speculations. See pp. 235–39. Calvin is quite clear that Christ's essence is not "mingled with ours," *Institutes* III.11.5, 731.

42. Here he is debating with Osiander. Later in this section Calvin says again that it is "through the power of the Holy Spirit that we grow together with Christ, and he becomes our head and we his members . . ." (731). In his commentary on John 14:20 he also speaks of "that holy and spiritual union that is between Christ and us."

43. Cf. IV.17.12: "The bond of this connection [between Christ and ourselves in the Supper] is the Spirit of Christ, with whom we are joined in unity, and is like a channel through which all that Christ himself is and has is conveyed to us" (1373).

44. The British title for his book, which in its American edition is called *The Gospel and the Churches*.

45. Ibid., 181.

46. "The heart of Calvin's theology [is] union with Christ," van't Spijker, in *Calvin and the Holy Spirit*, 44. Cf. the fine study of this theme by Wilhelm Kolfhaus, *Christusgemeinschaft bei Calvin* (Neukirchen: Buchhandlung des Erziehungsvereins, 1939).

47. The facet of glorification, often overlooked, is noted by Jelle Faber in his essay "The Saving Work of the Holy Spirit," in *Calvin and the Holy Spirit*, 7–8.

48. Werner Krusche is one of the few exceptions (see *Das Wirken des Heiligen Geistes*, 288ff.), but his analysis is not altogether satisfactory.

49. In a lecture, "Governed and Guided by the Spirit—A Key Issue in Calvin's Doctrine of the Holy Spirit," given at Davidson College, North Carolina, in January 1990, I give examples from almost every type of Calvin's writings: sermons, commentaries, catechisms, tracts, and prayers. This paper was later reproduced in *Calvin Studies V*, ed. John H. Leith (Davidson, N.C.: Davidson College Presbyterian Church, 1990), and reprinted in the festschrift for Gottfried Locher, *Reformiertes Erbe*, Teil 2, ed. Heiko Oberman, Ernst Saxer et al. (Zurich: Theologischer Verlag, 1992).

50. Q. 128.

51. Sermon no. 29.

52. Comm. Acts 16:6.

53. Ibid.

INDEX OF NAMES

INDEX OF SUBJECTS